NORTH AMERICAN RAILROADS

RAILROADS

THE ILLUSTRATED ENCYCLOPEDIA

By Brian Solomon

Voyageur Press

NTENTS

INTRODUCTION

American railroading spans nearly two centuries. This intricate and complex network has made for fascinating and endless study. As railroads emerged, evolved, and matured, numerous companies provided a great variety of services to points across the continent. Railroads grew rapidly to become the predominant form of American transport in the nineteenth century because they offered greater speed, capacity, and efficiency than other modes of transportation. American railroads thrived as a result of the nation's underdeveloped road network and an intense desire for transport to interior points. Prior to the railroad, American commerce relied largely on waterways—coastal shipping, river navigation, and, to a limited degree, manmade canals—which reached most established population centers. Yet commerce beyond these corridors was slow, difficult, and costly. Railway construction faced a host of hurdles in its infancy, but once its advantages were clearly demonstrated, the mode was unstoppable and railway construction took off at an unprecedented rate. Thousands of railroad schemes were formulated and innumerable companies chartered. Some railroads were immediately successful.

▼ Using its domestically built *Best Friend of Charleston*, South 15, 1831. The locomotive was destroyed in a boiler explosion a few months later. At the 1939 New York World's Fair, Carolina Canal & Rail Road introduced America's first scheduled steam-hauled passenger service on January k World's Fair, a replica of the *Best Friend* is demonstrated alongside the *William Mason*, a 4-4-0 locomotive typical of the mid-nineteenth century. *H. W. Pontin photo, Solomon collection*

Others progressed slowly, while some faltered and many remained little more than stillborn visions. By the early twentieth century, railway lines connected virtually every population center in North America. Competitive interests produced numerous parallel schemes that vied for traffic. As a result, most major cities were served by two or more railway systems.

Most primary routes were in place by 1910, and while construction of new lines continued on a limited basis into the 1930s, the network reached its zenith in the 1920s. The growth of government-sponsored highways, combined with inexpensive petroleum, fostered automotive industries that eroded railway traffic. While railroads initially favored highway development, viewing improved local roads as feeders to their lines, the tide quickly changed, and as early as 1916 railroads were feeling the pinch of highway traffic. By the 1930s, highways had dramatically affected business. Highway competition, strict rate regulation, and inflexible labor arrangements caused the whole industry to stagnate and then contract. During this transition, railroads evolved from general-purpose transportation networks to primarily bulk-freight transport systems. As railroads became more specialized, they withdrew from public consciousness. Yet deregulation in the 1980s, combined with rising fuel prices and improvements to railroad technology, have facilitated a railroad renaissance for freight and, to a limited extent, passengers.

In the course of this 200-year history, railroads have undergone a multitude of changes, some subtle, some dramatic. Companies have come and gone, and most railroads operating today are the result of waves of mergers and consolidations, spin-offs, and reorganizations. Every railroad has a unique history, and while generalizations can be applied to the industry as a whole, to understand the particulars of an individual railroad, a careful examination of its background is necessary.

THE FORMATIVE YEARS

The railway originated in Britain. The technology evolved in the early nineteenth century, from simple animal-drawn tramways serving collieries and quarries to steam-powered common carriers. Steam locomotives developed from stationary pumping engines into efficient pulling machines. The opening of George Stephenson's Stockton & Darlington railway in 1825 established a prototype for most later railway development and quickly attracted the attention of American engineers and entrepreneurs. Stephenson further refined the railway concept with his Liverpool & Manchester line that opened in 1829. These early railways combined locomotive haulage with a fixed-railed tramway, connecting established population centers and carrying both people and freight on a scheduled basis for published rates.

Early railways sought improved efficiency. This sparked Liverpool & Manchester to hold a locomotive competition with a view toward producing more effective and more powerful locomotives. Interestingly, George Stephenson's son, Robert, produced the winning locomotive, a cleverly designed machine called the *Rocket* that attained a top speed of 29 miles per hour, extraordinarily fast at the time. Combining the three principal elements of a successful locomotive—a multi-tube (fire tube) boiler, forced draft from exhaust steam, and direct linkage between the piston and drive wheels—the *Rocket* rendered all other designs obsolete and set the pattern for most future steam locomotive designs, not just in Britain, but in the United States and around the world.

The classic 4-4-0 wheel arrangement was by far the most common in North America in the second half of the nineteenth century, with many railroads continuing to use them well into the twentieth century. While the wheel arrangement was standard, there was considerable variation in other elements of 4-4-0 design. The *America*, pictured here (later Monon's No. 109), was an experimental type with an unusual Coventry boiler. *Solomon collection*

The tracks were barely in place on the Stockton & Darlington when the concept was exported to the United States. America was ripe for railway development. Prior to the British pioneers, American visionaries had been agitating for railways. As in Britain, the first American lines were industrial tramways. In Quincy, Massachusetts, Gridley Bryant built a 3-mile line to move granite from a quarry to a pier, while in Pennsylvania, coal-hauling tramways were built to move mine products to canal heads.

Most significant of the early lines was Delaware & Hudson (D&H), which as early as 1825 had considered a railway to augment its canal. D&H planned to move anthracite coal from mines at Carbondale, Pennsylvania, to New York City. In January 1828, the company's chief engineer, John B. Jervis, dispatched engineer Horatio Allen to Britain to learn about railway practice and to purchase both iron rails and complete locomotives for import to the United States. As built, D&H's 17-mile-long railway connected Carbondale with the canal head at Honesdale, Pennsylvania, using a mix of level sections, where coal wagons were horse-drawn, and steeply inclined planes that were hauled by cables drawn by stationary engines. History was made on August 8, 1829, when Allen fired up Foster, Rastrick & Company's *Stourbridge Lion* at Honesdale and operated it over 3 miles, making it the first commercially built steam locomotive operated in the United States. Unfortunately, this test demonstrated that the locomotives were too heavy for day-to-day operation and so they were never used as intended. D&H would later grow into a full railway, while its early achievements established important precedents in the United States and provided a learning ground for railway engineers. Both Jervis and Allen moved on to build and operate many of America's early successful railways.

While D&H began as commodity-specific industrial line, other early American railway plans embraced bolder concepts. In 1825, completion and opening of New York's famed Erie Canal fuelled fierce rivalry between East Coast ports. The canal bridged the gap between the navigable waters of the Hudson River and the Great Lakes, thus allowing New York City to become the gateway to the American interior and the nation's premier port. Other port cities reacted by proposing a host of similar transport schemes. New York was blessed with a low crossing of the Appalachian range via the Mohawk River Valley, facilitating canal construction, while other states faced difficult mountain crossings. Baltimore was among the ports threatened by New York. On February 28, 1827, the Baltimore & Ohio Rail Road (later shortened to the more modern "Railroad") was granted a charter to connect the city of Baltimore with the Ohio River. It was among the most ambitious transport schemes ever considered. Railroad construction across a mountain range hadn't been previously attempted. The Baltimore & Ohio (B&O) route through the Appalachians was purely conceptual; its line hadn't yet been surveyed, nor had B&O's proponents ever seen a railroad. Following D&H's lead, B&O looked to learn railroading from those who invented it. The company dispatched a team of engineers to Britain to meet with the Stephensons and other early railway engineers. They inspected railways and learned the required know-how. B&O completed its first 13 miles by May 1830. Using horse-drawn rail carriages, it inaugurated scheduled passenger services to the village of Ellicott Mills. A successful New York glue maker named Peter Cooper demonstrated a diminutive, experimental, domestically built locomotive on the B&O, and on August 28, 1830, he successfully hauled 13 tons at 4 miles per hour. Cooper's design was derived from marine practice. While it inspired a generation of homegrown American locomotive technology, ultimately machines derived from Stephenson's *Rocket* prevailed among U.S. locomotive builders. Of these, one of the earliest and ultimately the largest was Philadelphia-based Baldwin, which began production in 1833 and continued until the 1950s.

Once early lines demonstrated the possibilities and benefits of railroad transport, the concept expanded rapidly. America was ripe for industrial development, and the railroad proved the ideal vehicle with which to connect the nation. Meanwhile, the locomotives, carriages, and track developed in Britain was refined and adapted to suit American applications. From this formative time on, American technologies followed their own developmental path.

SHORT LINES TO TRUNK LINES

While a few early railroads, such as the B&O and New York's Erie Railroad, projected relatively long lines, most embraced modest ambitions at first, often running less than 100 miles between established population centers. For example, the Boston & Lowell, which was chartered in 1831, connected its namesakes by 1835. As railroads extended across the landscape, smaller companies consolidated into ever larger ones. A classic example is the string of short railroads that formed links in a chain spanning central New York from Albany to Buffalo, running roughly parallel to the Erie Canal. Initially, passengers had to change trains at each interface between lines, and in some places railroads didn't even have adjacent stations, let alone through-track connections. Gradually, these railroads moved toward greater cooperation, first by coordinating services and then by running through trains. In 1853, they finally consolidated into the original New York Central (NYC).

Through lines between major cities commanded ever-greater volumes of traffic. Increased business led to development of powerful trunk routes that vied fiercely for traffic on major corridors. The most important were the four principal east–west trunks between East Coast cities and Chicago. In the 1860s, NYC came under control of steamboat mogul and self-made millionaire Cornelius Vanderbilt, who combined NYC with New York–Albany routes, while securing connections west to Chicago. Erie Railroad, after eluding Vanderbilt's control, gradually extended west to Chicago, while B&O and Philadelphia-based Pennsylvania Railroad (PRR) extended their reaches to

Chicago and other midwestern gateways. Although it was the last of the big trunks to get started, during the mid-nineteenth century PRR rapidly emerged as America's most powerful railroad company, followed closely by the Vanderbilt network. As PRR and NYC vied for territory and control of lines, they largely defined industrial development in the eastern states.

Midwestern railway development was only a decade behind that on the Eastern seaboard. By the late 1830s, a variety of lines were underway west of the Appalachians. The mountains limited railway growth because of the difficult construction required, but midwestern railways spread out across the prairies and plains unchecked. Here, limitations on railway construction were large rivers and the Great Lakes, which not only imposed physical boundaries but also served as the railroad's primary competition.

Among the characteristics of midwestern railways' growth was the parallel linking of principal traffic gateways. Logically, railways connected inland ports such as Cincinnati, Louisville, St. Louis, and Memphis, where the transfer of goods and passengers from one mode to another was well-established. Although lines reached established gateways, they also created new gateways.

The greatest railway gateway was (and still is) Chicago. Yet prior to the advent of the railroad, this city was little more than an obscure outpost. Ideally situated on the southwestern shore of Lake Michigan, Chicago facilitated transfer from railways to Great Lakes ships, while its vast and largely level landmass was well-suited for railway yards and industry. Chicago's first line was Chicago & North Western predecessor Galena & Chicago Union, chartered in 1836. By the 1850s, Chicago had emerged as the premier meeting point between lines coming from the east and those pushing west. By 1900, many of America's largest railroads had reached Chicago. It was the nation's premier point for interchange and one of the nation's largest cities. Railroad development had defined its urban growth. Only a handful of railroads passed through Chicago; most terminated there. By serving as a transportation hub, Chicago attracted numerous industries that stood to benefit from superior rail service, including railway suppliers.

Most gateway cities offered similar advantages. St. Louis, Kansas City, the Twin Cities of Minneapolis and St. Paul, Omaha–Council Bluffs, Memphis, and New Orleans all developed as important east–west gateways, where multiple lines connected to interchange cars and passengers.

GAUGE ISSUES

George Stephenson established the 4-foot-8½-inch track gauge as the British standard. Why such an unusual measurement? It was derived from a standard mine cart gauge that measured 5 feet between the outside faces of the two rails. In the railway's earliest days the wheel flange was changed from the outside to the inside of the rails, where the measurement between faces was 4 feet, 8½ inches. American engineers imported this standard, and many of the earliest U.S. lines adopted the British gauge as their own. Other track widths were also adopted; however, in the early days there was no universal standard, which led to incompatibilities. Regional preferences complicated matters: lines in the South tended to adopt 5-foot gauge, while some communities and states imposed nonstandard gauge restrictions in an effort to fend off competition from other regions' lines. A few railroads found the Stephenson gauge prohibitively narrow, believing that a

After 1870, narrow gauge lines were pushed to many areas where railroad construction was previously cost-prohibitive. While Colorado's narrow gauge lines were the most famous, narrow gauge routes were constructed across North America. The 3-foot gauge East Tennessee & Western North Carolina—known as the "Tweetsie"—is seen traversing Tennessee's scenic Doe River gorge circa 1910. *Photographer unknown, Solomon collection*

broader gauge would allow for construction of larger locomotives and cars. Proponents of New York's Erie Railroad adopted 6-foot gauge, and many of Erie's feeder lines, such as Delaware, Lackawanna & Western, built to broad gauge. Several systems adopted the 5-foot-6-inch gauge, including Maine's Atlantic & St. Lawrence, which became part of Canada's Grand Trunk System, and the Louisville & Nashville.

The folly of gauge incompatibility became unsustainable as railroads grew into a network and became less focused on the specifics of local transport. The ability to interchange cars easily and provide through services soon greatly outweighed any benefits offered by nonstandard gauges. Southern railroads, in particular, had suffered from myriad gauge problems and a general lack of network connectivity. As a result, these lines were less effective during the American Civil War.

After the war, most railroads reconciled their gauges, and by 1880, the American railroad network had largely adopted the 4-foot-8½-inch gauge. Yet, significant exceptions remained. Beginning around 1870, narrow gauge railways caught interest. Using much narrower tracks and smaller equipment, narrow gauge railways cost less to build and operate, and thus allowed the construction of lines to many places where railways were previously deemed cost-prohibitive. During the next two decades, lightweight narrow gauge lines sprouted across America like mushrooms after a rain. Most prominent were the mountain lines in Colorado, New Mexico, and Utah, of which the 3-foot-gauge Denver & Rio Grande Western was the first, the most extensive, and the longest lived. Meanwhile, 2-foot-gauge lines were constructed in Maine to tap timber and other natural resources, while specialized narrow gauge lines were built across Appalachia, the Midwest, and California. The narrow gauge moment cooled following the turn of the twentieth century, and many railroads built as slim gauge were either converted to standard gauge or abandoned. A few narrow gauge operations survived as common carriers into the mid-twentieth century, including selected Colorado lines, Pennsylvania's East Broad Top, and lines in California.

A locomotive trailing two cars crosses a wooden trestle during construction of the transcontinental railroad in 1866. *Otto Herschan/Getty Images*

TRANSCONTINENTAL AMBITIONS

As the railroad mode gained a toehold in America, men with vision anticipated railways spanning the continent to the Pacific. In 1852, Secretary of War Jefferson Davis was charged by Congress with employing the army to locate the best route for a railroad to the Pacific, thus facilitating surveys across the West. Yet, the real progress toward a transcontinental railroad was fuelled by Civil War politics and a desire to link California to the rest of the nation.

Homegrown efforts in California, led by Theodore D. Judah, greatly contributed to the construction of America's pioneer transcon. Judah engineered the Sacramento Valley Railroad, a 23-mile line reaching from Sacramento into the Sierra foothills. His vision of a railroad east over the spine of the Sierra overcame skepticism and financial impediments. He selected Donner Pass as the best crossing and surveyed much of the route himself. More important, he drafted the original Central Pacific charter and in 1861 convinced four successful Sacramento business owners—Collis P. Huntington, Leland Stanford, Charles Crocker, and Mark Hopkins (popularly known as the Big Four)—to support the railroad. Judah personally lobbied Congress and the president and helped draft the Pacific Railroad Act that authorized the building of the transcontinental railroad. In July 1862, President Abraham Lincoln signed the Pacific Railroad Act, which provided both federal land grants and cash to the Union Pacific (UP) and Central Pacific (CP) railroads to help fund transcontinental construction. Central Pacific laid the first rails eastward in late 1863. UP would build west from Council Bluffs, Nebraska.

The term *transcontinental* requires qualification. The UP–CP line only spanned about half the continent, yet it offered the necessary link to eastern railroads that connected the East to the largely unsettled expanse of the American West. It was this unsettled land that had posed the greatest hurdle. Most American railroad construction had been financed privately. Typically, short railroads that tapped local traffic had been able to sustain railroad construction. The West had lots of untapped potential but lacked population (or traffic) between the Missouri River and the Pacific, making construction difficult to finance. This is where government land grants and cash incentives made the difference, although some observers feared contractors would build railroads strictly for the land grants without any intent to operate. After six years of construction, however, and considerable squabbling among the parties involved, Union Pacific and Central Pacific joined west of Salt Lake City at Promontory, Utah, on May 10, 1869. A golden spike symbolically marked completion and a telegraph clicked to let the world know the link had been made. Yet, this first "transcontinental" was far from finished.

In its original configuration, the line reached only as far west as Sacramento; a boat journey was still needed to reach the Golden Gate. More significantly, UP and CP both aimed at a securing the largest portion of grant moneys possible with little consideration for the quality of construction. As built, their railway line was in poor shape, and years passed before it was up to the standards of main lines in the eastern United States. Also, while the transcontinental railway had enormous symbolic importance, and effectively cut travel time to the Pacific from weeks to just a few days, it took years for significant volumes of transcontinental traffic to develop.

Yet, the Golden Spike spurred a flurry of development. The Big Four refocused their efforts toward securing feeders for their system and built, bought, and leased virtually every railway project in their territory. Their aims were rarely transparent, and it often appeared that they looked to maintain a complete monopoly on transcontinental traffic. However, during the next 50 years, a variety of transcontinental routes were completed, linking the West with lines in the East. In addition, crucial links were constructed across Canada and Mexico.

GIANT NETWORKS

By 1900, although hundreds of railroad companies operated across North America, most major railroads were grouped into just a few powerful systems. Methods of control were complex and varied; some systems were highly leveraged, others involved tight personal or familial connections, or convoluted networks of subsidiaries, leases, and other business affiliations.

◀ In its heyday, railroad transport was almost universal, with trains serving most American communities. In this view, probably made in the 1880s, wooden boxcars lettered for New York, Ontario & Western and Rome, Watertown & Ogdensburg are spotted in a pastoral village in central New York State. Boxcars carried virtually every kind of general freight, from grain to merchandise. *Solomon collection*

Pennsylvania Railroad and New York Central System dominated the East. In the West, Edward H. Harriman controlled the Union Pacific, Southern Pacific, and Illinois Central systems. James J. Hill, who had pushed his Great Northern to the Pacific using largely private capital, moved to control Northern Pacific (NP) and Chicago, Burlington & Quincy (CB&Q). Meanwhile, George Gould, the playboy railroad magnate, inherited a network of lines from his shrewd empire-building father, Jay Gould, and set about assembling a true transcontinental system that he hoped would connect Baltimore and San Francisco.

Yet the growing importance of commercial transportation, combined with fears of power abuse (real and imagined) by large corporations, led to a public backlash against big businesses and a growth in government regulation and involvement in railroad affairs. Efforts to impose rate regulation began in the 1870s. The Interstate Commerce Act of 1887 created the Interstate Commerce Commission (ICC), Congress' first step in regulating railroads nationally. Yet in its early form, the ICC wasn't sufficiently empowered. The clashes between Hill and Harriman in the West spurred some of the most significant changes to affect the industry, including the Elkins Act of 1903 and the Hepburn Act of 1906. These and court actions forever changed the railroad playing field.

Harriman had tried to wrest control of NP and CB&Q from Hill by quietly buying large stakes in NP. In November 1901, to fend off Harriman, Hill created an enormous holding company called Northern Securities, putting GN, NP, and CB&Q under common management. This consolidation was too radical for the time and alarmed many important people. Not only did Northern Securities represent the largest railroad consolidation in the United States, but it appeared Hill and Harriman had formed a stranglehold on western railroading, as Harriman and his bankers were significant stockholders in NP. About the time Northern Securities was formed, the public's opinion of big business had reached an all-time low. The tide changed against the railroads when President William McKinley was assassinated and his progressive vice president, Theodore Roosevelt, took charge. Among Roosevelt's first actions as president was to press a case against Hill's Northern Securities. Over the next few years it worked its way through the courts, and in 1904, the U.S. Supreme Court ruled that Northern Securities was in violation of the Sherman Antitrust Act and must be broken up. While Hill's lines could retain a familial relationship, merger was out of the question. The decision set the tone for further actions over the next dozen years. Harriman's Union Pacific and Southern Pacific were separated, and numerous other railroad affiliations across the country were either broken up by court action or voluntarily severed. Among other changes brought about by regulation was the separation of railroads and industries with which they had been closely linked. This forced coal railroads to sell off mines and coal-yielding lands.

On one hand, regulation hindered the ability of some railroads to do business; on the other it fostered railroads in other areas. Ultimately, though, regulatory changes would contribute to the end of the railroad's North American dominance.

STAGNATION AND DECLINE

Antitrust actions and government regulation, combined with large public investment in paved intercity highways and the dramatic rise in the cost of labor during World War I, hit American railroads hard. A long period of stagnation and decline began in the early decades of the twentieth century. While the resulting changes were significant and may seem obvious in retrospect, the results of decline took years to be fully appreciated. Railroads had been viewed with mistrust, but immediate changes were largely imperceptible to observers. So, despite the beginnings of a modal shift, through the 1920s, mainline traffic continued to rise; railroads generally carried more, yet lost market share to highways.

Significantly, railroads lost the ability to make necessary changes to their essential route structure. New construction had become cost-prohibitive in all but exceptional circumstances. Few new lines were built after World War I, and in general the North American railroad network remained as a legacy of nineteenth-century transportation needs. As the economy changed, railroads suffered from the inability to react. There were a few exceptions, but in general the industry became increasingly ill-equipped to adapt.

One episode that had profound implications was the United States Railroad Administration's (USRA) control of the industry during World War I. At the time railroads were suffering from intolerable congestion, partially a result of dramatic traffic increases during the war. However, inherent operational inefficiencies had been complicated by the recent financial burdens imposed by regulation. In an effort to make American railroads more fluid, the USRA took control at the end of 1917 and gained additional powers in early 1918. Under William G. McAdoo, the USRA aimed to increase efficiency while minimizing problems caused by unconstructive competition and incompatibility, a result of fiercely individualistic practices. Among the USRA's contributions was the development of a family of standardized steam locomotives and the integration of key portions of the railroad network. The railroads were returned to private control in March 1920. While the USRA was nominally successful, it left a legacy of distrust in government intervention in railroad affairs and a general ambivalence toward cooperation with government-sponsored initiatives.

Rate regulation, rising labor costs, and highway competition hit branch lines first. As early as 1910, railroads began seeking means to cut branch-line costs. By 1920, railroads began to trim and consolidate branch networks. The more serious implications of the railroad's loss of status became evident with the onset of the Great Depression. As industrial output declined, and individual personal income shrank, railroad traffic evaporated. Many big railroads declared bankruptcy and required reorganization. A few smaller railroads quit running altogether. During the Depression, railroads were incapable of adequately investing in their lines, locomotives, or facilities. In rare instances, improvements were facilitated through government loans or grants, such as Pennsylvania Railroad's mainline electrification between New York and Washington, D.C., but most railroads were reluctant to consider public money as a means of improvement. By the late 1930s, as conflict began to heat up in Europe, railroad traffic was again on the rise. The United States entered World War II after the attack on Pearl Harbor in December 1941, and freight and passenger traffic blossomed to levels never before experienced on American lines.

RENAISSANCE, CONSOLIDATION, AND REFORM

For a few years, wartime fuel rationing and an enormous demand for transport flooded American lines with traffic. Passenger traffic increased fourfold from 1940 to 1944, exceeding even pre-Depression levels. Freight reached a modern high-water mark in 1943 when railroads claimed a 73 percent market share. In 1944, the industry broke all previous records for freight moved. Riding high on these wartime gains, the railroad industry hoped to retain high traffic levels after the war. Nationwide, railroads invested heavily in new diesel-electric locomotives, largely to replace tired fleets of pre-Depression steam locomotives, improve efficiency, and reduce labor costs. Lines installed miles of Centralized Traffic Control to speed operations and reduce the number of people involved in the control of train movements.

Many lines remained committed to the long-distance passenger business and, based on the success of prewar streamlined trains and heavy wartime travel, invested in fleets of new diesel streamliners. By the mid-1950s, the steam locomotive was nearly finished, yet railroads were suffering from rapidly declining traffic. While some western lines remained healthy, lines in the East, particularly those wedded to the movement of anthracite coal and old smokestack industries, were in deep trouble. Plans for consolidation, which had been considered in the 1920s, were reconsidered and revised. With increased highway competition and declining traffic, railroads viewed mergers as the best means to lower operating costs, minimize interline rivalries and competition, and consolidate redundant routes and infrastructure. So-called end-to-end mergers were thought to allow lines to simplify interchange and eliminate yards (and associated costs), while it was hoped that parallel mergers would eliminate redundant routes and facilities, as well as wasteful competition.

The Interstate Commerce Commission oversaw the merger process, but it didn't always agree with merger proposals and often prevented some combinations and imposed difficult conditions on others. Despite complications and impediments, modern railroad systems began to coalesce, resulting in new railway combinations and the disappearance of many familiar names. Some combinations, such as the 1964 merger of Norfolk & Western, Nickel Plate Road, and Wabash, produced strong railroads. Others were not so successful, and some were disastrous. In 1968, after more than a decade of discussions, America's

▶ Often called America's railroad capital, Chicago is the United States' premier railroad interchange. Here, eastern railroads meet those from the West. Unusual among railroads that have plied Chicago rails was the Wabash, which ran from Buffalo and Detroit to St. Louis and Kansas City, and was one of the few lines running *through* this busy gateway rather than simply terminating there. On July 21, 1958, Wabash E8A No. 1000 rolls beneath a New York Central E7A/E8A pair, as two Rock Island diesels wait in a yard on the left. *Richard Jay Solomon*

two eastern giants, Pennsylvania Railroad and New York Central, merged to form Penn Central. The move was viewed through rose-colored glasses as a panacea to the railroads' problems, but in practice it failed and introduced new difficulties to an already untenable situation. Penn Central's planners failed to prepare adequately for the practicalities of merger on the most basic levels. Incompatibilities between the railroads stemming from more than a century of fiercely competitive practices were not easily glossed over. Complicating matters were employee loyalties that resulted in management conflicts and a lack of cooperation. Adding to Penn Central's woes, it had been forced by the ICC to absorb the chronically weak New Haven Railroad, which suffered from high terminal costs, a worn-out physical plant, and an extraordinarily high passenger deficit.

As Congress considered ways to relieve Penn Central of its long-distance passenger burden, the company declared bankruptcy on June 21, 1970. It was the largest bankruptcy ever. Other northeastern lines already on the brink of financial collapse followed suit. Worse, other railroads had preceded Penn Central into bankruptcy. Central Railroad of New Jersey (CNJ), for example, once a rich anthracite line, had been in terminal decline since the loss of its coal traffic and other key business. The Penn Central bankruptcy seemed to signal an end of days; railroading across the Northeast had ceased functioning as a profitable business. Yet, despite waves of bankruptcies and the inability of railroads to make basic investments in their lines, freight traffic remained strong in some areas.

In the late 1960s, Congress and the newly created U.S. Department of Transportation (USDOT) began developing a government solution to passenger-rail problems. There were two distinct challenges: relieve the railroads of their passenger burden as quickly and as painlessly as possible, and preserve a core passenger-rail network by curbing the decline in ridership. In January 1970, USDOT announced Railpax, a plan to develop a quasi-public corporation to run a national intercity passenger network. Penn Central's collapse in June accelerated the need for a solution. Congress acted and on October 29, 1970, President Richard Nixon signed the Rail Passenger Service Act, creating the National Railroad Passenger Corporation, better known by its trade name: Amtrak. When Amtrak came into existence on May 1, 1971, it assumed operation of most intercity passenger services. Yet, in the process, America lost about half of its remaining intercity passenger route miles. Railroads had the option to join, and not all railroads joined Amtrak right away. The last of the classic, privately operated American trains was Rio Grande's Denver–Salt Lake City *Rio Grande Zephyr*, which made its final runs in 1983.

During the 1970s and early 1980s, suburban passenger services, some of which had received a degree of public funding since the late 1950s, gradually made the transition from services provided by private railroad companies to services funded, subsidized, and operated by public agencies, such as Boston's Massachusetts Bay Transportation Authority and New York City–based Metro-North.

CONRAIL, DEREGULATION, AND NEW RAILWAYS

Amtrak didn't solve Penn Central's woes, and eastern freight railroading was still in deep trouble, so Congress created the Consolidated Rail Corporation (Conrail) to bail out the ailing eastern freight industry. In addition to Penn Central, operations of CNJ, Erie Lackawanna, Lehigh & Hudson River, Lehigh Valley, Reading Company, and some smaller lines were melded into Conrail on April 1, 1976. Planning had taken several years, and many routes were not included in Conrail's operation; some lines were abandoned, others sold. Lightly used branches were hacked mercilessly from the network. The creation of Conrail, and its subsequent pruning, completely changed the northeastern route map.

In the mid-1970s, fundamental problems continued to plague freight railroading. In addition to Conrail, several midwestern carriers were also in serious financial trouble, notably the Chicago, Rock Island & Pacific (Rock Island), and Chicago, Milwaukee, St. Paul & Pacific (Milwaukee Road). In 1980, Rock Island was liquidated, while Milwaukee Road reorganized and was drastically trimmed back.

To address the railroads' problems as well as other transportation issues, legislation in the late 1970s, culminating with the Staggers Act of 1980, aimed to deregulate the transportation industry and make railroading profitable again. One of the key provisions of Staggers was the dismantling of rigid rate regulation that had saddled railroads for decades. In fact, Staggers spurred many changes to American railroading. While it opened railroads to innovation, it also brought about an end to the structure that had supported many traditional companies. Some railroads that had subsisted on bridge traffic (cars they neither originated nor terminated, but carried from one gateway to the next) saw their traffic dry up overnight.

The effects of deregulation were widespread. Railroads were forced to reduce labor costs, resulting in dramatic changes to crewing agreements. Freight crews went from five and six men in the mid-1970s to just two or three by the early 1990s, while crew districts were greatly lengthened and craft distinctions liberalized. Many railroads shed unprofitable and marginally profitable lines, resulting in the creation of hundreds of new short lines and regional railroads. Conrail was among the lines that actively fostered short-line feeders, acknowledging that small, locally owned and managed railroads with lower labor costs were in a better position to develop traffic. Other companies trimmed secondary main lines to form significant regional systems. Illinois Central Gulf carved up much of its network and sold off most routes outside of its principle north-south corridor.

More significant was the new wave of mergers that began in 1980 with Burlington Northern's acquisition of Frisco and the melding of the Seaboard Coast Line railroads and Chessie System into the gigantic CSX. In response, Norfolk & Western and Southern Railway merged in 1982 to form Norfolk Southern, and Union Pacific swelled to include Western Pacific in 1981, Missouri Pacific in 1982, Missouri-Kansas-Texas in 1988, Chicago & North Western in 1995, and the Southern Pacific system in 1996. Canadian lines bought up railroads in the United States, while spinning off marginal lines in Canada. In 1995, Santa Fe and Burlington Northern merged to form Burlington Northern Santa Fe (later shortened to BNSF Railway). Conrail, which had struggled through the 1970s, flourished in the 1980s and early 1990s, but in 1996–1997, CSX and Norfolk Southern agreed to divide between them the much slimmed-down and profitable Conrail network.

During the 1990s, short lines were gobbled up by railroad companies specializing in short-line management. Traditional short lines such as New York's Genesee &

▼ Chicago, Rock Island & Pacific, or the Rock Island Line, was among the best-known names in American railroading. In the 1970s, as its visions of merging with Union Pacific evaporated, its physical plant deteriorated. In 1980, it gave up the ghost. Many of its routes were sold to other lines, but the Rock was no more. Lines of dead locomotives are seen stored at the defunct railroad's Silvis, Illinois, shops. *Mike Abalos photo, courtesy Friends of Mike Abalos*

Wyoming grew into multinational railroad operators with dozens of railroad operations under their management, while other companies such as Rail America grew to control a variety of short and regional lines across the continent. Some of the regional systems created in the 1980s were reabsorbed by the largest railway systems during the 1990s and 2000s. Chicago, Central & Pacific, which had been spun off by Illinois Central Gulf in 1985, was bought back by Illinois Central (sans Gulf) in 1996. Illinois Central itself was absorbed by Canadian National in 1998. By 2008, most mainline freight railroading in North America was controlled by just six large networks: BNSF, Canadian National, Canadian Pacific, CSX, Norfolk Southern, and Union Pacific. Several significant regional systems remain, including a much expanded Kansas City Southern network, New England's Pan American Railways, and the historic Florida East Coast, while hundreds of short-line companies, dozens of suburban commuter agencies, and nostalgic tourist and preserved lines add variety to the North American network.

100 CONCISE PROFILES

The bulk of this book consists of 100 concise railway profiles arranged alphabetically. This includes a variety of historic and contemporary railroad companies spanning the range of short-line, regional, and Class 1 lines, as well as a few preserved railways with historical connections. By design, the format for the profiles is limited to cover the railroads in two-, four-, and six-page spreads intended to provide each line's essential history, illustrated with sidebars listing key facts, and a few iconic images. These are intended to both provide vital facts while conveying the character of the railroad profiled.

Many of the railroads profiled were historic Class 1 mainline carriers that were absorbed by merger decades ago (e.g., the Erie Railroad, Northern Pacific, and Western Pacific). Others are more contemporary operations, including all of the "Super Six" freight railroads, various modern-day regional and short lines, and Amtrak. Although this is a big book, space limitations have not allowed for a complete listing of North American railways. A great many modern short lines have been left out. Furthermore, it would have been impossible to give justice to many of the small classic railways listed in the traditional *Official Guide of the Railways*, a book that in 1946 consisted of 1,440 pages and listed more than 1,200 transportation companies and affiliates, ranging from North Carolina's Aberdeen & Rockfish Railroad to Arizona's Yuma Valley Railroad. Among lines not included were strictly industrial railroads, most nineteenth-century antecedents of twentieth-century systems, paper railroads, and the majority of modern suburban commuter rail operators, such as Chicago's Metra and San Francisco–based Cal-Train. Each of these categories could easily fill their own volumes.

Regarding the statistics provided for railroad locomotives fleets, working from the most reliable data available to me, I selected fleet statistics that I felt best represented individual railroads at relevant times in their histories. With many railroads, I selected a steam figure from a time prior to wide-scale dieselization, yet near the zenith of steam operations, often in the late 1920s. In many situations, a figure from the World War I era may have yielded a larger number of steam locomotives. However, because the steam locomotive was still being refined during this period, a great many locomotives at the time had been built to older standards, lacked important innovations such as superheating, and were built with smaller wheel arrangements, which required more locomotives to compensate for lower efficiency. By the late 1920s, many railroads had displaced large numbers of antique steam locomotives with more modern machines, resulting in slightly smaller, but more efficient, fleets. While steam continued to be refined during the 1930s, fleet sizes were much reduced during the Great Depression.

In regard to diesels, depending on the railroad, I provided a figure from one of several periods: shortly after complete dieselization (typically in the late 1950s), at the end of the railroad's independence prior to being absorbed by merger, or a contemporary total if the railroad remains in operation today. In some circumstances I felt it was beneficial to show more than one year's diesel fleet, where mergers or dramatic changes in operation and improvements to technology resulted in significantly different numbers. In many instances, I chose to represent a period during the steam-to-diesel transition (in the early 1950s) to give a sense of the fleet changes during this critical time. On railroads that operated electrified lines, I've also listed electric equipment, including electric locomotives (described as "motors" on many lines) and multiple-units (self-propelled passenger cars). On a few lines, I've also listed self-propelled gas-electric and rail diesel cars.

Regarding mileage, I've likewise selected significant periods in each railroad's history. For the classic railroads, I've provided one or more of the following: pre-Depression mileage, post–World War II mileage, a listing from near the end of independent operations, or a contemporary figure. In each case, I've tried to select figures that would best represent individual railroads, but I've not necessarily chosen peak mileage figures, since these were often short-lived and not necessarily representative of a railroad over a longer period of operation. In a few situations, such as Illinois Central, I've shown figures that illustrate the effects of growth as result of mergers or line reductions.

In regard to the sidebar listings "major cities served," many are historic railroad gateways, key to interchange and operations; in some instances railroads served cities without actually entering traditional city limits. In a railroad context, cities such as Buffalo, Chicago, Cincinnati, and St. Louis consist of the greater metropolitan area, and there should be an understanding that some railroads had or have yards in suburbs beyond the city limits. In the case of Kansas City, references are to the railroad gateway that

encompasses adjacent cities of that name in both Kansas and Missouri. Where space allows, clarification and details are provided. Yet, simplification is necessary, because to fully elucidate details and particulars of American railroading would often require far more space than allotted for each railroad entry. This is especially true regarding railroad terminal arrangements where the degrees of complexity are well beyond the scope of this book.

Readers should also be aware that many railroad names can be deceiving. Historic lines often included places well beyond their service areas. The Chicago, Rock Island & Pacific never reached farther west than Texas or Colorado; Spokane, Portland & Seattle only directly served the first two of its namesake cities; and the Belfast & Moosehead Lake's ambitions were never fully realized. Other names draw references that made sense in their time period but may seem confusing today. The Delaware, Lackawanna & Western referred to the Delaware River, and not the state, while the Seaboard Air Line existed many years before the first airplane and decades before commercial aviation (its name used the term *air line* when this was loosely synonymous with *tangent*).

The railroad industry is continually changing. Some railroads that have existed for decades may disappear as result of mergers, while other traditional names, long erased from the map, may be revived. It is for this reason that this book should be a valued resource and can serve as a guide to railroads past, present, and future.

ALASKA RAILROAD

The Alaska Railroad is an unusual American railroad for a variety of reasons: (1) it is nearly entirely a twentieth-century construction; (2) where most American lines were built and operated by private companies, much of the line was built by the federal government and federally operated until 1985, when the state of Alaska bought the operation; (3) the route is isolated from the rest of the North American network, relying on ships to ferry cars to and from its system; (4) the line still operates its own passenger service over most of its route mileage; and (5) as of 2011, it is the only line regularly to assign Electro-Motive SD70MACs to passenger trains.

▼ A pair of Alaska Railroad SD70MACs leads a northbound *Denali Star* across the Riley Creek trestle in Denali National Park, less than a mile from the park's scheduled station stop. *Scott R. Snell*

The antecedents of the ARR were privately funded lines, namely the 71-mile Alaska Northern that had built north from Seward and the narrow gauge Tanana Valley line. Both were taken over and melded into the federally sponsored ARR, which constructed more than 300 miles of line to connect Seward and Whittier with Fairbanks. President Warren G. Harding presided over the ceremony marking the line's completion in July 1923.

Today, the Alaska Railroad remains a vital freight and passenger artery. Passenger trains are popular with tourists and operate year-round on regular schedules. A more intensive service operates between May and September, and includes the *Denali Star* (Anchorage–Denali–Fairbanks) and *Glacier Discovery* (Anchorage–Whittier–Grandview) services.

ARR was noted for its late use of Electro-Motive E- and F-unit diesels, several of which are preserved in the lower 48 states.

Headquarters: Anchorage, AK
Years operated: 1914–present
Route mileage: 525 (c. 1997)
Locomotives
  Steam: 34 (c. 1950)
  Diesel: 54 (c. 1950); 60 (2005)
  Reporting mark: ARR
Emblem: Letters ARR in gold circle
Primary locomotive shop: Anchorage, AK
Notable feature: Mears Memorial Bridge (Tanana River, near Fairbanks), 700-ft. through-truss
Cities served: Anchorage and Fairbanks

▲ This timetable cover trumpeted Alaska's great outdoors and newly acquired statehood. *Solomon collection*

◀ Passenger timetable, 1961. *Solomon collection*

ALGOMA CENTRAL RAILWAY

Algoma Central Railway's name dates to 1899, but early on the name was changed to Algoma Central & Hudson Bay and then converted back in 1965. Construction began just after the turn of the twentieth century. From Sault Ste. Marie, Ontario, it reached northward 296 miles to Hearst, Ontario, arriving there in 1914. In addition, a 26-mile branch was extended from Hawk Junction (165 miles from Sault Ste. Marie) to Michipicoten. The railroad is believed to have been the first Canadian line to complete dieselization, achieving that feat in 1952, significantly ahead of the larger roads.

Unlike many of it counterparts south of the border, Algoma Central never gave up on its passenger trade. In addition to regularly scheduled all-stops passenger trains, during the 1960s it began to develop the tourist trade. This flourished in the 1970s, focused on daytrips between Sault St. Marie and the scenic Agawa Canyon, a 1.2 billion-year-old gash in the earth at AC's milepost 102.

▼ In June 1961, Algoma Central GP9 No. 165 leads a scheduled passenger train. Algoma Central was unusual in that it continued to order Electro-Motive GP9s several years after more powerful types had been in regular production. *Richard Jay Solomon*

Wisconsin Central acquired the line in 1995, operating it as a subsidiary and purchasing secondhand Electro-Motive F-units for Algoma's passenger services, while transferring many Algoma freight units south of the border to work in Wisconsin and Illinois. Algoma Central passed to Canadian National control in 2001 when CN acquired Wisconsin Central. In addition to freight services, the line continues to host triweekly passenger trains over the length of its mainline, as well as seasonal Agawa Canyon tour trains from Sault Ste. Marie.

Headquarters:
Sault Ste. Marie, ON
Years operated: 1899–1995
Disposition: Acquired by
Wisconsin Central (c. 1995),
which became part of
Canadian National (2001)
Route mileage: 322 (c. 1950)
Locomotives
Steam: 30 (c. 1950)
Diesel: 22 (c. 1990)
Reporting mark: ACIS
Emblem: Silhouette of
black bear encircled by
railroad name within
concentric circles
Notable feature:
Agawa Canyon

◀ System map, 1960.
Richard Jay Solomon collection

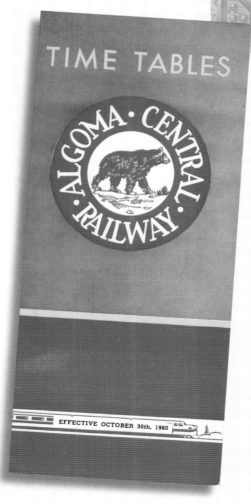

◀ Timetable, October 1960.
Richard Jay Solomon collection

AMTRAK

By the mid-1950s, American railroads concluded that unsubsidized passenger trains were no longer viable. The economics of operating trains had changed and as the country devoted more national resources to highway development, passenger trains had gone from marginally profitable to a drain on corporate resources. The Transportation Act of 1958 eased the process for dropping trains, and over the next decade most railroads drastically curtailed service. The downward spiral coincided with the growth of suburbia and highway culture, and the deterioration of traditional city centers and urban transit operations. The death knell for many trains came in 1967 when the U.S. Post Office did not renew most railroad mail contracts, historically a staple source of revenue for many intercity passenger trains. Without the mail revenue the trains were doomed.

▼ Amtrak began operations with a variety of equipment inherited from private railroads in 1971. On October 12, 1976, a pair of E8s roars west with train No. 63, *The Niagara Rainbow*, on the former New York Central Water Level Route at Yosts, New York. *George W. Kowanski*

Railroad woes went beyond the ailing passenger sector. By 1970, many railroad companies in the Northeast were teetering on insolvency. Penn Central was America's largest passenger carrier and in dire need of relief; to aid Penn Central and other railroads of intercity passenger obligations, Congress created the National Railroad Passenger Corporation (NRPC, subsequently known by the trade name Amtrak). Among other things, the act was designed "to provide financial assistance for and establishment of a national rail passenger system, to provide for the modernization of railroad passenger equipment, to authorize the prescribing of minimum standards for railroad passenger service." Railroads had the option of joining NRPC and providing it with cash, equipment, or the equivalent, or staying out of it. Those that opted out had to continue providing their own intercity passenger services.

▲ The 1970s and 1980s logo on the Rochester, New York, station. *Brian Solomon*

Initially, 17 railroads signed contracts with Amtrak. The names of most of those railroads have since been swept away by mergers. Today, Amtrak is among the oldest larger railroad companies in the United States continuously operating under the same name. In its early days, Amtrak neither owned any railway lines nor employed its own operating crews. Gradually this changed as Amtrak assumed responsibility for portions of its most important routes and in the 1980s began using its own train crews, though today many Amtrak trains still operate as tenants on freight railroads.

▲ With a top service speed of 150 miles per hour, Amtrak's custom-built high-speed trainsets in *Acela Express* service are the fastest trains in North America. One of the streamlined HSTs blitzes Old Saybrook, Connecticut, on the former New Haven Railroad. *Brian Solomon*

▶ Amtrak No. 5, the westward *California Zephyr* led by F40PH-2 No. 277, makes its station stop at Davis, California, on the former Southern Pacific in October 1989. The *CZ*, like most of Amtrak's long-distance services in the West, largely comprises bi-level *Superliner* cars, although this consist also features a former Santa Fe Budd-built car, identified by its slightly lower profile. *Brian Solomon*

Headquarters: Washington, D.C.

Years operated: 1971–present

Route mileage c. 1950: 19,366 (1971), 21,225 (2011)

Locomotives:

Diesel: 286 (1971 incl. railroad-owned locos) and 333 (2011)

Electric: 40 (1971, incl. railroad-owned locos) and 63 (2011)

Self-propelled: 1971 data inconclusive; 20 (2011)

Reporting marks: AMTK

Emblems: Traditionally red-and-blue "pointless arrow"; currently stylized shield comprising three vanishing bars and wordmark

Primary locomotive shops: New Haven, CT; Wilmington, DE; Beech Grove, IN; Rensselaer, NY

Notable features: B&P tunnels (Baltimore), 4,962 and 2,190 ft.; Hell Gate Bridge (New York City), 19,233 ft. long, 135 ft. high; Penn Station with East River and North River (Hudson) tunnels (New York City); Susquehanna River Bridge (Havre de Grace, MD); Union Station (Washington, D.C.); Zoo Junction (Philadelphia)

States and provinces served: Most of the continental U.S., except SD and WY, plus BC, ON, QC

Major cities served: Most in the continental U.S., plus Montreal, Toronto, Vancouver

Trains and Traffic

Flagship passenger train: *Acela Express* (Boston–New York–Philadelphia–Washington, D.C.)

Other name passenger trains: *Adirondack, Auto Train, California Zephyr, Capitol Limited, Capitols, Cardinal, Carolinian, Cascades, City of New Orleans, Coast Starlight, Crescent, Blue Water, Downeaster, Empire Builder, Ethan Allen Express, Heartland Flyer, Hiawatha Service, Hoosier State, Keystone, Lake Shore Limited, Maple Leaf, Missouri River Runner, Northeast Direct, Pacific Surfliner, Palmetto, Pennsylvanian, Pere Marquette, Piedmont, San Joaquin, Silver Star, Silver Meteor, Southwest Chief, Sunset Limited, Texas Eagle, The Carl Sandburg, The Illinois Zephyr, The Illini, The Saluki, Vermonter*

Notable freight commodities: Mail and express

▼ Eastern Corridor schedules, 1972. *Richard Jay Solomon collection*

▲ Detail of *Superliner* dining car on train No. 5 *California Zephyr* in October 1989. *Brian Solomon*

ATCHISON, TOPEKA & SANTA FE RAILWAY

Born out of a romantic dream to span the American West, the Atchison, Topeka & Santa Fe grew to be one of the great railway systems. It was the only traditional railway to connect Chicago directly with California. In steam days, the Santa Fe, as it was more commonly known, pursued unusual paths of development, driven largely by lack of online coal reserves, long stretches of desert running, and a desire to run both long, heavy freights and fast passenger trains.

As the twentieth century dawned, Santa Fe developed unusual wheel arrangements and novel technologies. It experimented with and refined oil-burning steam locomotives. For helper service over the 7,834-foot Raton Pass on the Colorado–New Mexico border, it developed the 2-10-2, christened the "Santa Fe type," which initially used the trailing truck to aid in long reverse moves. The need to conserve fuel and water led to a fanatical

▼ Santa Fe was the only freight railroad to order modern four-motor diesels with North American Safety Cabs. All were delivered in its famous "warbonnet" livery designed by Electro-Motive's Leland Knickerbocker in the 1930s for E-units built to haul the *Super Chief*. *Brian Solomon*

interest in compound designs, including curious Mallets with jointed boilers. Santa Fe even contemplated preposterous Quadruplex and Quinteplex articulated locomotives, which would have placed four and five sets of running gear under one throttle.

Late in the steam era, Santa Fe had some of the longest regular runs in the United States, with some engines working through from Kansas City to Los Angeles. Santa Fe's difficult operating territory and speed and power requirements led to pioneer applications of diesel-electric locomotives. It had the first big fleet of road freight diesels: Electro-Motive Division's acclaimed FT. A four-unit set of these powerful diesels accomplished what Santa Fe's fanciful steam designs had anticipated a generation earlier.

Santa Fe's mainline offered the fastest route to Los Angeles, and its fleet of luxury passenger trains was among the best known in the nation. In 1937, its Budd-built, General Motors diesel–hauled, streamlined *Super Chief* set a new standard for American long-distance passenger trains. The railroad operated a full schedule of long-distance passenger services longer than many lines, but joined Amtrak in 1971, nevertheless. It honed

▲ Santa Fe's streamlined *Super Chief* was the railroad's flagship passenger train and arguably one of the best-known American trains of the streamlined era. In this posed publicity photo, the *Super Chief* passes the Coconino National Forest near Flagstaff, Arizona. *Frank E. Meitz photo, Solomon collection*

Headquarters: Chicago, IL

Years operated: 1860–1995 (began as Atchison & Topeka)

Disposition: Merged with Burlington Northern (1995)

Route mileage: 13,074 (c. 1950); 8,359 (c. 1995)

Locomotives

Steam: 1,055 (c. 1950)

Diesel: 508 (c. 1950); 1,646 (c. 1995)

Gas-electric railcars: 41 (c. 1950)

Reporting mark: AT&SF

Emblem: Circle with cross

Trade name: Santa Fe Railway

Slogan: Santa Fe All the Way

Primary locomotive shops: Albuquerque, NM; Barstow, CA (diesel shop); Cleburne, TX; San Bernardino, CA; Topeka, KS

Notable features: Canyon Diablo Bridge (AZ), 542 ft. long, 222 ft. high; Colorado River Bridge (near Topock, CA), 1,506 ft. long; Mississippi River Bridge (Fort Madison, IA), 3,347 ft. long; Missouri River Bridge (Sibley, MO), 4,082 ft. long; Raton Pass tunnels, 2,041 and 2,789 ft.; Tunnel 1 (Franklin Canyon, CA), 5,596 ft.

States served: AZ, CA, CO, IL, IA, KS, LA, MO, NM, OK, TX

Major cities served: Chicago, Dallas/Ft. Worth, Denver, El Paso, Houston, Kansas City, Los Angeles, Phoenix, San Diego, San Francisco

▲ Santa Fe 2-10-4 No. 5001 leads a westward freight at Friona, Texas, on August 31, 1952. The dearth of coal on its far western lines, combined with ample supplies of cheap petroleum, encouraged Santa Fe to pioneer oil-fired steam locomotive designs. *John E. Pickett*

▲ A westward Santa Fe freight led by C30-7 No. 8140 winds around Southern Pacific's famed Tehachapi Loop at Walong, California, at 3:30 p.m. on June 18, 1984. Santa Fe was a tenant on SP's rugged Tehachapi crossing. *George W. Kowanski*

its transcontinental mainline into the nation's premier intermodal corridor, which contributed to its success in the modern era. In fact, Santa Fe was the only U.S. railroad to buy fleets of high-horsepower, four-motor Safety Cab locomotives for fast freight work.

By the mid-1990s, however, Santa Fe, which had been the country's longest traditional railroad in terms of route miles, was dwarfed as lines merged all around it. Its attempt to merge with Southern Pacific in the 1980s was denied by the Interstate Commerce Commission. In 1995, it succeeded in merging with the giant Burlington Northern system to form Burlington Northern Santa Fe, now BNSF Railway.

Flagship passenger train: *Super Chief* (Chicago–Los Angeles)

Other name passenger trains: *California Limited*, *Chief*, *El Capitan* (Chicago–Los Angeles); *Golden Gate* (Bakersfield–Oakland with Los Angeles and San Francisco bus connections); *San Diegan* (Los Angeles–San Diego); *San Francisco Chief* (Chicago–Oakland with San Francisco bus connection); *The Grand Canyon* (Chicago–Belen, NM–Los Angeles/Oakland with Grand Canyon connections); *The Kansas Cityan* (Chicago–Kansas City, MO); *The Scout* (Chicago–Los Angeles); *The Texas Chief* (Chicago–Tulsa/Ft. Worth–Galveston); *The Tulsan* (Chicago–Tulsa)

Notable freight commodities: Coal, grain, intermodal, general freight, perishables

Principal freight yards: Argentine (Kansas City), KS; Barstow, CA; Corwith (Chicago); Hobart (Los Angeles) and Richmond, CA

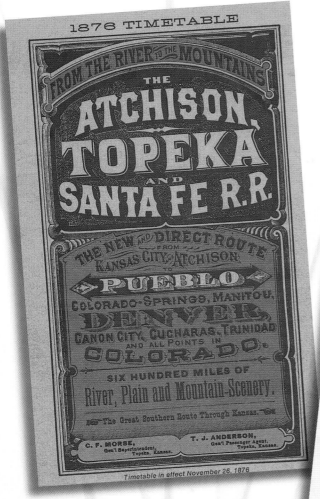

▲ Facsimile cover of 1876 timetable. *Voyageur Press collection*

▶ Public timetable, 1960. *Solomon collection*

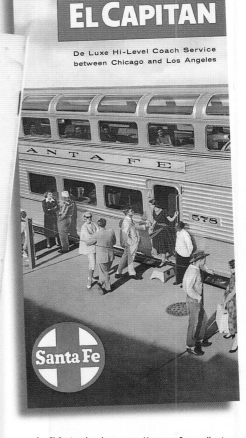

▲ *El Capitan* brochure, 1962. *Voyageur Press collection*

ATLANTIC COAST LINE

Following the Civil War, Atlantic Coast Line was among those southern railways developed by opportunistic northern capitalists. Initially connecting Richmond, Virginia, and Charleston, South Carolina, ACL comprised several significant components, including Virginia's Petersburg Railroad, chartered in 1830; North Carolina's Wilmington & Weldon Railroad; and the Wilmington & Manchester Railroad.

At its beginning in the 1870s, "Atlantic Coast Line" served strictly as a marketing name. Later, in 1893, under the direction of William T. Walters, the system was consolidated as the Atlantic Coast Line Company. In about 1900, it was renamed the Atlantic Coast Line Railroad Company and ran from Richmond to Charleston and Augusta, Georgia. In 1902, ACL absorbed Henry B. Plant's 2,100-mile railway system in Florida, Georgia, and South Carolina and acquired a majority interest in the Louisville & Nashville, although it didn't exercise direct control over the L&N. ACL continued to grow, adding the Birmingham & Atlantic in the 1920s and by World War II operated more than 5,300 route miles. Its primary routes benefited from low-grade profiles, although ACL's Charleston & Western Carolina subsidiary face tough grades on its run to Spartanburg, South Carolina (where it connected with Clinchfield, another ACL affiliate). Historically the railroad's corporate headquarters were located in Wilmington, North Carolina, but relocated to Jacksonville, Florida in 1960.

▼ A Budd-built buffet-lounge-observation car was photographed on the back of the Chicago–Miami *South Wind* at Louisville, Kentucky, in 1942. ACL was an important link for Florida-bound passenger trains from both the East Coast and Midwest. *H. R. Blackburn photo, Jay Williams collection*

▲ Considering the large numbers of long-distance passenger trains that ACL moved, it should be no small surprise that the railroad had 345 of the common Pacific type on its roster by the end of 1926. This P5a Pacific was photographed at Emporia, Virginia. *R. W. Legg photo, Bob Buck collection*

ACL developed Florida vacation traffic and was a key south–north corridor for perishable traffic carried in insulated boxcars called reefers from southern citrus groves. Richmond, Virginia, became ACL's most important interchange point. Much of ACL's freight and passenger traffic was forwarded from Richmond over the Richmond, Fredericksburg & Potomac, of which ACL was a part owner. ACL double-tracked much of its Richmond–Jacksonville route to accommodate fast freight and relatively dense passenger traffic. It was early to equip the line with automatic block signals to increase capacity and improved safety. Following World War II, ACL invested in Centralized Traffic Control and modern diesels, and by 1954 its steam operations had concluded.

In the 1950s, ACL and its north–south rival, Seaboard Air Line, discussed a merger to reduce costs and more effectively compete with non-rail modes. Finally in 1967, after a decade of planning and regulatory hurdles, ACL and Seaboard merged to become Seaboard Coast Line. The merger allowed for some consolidation of duplicate routes and facilities. SCL eventually became a component of Seaboard System, one of the primary CSX companies.

Headquarters: Wilmington, NC

Years operated: 1900–1967

Disposition: Merged with Seaboard Air Line to form Seaboard Coast Line (1967); most routes now operated by CSX

Route mileage: 5,379 (c. 1953)

Locomotives

Steam: 1,033 (1928)

Diesel: 609 (1966)

Reporting mark: ACL

Emblem: Circles surrounding name in script

Primary locomotive shops: Emerson (Rocky Mount), NC, and Waycross, GA

Notable feature: James River Bridge (Richmond, VA), 2,278 ft.

States served: AL, FL, GA, NC, SC, VA

Major cities served: Atlanta, Birmingham, Orlando, Richmond, Savannah, St. Petersburg, Tampa

Flagship passenger trains:
East Coast Champion (New York–Miami via Florida East Coast [FEC]) and *West Coast Champion* (New York–St. Petersburg)

Other name passenger trains:
Operated via Pennsylvania Railroad and Richmond, Fredericksburg & Potomac (New York–Washington, D.C.); *Everglades* (New York–Miami via FEC); *Florida Special* (New York–Miami via FEC); *Havana Special* (New York–Miami via FEC); *Miamian* (New York–Miami via FEC); *Palmetto* (New York–Savannah)

Notable freight commodities:
Aggregates, coal, general freight, grain, perishables, phosphates

Principal freight yards:
Jacksonville, FL; Southover (Savannah), Tifford (Atlanta), Waycross, GA

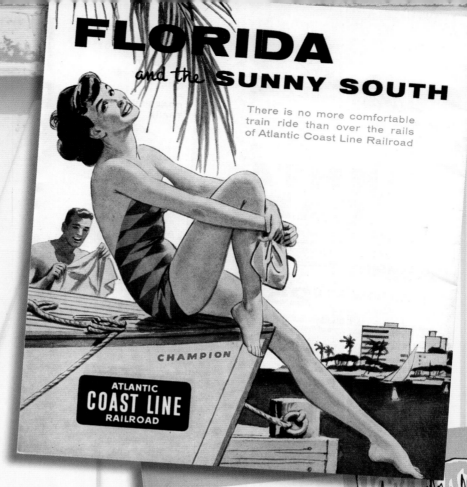

▲ Public timetable, 1957. Today, Amtrak continues to serve former ACL routes with popular runs, including its *Auto Train*. *Solomon collection*

▶ ACL was a preferred route for snowbirds heading for winter sun. *Solomon collection*

▲ ACL Florida routes, 1957. *Solomon collection*

BALTIMORE & OHIO RAILROAD

Baltimore & Ohio holds a special place in the annals of American railroading. It was the first line chartered as a common carrier and helped set the pattern for American railroad development. Its 1827 charter was intended to enable Baltimore to compete with the Erie Canal by building west to the Ohio River. B&O began construction on July 4, 1828, and on May 24, 1830, it began scheduled passenger service on 13 miles of line between Baltimore and Ellicott Mills. Its early trains were horse-drawn, but experiments with steam in August 1830 encouraged it to use domestically built locomotives when many other early lines still relied on British imports. Construction was slow, and it wasn't until 1852 that B&O finally reached its namesake river at Wheeling, Virginia (today West Virginia). B&O expanded with line acquisitions and new construction, eventually reaching west

▼ During World War II, B&O was denied road freight diesels and instead bought compact 2-8-8-4s designated EM-1s. In their final years, these largely worked lines in eastern Ohio. *Photographer unknown Solomon collection*

to Chicago and St. Louis. Pushing eastward, B&O rails reached Philadelphia, and then tapped the New York market via connections over Reading Company and Central Railroad of New Jersey to the Hudson River.

In its early days, B&O took a distinct approach to railroading. It was an innovator and boasted of many firsts. In the 1850s, it pioneered applications of Bollman and Fink iron truss bridges; its Baltimore Belt Line, opened in June 1895, featured America's first mainline electrification. In 1900, Frederick U. Adams' wood-clad streamliner was the first wind-resistant train. In 1904, it was the first American railroad to adopt the articulated Mallet compound locomotive.

B&O was also among America's most familiar railroads, thanks in part to its pioneering efforts and later to its place on the Monopoly board game. In fact, several clever self-promotions over the years helped B&O become a household name. In 1927, for example, to celebrate its 100th anniversary, it sponsored the widely attended "Fair of the Iron Horse" in Baltimore.

B&O's passenger trains were among the finest. Its *Royal Blue* and *Capitol Limited* were choice means of travel in the golden age of the passenger train. Yet, freight traffic paid B&O's bills. Coal was the railroad's lifeblood, and it flowed in tides over B&O lines from its early days.

In 1962, Chesapeake & Ohio assumed control of B&O, leading to creation of the C&O-managed Chessie System in the 1970s, which also included the Western Maryland. In 1980, the Chessie System became a component of CSX. In 1987, after a quarter-century in a secondary role, B&O was quietly merged out of existence, though many of its lines remain an important part of CSX's route structure.

Scenery...Unlimited from B&O's STRATA-DOMES

Completely relaxed in a comfortable seat, you'll enjoy Nature's everchanging panorama of colorful scenery, from every angle as you glide along in B&O's thrilling Strata-Dome between Washington and Chicago. *And there's no additional charge.*

FLOODLIGHTS AT NIGHT
Powerful beams of light turn the landscape into a panorama of novel attractions!

Strata-Dome Dieseliners between
CHICAGO • AKRON
PITTSBURGH • WASHINGTON
The Capitol Limited
(All-Pullman with Stewardess-Nurse)
The Columbian
(Deluxe Coach with Stewardess-Nurse)
The Shenandoah*
(Pullman and Coach with Stewardess-Nurse)
Through service to and from Baltimore, Wilmington, Philadelphia and New York.
*On the Shenandoah, Strata-Dome is operated on alternate dates. Available only to Pullman passengers on the Shenandoah.

NEW FEATURES on the CAPITOL LIMITED

LARGE, ULTRA-MODERN DINING CAR—B&O's fine food, moderately priced, courteously served in a relaxing atmosphere.

STEWARDESS SERVICE—The courteous, efficient B&O Stewardess-Nurse will be happy to assist you in dozens of ways, without obligation.

Strata-Domes are a B&O exclusive in the East

◀ B&O was among the only railroads in the eastern United States to run dome cars. *Richard Jay Solomon collection*

Headquarters: Baltimore, MD

Years operated: 1827–1987

Disposition: Melded into CSX, most surviving routes operated by CSX

Route mileage including subsidiaries:
6,289 (c. 1953)

Locomotives (1953)
  Steam: 1,017
  Diesel: 758
  Gas-electric railcars: 1

Reporting mark: BO

Emblem: Capitol dome in circle

Slogan: Linking 13 Great States with the Nation

Nickname: The Bando

Primary locomotive shops:
  Cumberland, MD; Mt. Clare (Baltimore); Galeton, PA

Notable features: Howard Street Tunnel (Baltimore), 7,341 ft.; Sand Patch Tunnel (near Meyersdale, PA); Staten Island Drawbridge (New York City); Susquehanna River Bridge (Havre de Grace, MD), 6,108 ft.; Tray Run Viaduct (Cheat River Grade, WV)

States served: DE, IL, IN, KY, MD, MI, MO, NJ, NY, PA, OH, VA, WV

Major cities served:
  Baltimore, Buffalo, Cleveland, Chicago, Cincinnati, Columbus, Detroit, Indianapolis, Louisville, New York, Philadelphia, Pittsburgh, St. Louis, Toledo, Washington, D.C.

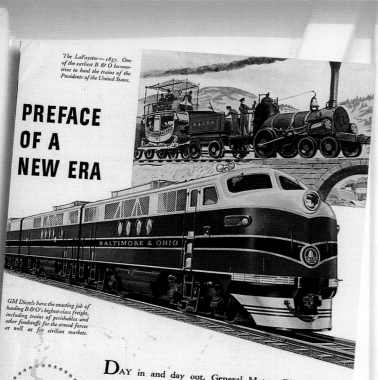

The LaFayette—1837. One of the earliest B & O locomotives to haul the trains of the Presidents of the United States.

PREFACE OF A NEW ERA

GM Diesels have the exacting job of hauling B&O's highest-class freight, including trains of perishables and other foodstuffs for the armed forces as well as for civilian markets.

KEEP AMERICA STRONG BUY WAR BONDS

DAY in and day out, General Motors Diesel Locomotives are proving their ability to haul huge loads far, fast, with little attention and at low cost. In any vision of the future of transportation, these tireless giants must loom large. Already they have won a place of rare importance by their unprecedented performance in the work of the railroads at war.

GM
GENERAL MOTORS
DIESEL POWER

LOCOMOTIVES........ELECTRO-MOTIVE DIVISION, La Grange, Ill.
ENGINES...150 to 2000 H.P...CLEVELAND DIESEL ENGINE DIVISION, Cleveland, Ohio
ENGINES.....15 to 250 H.P......DETROIT DIESEL ENGINE DIVISION, Detroit, Mich.

▲ Electro-Motive Division tapped B&O's long history to stir patriotic fervor during World War II. *Voyageur Press collection*

▶ B&O train check.
Richard Jay Solomon collection

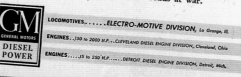

TRAIN CHECK

Jan.	1	2
Feb.	3	4
Mar.	5	6
	7	8
April	9	10
May	11	12
	13	14
June	15	16
July	17	18
	19	20
Aug.	21	22
Sept.	23	24
Oct.	25	26
Nov.	27	28
	29	30
Dec.		31

Issued by BALTIMORE & OHIO RAILROAD

Flagship passenger trains: *The Capitol Limited* (Washington, D.C.–Chicago); *The National Limited* (Jersey City–Washington, D.C.–St Louis); *The Royal Blue* (Jersey City–Washington, D.C.)

Other name passenger trains: *The Ambassador* (Baltimore–Detroit); *The Diplomat* (Jersey City–Washington, D.C.–St. Louis); *Metropolitan Special* (Jersey City–Washington, D.C.–St Louis)

Notable freight commodities: Coal and merchandise

Principal freight yards: Baltimore and Cumberland, MD; Barr (Chicago); Cone (East St. Louis), IL; Connellsville and Newcastle, PA; Benwood, WV; Grafton and Keyser, WV; Mill Creek (Cincinnati); Willard, OH

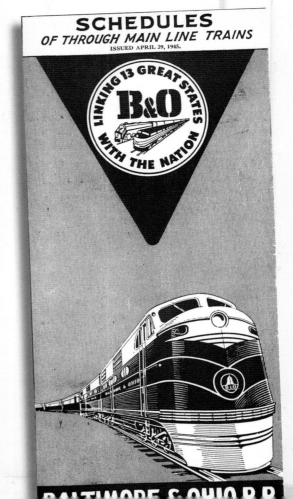

SCHEDULES
OF THROUGH MAIN LINE TRAINS
ISSUED APRIL 29, 1945.

LINKING 13 GREAT STATES WITH THE NATION

B&O

BALTIMORE & OHIO R.R.

▶ B&O's World War II–era public timetable featured its prewar streamlined train with an Electro-Motive Corporation model EA diesel. *Richard Jay Solomon collection*

▲ Before their run, the crew of B&O's *Cincinnatian* discusses logistics on the platform at Cincinnati Union Station.
Wallace W. Abbey, Center for Railroad Photography & Art

BANGOR & AROOSTOOK RAILROAD

Bangor & Aroostook was incorporated in 1891 and obtained an exclusive charter in northern Maine, allowing it to absorb two existing lines while building a north–south route free of interference from competing schemes. Construction began from a connection with Canadian Pacific's transcontinental mainline at Brownville Junction and progressed northward. Over the next two dozen years, it built lines across the top of the state, reaching Fort Kent, in far northern Maine in 1902 and concluding its expansion in 1915 by bridging the St. John River between Van Buren, Maine, and St. Leonard, New Brunswick, to reach a connection with a CN predecessor. The railroad also pushed southward, establishing connections with Maine Central (initially at Old Town and later at Northern Maine Junction west of Bangor), and culminating with an Atlantic port at Searsport.

Through most of the twentieth century, the railroad thrived by hauling forest products and potatoes (which at one time accounted for one-third of its traffic, up to 50,000 carloads annually), and through the 1950s maintained a tidy, well-run passenger service, exemplified by its *Aroostook Flyer*. The line was fully dieselized by 1952, primarily operating Electro-Motive products. In the 1980s, it caught the attention of locomotive enthusiasts as the last to operate EMD's F3A and unusual model BL2 in road service.

▼ Northern Maine Junction, west of Bangor, served as BAR's primary operations hub and locomotive shop. The railroad continued to operate 1940s-vintage F3s and BL2s longer than most other railroads in the United States. *George S. Pitarys*

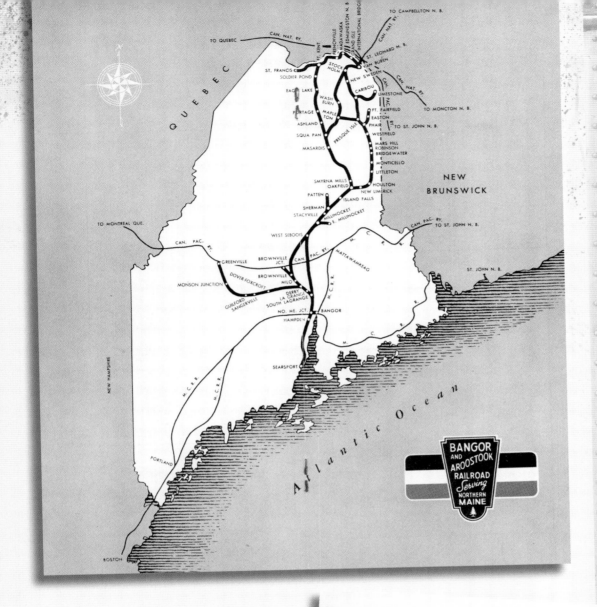

Headquarters: Bangor, ME

Years operated: 1891–2003

Disposition: Lines acquired by Rail World's Maine, Montreal & Atlantic in 2003; south of Millinocket operated by MM&A; since 2011, lines north of Millinocket owned by the state of Maine and operated by Maine Northern Railway

Route mileage: 616 (c. 1949); 420 (c. 1993)

Locomotives
  Steam: 88 (c. 1927)
  Diesel: 43 (c. 1953)

Reporting mark: BAR

Emblem: Shield with company name in script

Nicknames: State of Maine Route and The Potato Road

Primary locomotive shop: Northern Maine Junction

Major cities served: Bangor

Flagship passenger train: *Aroostook Flyer* (Bangor–Van Buren, ME)

In 1994, the Bangor & Aroostook was acquired by Iron Road, which grouped it into a regional network of lines that included former Canadian Pacific lines in Maine, Vermont, and Quebec. Never prosperous, Iron Road's network was sold to Rail World's Montreal, Maine & Atlantic in 2003. Declining revenue on lines north of Millinocket led MM&A to sell these routes to the state of Maine in 2011, which contracted Maine Northern Railway as an operator.

▶ System map, 1958. *Richard Jay Solomon collection*

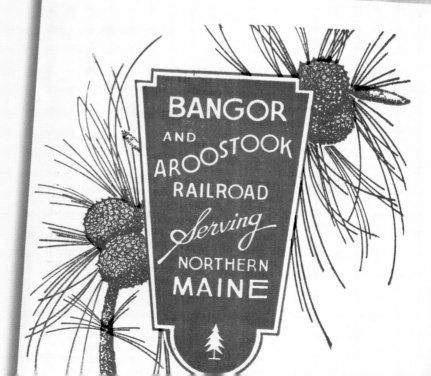

BELFAST & MOOSEHEAD LAKE RAILROAD

The 33-mile Belfast & Moosehead Lake Railroad is an unusual short line that has been described as "quintessentially Maine." Chartered in 1867, it was promoted by the Penobscot Bay village of Belfast, which owned the line and built across Waldo Country to a connection with the Maine Central at Burnham Junction, reaching there in 1870. Visions of reaching Maine's largest lake remained illusory, and in 1871 Maine Central leased the B&ML, operating it for more than five decades as its Belfast Branch.

Due to high operations costs and declining traffic, Maine Central looked to abandon the line. In 1926, Belfast businessmen took over the operation, resulting in a rare example of a municipally owned and operated U.S. common carrier until the city sold the line in 1991.

Traffic consisted of fish products, lumber, potatoes, and chicken feed for Waldo County's thriving poultry business, as well as nominal passenger traffic. The line dieselized in 1946, acquiring a small fleet of General Electric 70-ton switchers. Freight traffic

▼ B&ML acquired its steam locomotives secondhand from other lines in the region. No. 20, a 2-6-0, is turned on the "armstrong" table in front of the Belfast roundhouse. *Linwood Moody photo, Solomon collection*

▲ B&ML dieselized in the 1940s with a small fleet of General Electric 70-ton switchers that characterized its freight operations going forward. Old No. 54 works in the snow with a two-car freight at Unity. *George S. Pitarys*

largely dried up in the 1980s, and in 1988 it initiated tourist excursion services. Excursions were primarily based at Unity and worked the north end of the line, due to growing hostility toward the line in Belfast; gentrification forced B&ML to exit the city waterfront in 2005.

In 1995, B&ML imported a Swedish 4-6-0 and passenger cars to boost its excursion business. While many assets, including the 4-6-0, were sold at the end of 2010, in 2011 B&ML offered limited excursion service at the Belfast end of the line.

Headquarters: Belfast, ME

Years operated: 1867–2010

Disposition: Many assets sold at the end of 2010, yet very limited excursion service still offered in 2011

Route mileage: 33

Diesel locomotives: 3 (c. 1953)

Reporting mark: B&ML

Emblem: Circle around moosehead

Primary locomotive shop: Belfast

BELT RAILWAY OF CHICAGO

Belt Railway of Chicago is among America's most unusual freight railroads. Although short in route mileage, it serves a crucial link between major freight carriers at the nation's largest freight gateway. The line was built by the Chicago & Western Indiana in the early 1880s. By the time the new belt line was completed in 1883, the new line was reorganized as Belt Railway of Chicago with five significant major railroads as owners. Yet it remained affiliated with the C&WI for many years.

BRC's primary asset is Clearing Yard, a massive double-hump yard (uses gravity to sort freight cars by rolling them onto classification tracks). Clearing was among the earliest hump yards and for many years among America's largest.

▼ BRC operated America's most intact fleet of Alco C-424s through the late 1990s. Six of these 2,400-horsepower diesels worked in pairs on transfer runs and through moves on BRC's Chicago network. They were the last BRC Alcos. *Brian Solomon*

▲ Cover of Belt Railway of Chicago's system map, 1960s. *Solomon collection*

Headquarters: Chicago, IL

Years operated: 1882–present

Route mileage: 28 (2011)

Locomotives

   Steam: 86 (1929)

   Diesel: 44 (1972)

Reporting mark: BRC

Emblem: Circular belt around railroad name and centrally placed Y

Primary locomotive shop: Clearing, IL

Notable feature: Clearing Yard

▼ This pocket-size book issued by BRC in 1969 set out the railroad's governing safety rules for employees. *Voyageur Press collection*

Changes in Chicago-area operating agreements in 1912 led to more railroads becoming joint owners of BRC, including Burlington, Chicago & Eastern Illinois, Erie, Grand Trunk, Monon, Illinois Central, Pennsylvania, Rock Island, Santa Fe, Soo Line, and Wabash. By 1929, BRC was interchanging more than 1.5 million cars annually. It was among the last railroads in the United States to operate Electro-Motive transfer diesels—"cow-calf" sets consisting of semi-permanently coupled switchers with cab-less "B" units.

Today, in addition to serving as a primary interchange point and classification yard, BRC operates intensive switching services, reaching dozens of carload customers along its 28-mile route. As of 2011, BRC retained its primary functions and was owned by the six major North American railroads serving Chicago: BNSF, Canadian National, Canadian Pacific, CSX, Norfolk Southern, and Union Pacific.

THE BELT RAILWAY COMPANY
OF CHICAGO

SPECIAL INSTRUCTIONS NUMBER 107 and SAFETY RULES

Effective August 1, 1969

Superseding all previous Special Instructions, supplements thereto and Safety Rules. For Government and Information of Employes Only.

SAFETY ABOVE EVERYTHING

L. A. EVANS
President and General Manager

D. R. TURNER
Vice President & Assistant General Manager

J. OVERBEY
Superintendent

BESSEMER & LAKE ERIE RAILROAD

By Patrick Yough

Bessemer & Lake Erie traces its lineage back to 1869 and the formation of predecessor Shenango & Allegheny. In 1896, steel magnate Andrew Carnegie became involved, extending the S&A from Butler, Pennsylvania, to a connection with the Union Railroad in East Pittsburgh.

Carnegie aimed to break Pennsylvania Railroad's Pittsburgh stranglehold. The strategy resulted in his control of railroads and lake shipping, enabling Carnegie Steel to function as a completely integrated operation from mine to consumer. Iron ore from Minnesota's

▼ B&LE F7s cross the Allegheny River Bridge while southbound en route to North Bessemer, Pennsylvania. *Bessemer & Lake Erie Railroad, Lloyd Transportation Library*

Headquarters: Pittsburgh, PA (U.S. Steel/USX); Monroeville, PA (Transtar)

Years operated: 1869–2004

Disposition: Purchased by Canadian National in 2004

Route mileage: 214 (c. 1950)

Locomotives (c. 1950)

    Steam: 105

    Diesel: 1

Reporting mark: BLE

Emblem: Word *BESSEMER* in circle with rail cross-section between second *S* and *E*

Primary locomotive shop: Greenville, PA

Notable feature: Double-track steel bridge over Allegheny River (at river mile marker 14.3), 2,327 ft.

States served: OH and PA

Major cities served: Erie and Pittsburgh, PA (via sister Union Railroad)

Trains and Traffic

Notable freight commodities: Iron ore, coal, limestone, finished steel products, railroad cars

Principal freight yards: Albion and North Bessemer, PA; Conneaut, OH

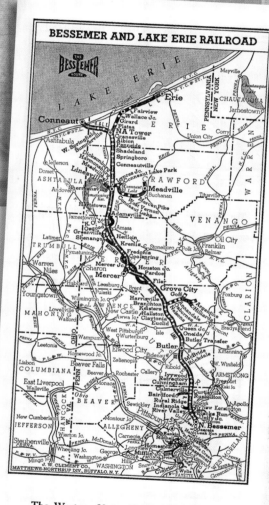

The Western Union Telegraph Company

Handles Messages at Public Telegraph

Offices on this Railroad

Mesabi Range was shipped by rail to Lake Superior docks, where it was transloaded into Carnegie-owned boats for shipment to Conneaut, Ohio. From there the ore was reloaded into B&LE rail cars for transport to Carnegie's steelworks in the Monongahela River Valley. When the first ship left Duluth for Conneaut, Carnegie famously wrote to his employee Henry C. Frick, "Today, Pittsburgh becomes a lake port." In addition, B&LE carried metallurgical coal from online mines to Bethlehem, Republic, and U.S. Steel coke ovens, while some moved northward to the Conneaut docks for export to Canada.

B&LE passenger service was insignificant, consisting of just two daily roundtrip services: Greenville to Erie and Greenville to North Bessemer. Passenger service was discontinued on March 5, 1955. In 1988, B&LE and other U.S. Steel (by now USX) subsidiary railroads were transferred to Transtar. In May 2004, the B&LE, the Duluth, Missabe & Iron Range, and USX's Great Lakes fleet were sold to the Canadian National.

▲ System map, 1940s. *Richard Jay Solomon collection*

BNSF RAILWAY

Burlington Northern Santa Fe was created in September 1995 through the merger of Burlington Northern and Santa Fe. Since 2005, it has been officially known as the BNSF Railway. This giant North American railway has vied with Union Pacific for dominance of freight transport in the West. Among its most prominent traffic corridors are the former Santa Fe Chicago–Kansas City–Los Angeles "transcon" (one of America's premier intermodal routes); the former Chicago, Burlington & Quincy/Great Northern Chicago–Twin Cities–Pacific Northwest transcon; and low-sulfur coal traffic originating in Wyoming's Powder River Basin that flows in tides to generating stations across the Midwest and Southeast. In 2009, BNSF employed an estimated 38,000 people on its network spanning 28 U.S. states and two Canadian provinces.

▼ A westward intermodal train races along the former Chicago, Burlington & Quincy at Chana, Illinois. BNSF assigns a high-horsepower-per-ton ratio to priority intermodal trains, which allows them to get up to speed quickly and keep moving fast. *Brian Solomon*

▲ BNSF General Electric Dash 9 at Colorado's Palmer Divide in 2001. *Brian Solomon*

BNSF benefits from large fleets of modern high-horsepower locomotives. It has operated two largely separate road fleets, assigning exclusively three-phase, alternating current, six-motor units to heavy-haul mineral and unit-train service, and various more traditional direct-current models on intermodal services. Use of distributed power technology (DPUs) has become standard on many through freight runs, resulting in remote-control locomotives located in the middle or at the back of the train. BNSF has also been a pioneer in large-scale application of hybrid genset locomotives in yard service, primarily in California and Texas.

Unlike mergers of the 1960s and 1970s that tended to result in consolidation and mass line reduction, the BNSF has focused on building traffic and increasing business. Few lines have been abandoned, although changes in operations have maximized the use of parallel infrastructure. In recent years, the railroad has made significant investment in its lines to eliminate traffic bottlenecks and increase capacity. Of special interest has been the former Santa Fe Chicago–L.A. route, which has received extensive double-tracking and installation of bi-directional signaling to better accommodate the tide of long-distance fast freights.

In November 2009, American billionaire Warren Buffett bought BNSF through his Berkshire Hathaway conglomerate, setting important precedents regarding the future viability of the American railroad industry and potentially providing the railroad with necessary capital for further investment.

Headquarters: Ft. Worth, TX

Years operated: 1995–present

Route mileage: Approx. 32,000 (2011)

Diesel locomotives: Approx. 6,000 (2011)

Reporting mark: BNSF

Emblem: Italicized *BNSF* with stylized angled line below

Primary locomotive shops: Barstow, CA; Argentine (Kansas City) and Topeka, KS; Northtown (Minneapolis); Havre and Glendive, MT; Alliance and Lincoln, NE

Notable features: Canyon Diablo Bridge (AZ), 542 ft. long, 222 ft. high; Cascade Tunnel (WA), 7.8 mi.; Colorado River Bridge (near Topock, CA), 1,506 ft.; Crooked River Gorge arch bridge (OR), 350 ft. long, 320 ft. high; Tunnel 1 (Franklin Canyon, CA), 5,596 ft.; Flathead Tunnel (MT), 7 mi.; Mississippi River Bridge (Fort Madison, IA), 3,347 ft.; Missouri River Bridge (Sibley, MO), 4,082 ft.; Raton Pass Tunnels, 2,041 and 2,789 ft.; Stampede Tunnel (Washington Cascades), 9,834 ft.

States and provinces served: 28 states and 2 provinces

Major cities served: Chicago, Dallas/Ft. Worth, Denver, Houston, Kansas City, Los Angeles, Minneapolis, New Orleans, Phoenix, St. Louis, St. Paul, Seattle, Vancouver

Notable freight commodities: Coal, grain, intermodal, timber products

Principal freight yards: Argentine (Kansas City), KS; Barstow, CA; Corwith and Cicero (Chicago) and Galesburg, IL; Hobart (Los Angeles); Tennessee (Memphis); Northtown (Minneapolis); Pasco, Balmer (Seattle), Spokane, WA; Tulsa, OK

▼ The high volume of coal traffic originating in Wyoming's Powder River Basin has led BNSF to increase line capacity by adding second, third, and, in a few places, fourth main tracks to its 1970s-built Orin Line shared with Union Pacific. Here, a pair of BNSF Electro-Motive SD70ACe diesels leads a Powder River unit coal train. *Patrick Yough*

BNSF's northward HRRBVAW (high-priority manifest, Riverbank, California, to Vancouver, Washington) negotiates Trout Creek Canyon on the Oregon Trunk near South Junction, Oregon, on August 9, 2009. With the UP-SP merger of 1996, BNSF was granted extensive trackage rights over the former Western Pacific, allowing the old Oregon Trunk to function as a through north–south route between the Pacific Northwest and Central California. *Philip A. Brahms*

BOSTON & ALBANY RAILROAD

The opening of the Erie Canal across central New York in 1825 encouraged the development of a trans-Massachusetts transportation scheme to connect Boston, the state capital, and the canal head near Albany, New York. Initially a canal through the Berkshires was considered, but by the late 1820s, proponents urged construction of a through railroad. Boston & Worcester began construction in 1832 and connected its namesakes on 44 miles of line in July 1835. In the meantime, in 1833, B&W directors incorporated the Western Railroad (of Massachusetts) to build west from Worcester, via Springfield, over the Berkshires to the New York state line. Major George Washington Whistler was hired to survey and engineer the line. He located a low summit of the Berkshires, near the village of Washington, Massachusetts, 1,459 feet above sea level, and constructed the world's first mountain main line. With connections at the Massachusetts–New York state line, the B&W and Western formed a through link between Boston & Albany in 1841.

▼ In the mid-1920s, Lima used the B&A as a proving ground for its new superpower steam concept. The success of the 2-8-4 on the B&A route resulted in this wheel arrangement being named for the Berkshire Mountains. B&A bought three classes of Lima Berkshires beginning in 1926. On October 14, 1947, B&A A1a No. 1421 works east through Warren with tonnage freight. *Robert A. Buck*

B&W and Western merged in 1867 to form the Boston & Albany, which at the time had a virtual monopoly on trunk traffic to southern New England. B&A prospered through the nineteenth century and was among the first railroads to adopt automatic block signaling. In 1900, the New York Central & Hudson River leased the B&A. While the New York Central System image predominated for a few years, local demand restored the B&A name, and from 1912 through the end of the steam era, equipment was lettered thus.

Today the route survives as CSX's main line to New England and serves as a Massachusetts Bay Transportation Authority commuter line between Boston and Worcester.

▼ This period postcard, circa 1910, depicts an eastward B&A express running through the valley of the West Branch of the Westfield River between the villages of Huntington and Russell, Massachusetts. *Solomon collection*

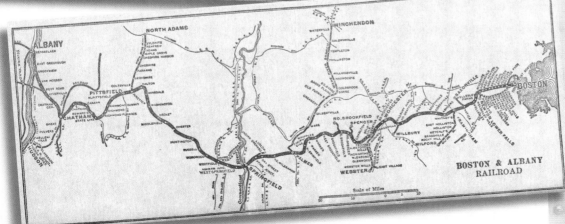

▲ Route map, 1942. *Bob Buck collection*

Headquarters: Springfield, MA

Years operated: 1867–1900 and 1900–1960 (New York Central lessee)

Disposition: Merged into NYC in 1960; passed to Penn Central in 1968, Conrail in 1976, CSX in 1999

Route mileage: 395 (1933)

Steam locomotives: 284 (1933)

Reporting mark: B&A

Emblems: Traditionally circle surrounding "Boston & Albany" in script; also rectangle around "BOSTON AND ALBANY"

Primary locomotive shop: West Springfield, MA

Notable features: Connecticut River Bridge (Springfield, MA); various early stone-arch bridges at West Warren, Chester, and Middlefield, MA

States served: MA and NY

Major cities served: Boston, Worcester, Springfield, Albany

Flagship passenger trains: The Boston section *20th Century Limited* (Boston–Chicago) and *New England States* (Boston–Chicago), both in the New York Central era

Other name passenger trains: *Boston Express* (Boston–Buffalo); *Boston Special* (Boston–Chicago); *Iroquois* (Boston–Chicago); *Lake Shore Limited* (Boston–Chicago); *Paul Revere* (Boston–Chicago); *Ohio State Limited* (Boston–Cincinnati); *Southwestern Limited* (Boston–St. Louis)

Notable freight commodities: General freight, milk, oil (during World War II), perishables

Principal freight yards: Beacon Park (Allston), West Springfield, and Worcester, MA

55

BOSTON & MAINE RAILROAD

Boston was the location of an early American railroad boom. During the 1830s and 1840s, myriad schemes projected lines radiating from the city, each eyeing other schemes as potential adversaries or partners. One of the earliest was Boston & Lowell, which connected its namesakes by 1835. The Andover & Wilmington was chartered to connect the B&L with Andover village and soon evolved quickly into a farsighted railroad called the Boston & Maine, one of the earliest lines with charters in three states. B&M reached Portland, Maine, using a link with Portland, Saco & Portsmouth in 1842. In its early years, B&M competed fiercely with the Eastern Railroad for supremacy of the Boston–Portland trade. Yet, gradually over the next six decades, B&M acquired control of most of the lines radiating north and west from Boston, except for the Boston & Albany, which was leased by New York Central in 1900.

Among the most important lines in the B&M fold was the Fitchburg Division running west via the Hoosac Tunnel, a 4.75-mile bore built largely by the Commonwealth of Massachusetts (later acquired by the Fitchburg Railroad). In the early years of the twentieth century, the B&M and New Haven Railroad systems were under common management. B&M and Maine Central had shared affiliation since the 1880s.

By the mid-1920s, B&M was carrying great volumes of tonnage and passengers. Its Boston-area suburban services were among the most intensely operated in the region, and it installed some of the earliest Centralized Traffic Control to accommodate the volume traffic on its main lines. In 1911 and with New Haven's help, it electrified its Hoosac Tunnel

▼ An A-B set of B&M F2s leads southward train No. 72, slowing to take orders and make its station stop at East Northfield, Massachusetts, on March 13, 1955. East Northfield was the junction with the Central Vermont. North from here, B&M and CV had parallel lines to Brattleboro, Vermont, and operated "paired track." B&M's line on the east side of the Connecticut River was the northward track, while CV's on the west side served as the southward track. *Jim Shaughnessy*

Headquarters: Historically Boston, MA; later North Billerica, MA

Years operated: 1830s–1983

Disposition: Freight operations melded into Guilford Transportation in 1983 (later Guilford Rail System, now Pan Am Railways); today main line west of Ayer, MA, run by Pan Am Southern (joint venture between Pan Am Railways and Norfolk Southern); Boston suburban lines and passenger service operated by MBTA

Route mileage: 1,702 (c. 1953)

Locomotives

    Steam: 166 (c. 1953)

    Diesel: 233 (c. 1953)

    Self-propelled railcars: 65 (c. 1954)

Reporting mark: B&M

Emblems: Traditionally a shield featuring minuteman soldier; later stylized, intertwined "B&M"

Nickname: Line of the Minute Man

Primary locomotive shops: North Billerica and East Deerfield, MA (modern); Fitchburg, MA; Concord and Keene, NH; Lyndonville, VT (steam era)

Notable features: Hudson River Bridge (near Mechanicville, NY); Hoosac Tunnel (near North Adams, MA), 25,081 ft.; North Station (Boston)

States served: CT (after 1982), ME, MA, NH, NY, VT

Major cities served: Boston, Springfield, and Worcester, MA; Portland, ME

Flagship passenger trains: *Minute Man* (Boston–Troy, NY, with through cars to/from Chicago via New York Central)

Other name passenger trains: *Alouette* (Boston–Montreal via Canadian Pacific); *Connecticut Yankee* (White River Junction, VT–Springfield–New York City via New Haven Railroad); *Flying Yankee* (Boston–Portland–Bangor via Maine Central); *Gull* (Boston–Bangor via Maine Central, with through cars to Calais, ME, and Halifax, NS; *Montrealer/Washingtonian* (Washington, D.C.–Montreal via Pennsylvania Railroad, New Haven Railroad, Boston & Maine, Central Vermont, and Canadian National); *Red Wing* (Boston–Montreal via Canadian Pacific); *The Cheshire* (Boston–Bellows Falls, VT)

Notable freight commodities: Paper products and manufactured goods

Principal freight yards: East Deerfield and Somerville (Boston), MA; Mechanicville, NY; Rigby (Portland), ME

▼ Timetable, 1945.
Richard Jay Solomon collection

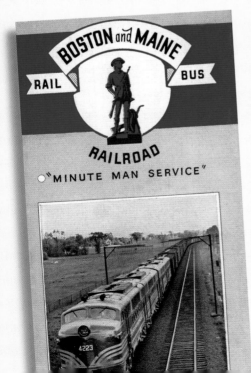

operations to reduce fumes within the bore. Yet B&M's decline had begun, and the gradual exodus of New England manufacturing and textile industries put the railroad in an early downward spiral. Secondary routes such as the Central Massachusetts line from Boston to Northampton were truncated in the 1930s. Further downsizing of the network occurred as traffic dried up or switched to highways over the next six decades.

Main lines were dieselized after the war (which also enabled B&M to discontinue Hoosac Tunnel electrification), yet some Boston-area suburban services survived in steam until 1956. Passenger services were scaled back with the advance of the automobile and improved roads (the Hoosac Tunnel route lost through passenger services in the 1950s). Boston suburban services survived and in the 1970s became the domain of the Massachusetts Bay Transportation Authority (MBTA). B&M's freight operations were acquired by Guilford Transportation in 1983.

▲ B&M FTs exit the Hoosac Tunnel's west portal with a westward freight on September 10, 1955. The railroad's early mainline dieselization enabled it to abandon Hoosac's high-voltage electrification. A few years after this image was made, B&M traded its FT fleet back to Electro-Motive for new GP9 road switchers. *Jim Shaughnessy*

BURLINGTON NORTHERN RAILROAD

In the early years of the twentieth century, James J. Hill envisioned merging his three primary properties—Chicago, Burlington & Quincy, Great Northern, and Northern Pacific—into a dynamic northern transcontinental line connecting Chicago, Omaha, and St. Louis with the Twin Cities and Pacific Northwest. His formation of the Northern Securities Company in 1901 was aimed at consolidation and fending off raids from competing interests. Much to Hill's dismay, President Teddy Roosevelt frowned upon his consolidation designs, and in a landmark decision, the U.S. Supreme Court ruled that Northern Securities be dismantled. Despite this, Hill's railroads retained a family relationship, and the Spokane, Portland & Seattle filled gaps in his network.

▼ In the 1970s, BN began buying large numbers of SD40-2s, which came to typify its locomotive fleet until its merger with Santa Fe in 1995. Here, five BN SD40-2s descend Marias Pass in the Montana Rockies, westbound on the former Great Northern transcon route. *Brian Solomon*

▲ BN safety sign at the former SP&S Wishram, Washington, yard. *Brian Solomon*

▲ This chrome-plated BN logo was fixed to the nose of executive F-unit BN-1. *Brian Solomon*

In 1956, four decades after Hill's death, CB&Q, GN, NP, and SP&S again planned for merger. After numerous hurdles, the union was sanctioned by the Interstate Commerce Commission in 1967. The U.S. Justice Department delayed merger, but the four "Hill" properties were finally joined as Burlington Northern in March 1970. Ten years later, BN expanded its operations in the South and Southwest by absorbing the St. Louis–San Francisco (Frisco).

Key to BN's success was its development of Wyoming's Powder River Basin coal territory using a mix of existing lines and its newly built Orin Cutoff to serve new mines. Coal traffic continued to grow during the 1980s and 1990s. In 1993, BN became the first North American railroad to adopt commercially developed AC-traction diesels to move unit coal trains more efficiently.

BN's success led its 1995 merger with Santa Fe to form BNSF.

Headquarters: Ft. Worth, TX

Years operated: 1970–1995

Disposition: Merged with Santa Fe; most routes now operated by BNSF

Route mileage: 23,609 (c. 1970)

Diesel locomotives: 1,973 (c. 1970) and 2,690 (c. 1995)

Reporting mark: BN

Emblem: Stylized BN

Primary locomotive shops: West Burlington, IA; Northtown (Minneapolis); Glendive and Livingston, MT; Alliance and Lincoln, NE

Notable features: Cascade Tunnel (WA), 7.8 mi.; Crooked River Gorge Bridge (OR), 350 ft. long, 320 ft. high; Flathead Tunnel (MT), 7 mi.; Lake Pend d'Orielle (ID), 4,767 ft. long; Sheyenne River Bridge (Karnak, ND), 2,742 ft. long, 160 ft. high; Hill Bridge over Mississippi River (Minneapolis), 2,100 ft.; Stampede Tunnel (Washington Cascades), 9,834 ft.; Valley City (ND) trestle, 3,856 ft. long, 165 ft. high

States and provinces served: 17 states and 2 provinces

Major cities served: Chicago, Dallas/Ft. Worth, Denver, Houston, Kansas City, Memphis, Minneapolis, Omaha, Portland, Seattle, St. Louis, St. Paul, Tulsa

15

CALIFORNIA NORTHERN RAILROAD

Initially affiliated with California & Arizona, which operated former Santa Fe secondary lines, California Northern began operations in September 1993 on three disconnected secondary routes in northern California that were spun off by the Southern Pacific. Initially these consisted of a portion of the former Northwestern Pacific (and connecting lines) between Willits, Schellville, and Napa Junction, and a connection with Southern Pacific at Fairfield; 58 miles of the northern portion of Southern Pacific's Westside Line between Southern Pacific's yard at Tracy and Los Banos; and the entire Southern Pacific West Valley Line between junctions at Davis and Tehama.

Historically, Northwestern Pacific had been a joint venture between Southern Pacific and Santa Fe, but was operated as a Southern Pacific subsidiary since the mid-1920s. Southern Pacific spun off the Willits–Eureka portion of Northwestern Pacific in 1985 to the short-lived Eureka Southern. This operation was later conveyed to a local authority working as the North Coast Railroad. California Northern's operation of the Willits–Schellville portion of Northwestern Pacific ended in 1996, when North Coast Railroad

▼ On July 7, 2005, a southward California Northern freight works toward Davis, California, on the former Southern Pacific West Valley Line. *Brian Solomon*

Headquarters: Davis, CA; previously American Canyon, CA

Years operated: 1993–present

Route mileage: 354 (c. 1993); 261 (2011)

Diesel locomotives: 10 (2006)

Reporting mark: CFNR

Emblem: Green rectangle around silhouette of evergreen with setting sun over words CALIFORNIA NORTHERN RAILROAD CO.

Notable feature: Brazos Drawbridge (Napa River near American Canyon)

▲ The distinctive bell on the nose of this California Northern GP15-1 No. 108 reveals its Chicago & North Western heritage. *Brian Solomon*

▲ Three former Chicago & North Western GP15-1s lead a California Northern freight from the Southern Pacific interchange at Fairfield to Petaluma, over the former Northwestern Pacific line west of Schellville, California. *Brian Solomon*

assumed operation of this segment as well, and briefly operated the unified Schellville–Eureka route under the revived Northwestern Pacific name until the Federal Railroad Administration shut the operation down, citing safety concerns.

Since then, California Northern has focused on its remaining line segments. In 2002, it was acquired by North American short-line operator Rail America. California Northern's operations have been largely handled by a small fleet of former Chicago & North Western EMD-built GP15-1 diesels, though in late 2009 Rail America announced an order for a fleet of modern genset locomotives.

16

CANADIAN NATIONAL RAILWAY

While most of the U.S. railroad network was in place by 1910, Canada experienced a late-era building boom in the second decade of the twentieth century. The recently formed Grand Trunk Pacific extended a line west to Prince Rupert, British Columbia, reaching there in June 1914. Meanwhile, Canadian Northern was expanding its network east and west, with its western extension reaching Vancouver, British Columbia, in early 1915. Canadian Northern finally reached Montreal on the eve of World War I, but was not afforded the best entry to the city, as premier routes had been taken by earlier railways. Its downtown Montreal terminal was reached by a 3-mile tunnel under Mount Royal, which required overhead electrification to avoid smoke problems. Electrification was later expanded to suburban services north and west of Montreal.

▼ A new CN SD70M-2 leads eastward empty coal cars at Swan Landing, Alberta. Where most of the large North American railroads have conceded to the advantages of modern three-phase AC traction, CN remains loyal to conventional DC-traction diesels.
George S. Pitarys

▲ In October 1964, CN Class U-2g 4-8-4 No. 6218 works an excursion in Quebec. CN and its American subsidiary, Grand Trunk Western, had the largest fleet of 4-8-4s in North America. *Richard Jay Solomon*

Canada's light population density and enormous distances, combined with financial difficulties as a result of World War I, failed to sustain the enormous investment in this duplicative infrastructure. The financial collapse of some routes resulted in nationalization of several key Canadian lines. This process began during World War I and took several years to complete, but by 1923 most of Canada's network, with the notable exception of Canadian Pacific, had been folded into the new government-controlled Canadian National Railways (CN). Complicating matters were lines south of the border owned and operated by CN constituents. CN created the Grand Trunk Western to operate former Grand Trunk Railway (GTR) routes in Michigan, Indiana, and Illinois, while operating other lines in the United States as subsidiaries, including the Central Vermont to New London, Connecticut. While CN's former GTR to Portland, Maine, was operated simply as the Grand Trunk, its route to Duluth, Minnesota, was operated as a CN subsidiary called Duluth, Winnipeg & Pacific. Long-distance passenger services were conveyed to VIA Rail in 1978.

Headquarters: Montreal, QC
Years operated: 1919–present
Route mileage (including affiliates): 24,178 (c. 1949); 20,421 (2011)
Locomotives (2009)
 Diesel: 1,912
Reporting mark: CNR
Emblems: Maple leaf with railroad name until 1960; since 1960, CN in stylized letters commonly referred to as the "toothpaste" or "wet noodle" logo
Primary locomotive shops: Homewood (former IC near Chicago); Battle Creek, MI (GTW shops); Port St. Charles (Montreal); Transcend (Winnipeg)
Notable features: Fraser River Bridge (BC), 813 ft. long, 220 ft. high; Mount Royal Tunnel (Montreal); Niagara Gorge arch bridge, 1,082 ft. long, 250 ft. high; Quebec Bridge (near Quebec City), cantilever structure, 3,239 ft. long, 164 ft. high; Victoria Bridge (Montreal), 10,284 ft. long
Provinces and states served (incl. American affiliates): 8 provinces and 16 states
Major cities served: Buffalo, Calgary, Chicago, Detroit, Edmonton, Halifax, Memphis Montreal, New Orleans, Ottawa, Quebec City, St. Paul, Toronto, Vancouver

Flagship passenger trains: *Continental Limited* (Montreal–Vancouver) and *Super Continental* (Montreal–Vancouver)

Other name passenger trains: *International Limited* (Montreal–Chicago) and *Ocean Limited* (Montreal–Halifax)

Notable freight commodities: Chemicals, coal, general freight, grain, intermodal, timber products

Principal freight yards: MacMillan (Toronto); Symington (Winnipeg); Taschereau (Montreal); Illinois Central yards at Champaign and Homewood, IL; Fulton, KY; Jackson, MS; and Memphis, TN; Wisconsin Central yards at North Fond du Lac and Stevens Point, WI

CANADIAN NATIONAL RAILWAYS
TOURIST'S MAP OF CANADA *and the United States*

THE SCENIC ROUTE ACROSS CANADA

CANADIAN NATIONAL *To Everywhere in Canada*

▲ Brochure, 1951. *Voyageur Press collection*

▶ CN General Electric Dash 9 diesels lead a westward tank-train against the backdrop of the Montreal skyline in October 2004. *Brian Solomon*

In the late twentieth century, CN began trimming its routes and sold off several American properties, including the Portland route, which sold to regional operator St. Lawrence & Atlantic in 1989 (now operated by Genesee & Wyoming). In 1995, Central Vermont was spun off as the New England Central. During the 1990s, CN continued to trim its branches and secondary lines, spawning a host of short-line and regional railways in Canada, including the Cape Breton & Central Nova Scotia, which assumed operations on lines east of Halifax.

More significantly, CN was privatized in 1995 and has since been publicly known by its initials, CN. It began a series of North American acquisitions that greatly expanded its reach beyond its traditional limits. In 1998, CN merged with Illinois Central, which brought it all the way to New Orleans, while opening up gateways to Texas and Mexico. In 2001, it bought the Wisconsin Central (WC) network, including Algoma Central (which WC had acquired several years earlier), as well as a stake in WC's overseas ventures, such as Britain's English, Welsh & Scottish Railway freight operation (subsequently sold to Germany's Deutsche Bahn AG in 2007). In 2003, CN took control of the BC Rail network in British Columbia, and a year later it bought former U.S. Steel/USX roads Bessemer & Lake Erie and Duluth, Missabe & Iron Range. While DM&IR provided a key link with CN's former Wisconsin Central lines, the B&LE remains isolated from the rest of the network. Most recently, CN consummated its purchase of Chicago-based Elgin, Joliet & Eastern (also a onetime U.S. Steel property), giving it a key connection between its other three properties serving Chicago, which in time will ease the movement of freight through this key gateway.

In modern times, CN mainline operations have been characterized by freight trains that are among the longest regularly operated in North America. Unlike most other large North American freight railroads, CN has shunned AC traction, instead preferring conventional DC-traction diesels.

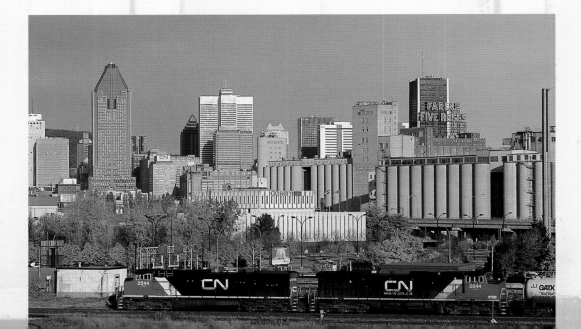

◀ CN predecessor Canadian Northern electrified its Mount Royal Tunnel and Montreal terminal in the World War I period using a 2,400-volt DC overhead system. On August 23, 1958, an outward CN electric multiple-unit pauses at the Montreal suburban station of Val Royal. *Richard Jay Solomon*

◀ Thirty-five years later at the same place, aged CN GE boxcab electrics pause at Val Royal with a suburban train on the evening of January 11, 1993. The original locomotives built between 1914 and 1916 served this system for the better part of 80 years. *Brian Solomon*

CANADIAN PACIFIC RAILWAY

Envisioned in the 1870s as the glue that would hold together the newly formed Dominion of Canada, the Canadian Pacific Railway remained an idealistic dream for a decade as progress was delayed by a host of political, financial, and geographical obstacles. In 1881, construction began and rapidly spanned the continent, climbing through the rocky and forbidding Canadian Shield, across the Great Plains, and over the Canadian Rockies to reach the Pacific coast in 1885. Despite its national prerogative, CP was a privately managed company that enjoyed a blend of government and private financing. It also was built under one management to avoid the inefficiencies of America's first transcontinental built competitively by Union Pacific and Central Pacific. Like the first American transcon lines, however, CP benefited from substantial land grants and financial rewards. It reached the Pacific years ahead of schedule, meanwhile extending eastward to the Atlantic Coast port of St. John, New Brunswick, by crossing the northern tier of Maine.

▼ CP's main line skirts the Canadian Shield along the north shore of Lake Superior. A pair of General Electric ES44AC diesels leads an eastward intermodal train at the Mink Tunnel, about a mile east of Coldwell siding on the Heron Bay Sub in Ontario. *George S. Pitarys*

▲ In the 1970s and 1980s, Canadian Pacific's SD40/SD40-2s painted in "Action Red" typified the railroad's western operations. On August 6, 1981, a westward coal train meets an eastbound freight at the Continental Divide (marked by the stone obelisk to the right of the trains). *Scott Muskopf*

Headquarters: Calgary, AB; previously Montreal, QC

Years operated: 1881–present

Route mileage: Approx. 17,000 (c. 1950)

Locomotives (c. 1950)

Steam: 1,670

Diesel: 190

Reporting mark: CPR

Emblem: Shield with beaver

Primary locomotive shops: Calgary, Montreal, Winnipeg

Notable features: St. Lawrence Bridge (near Montreal); Lethbridge Viaduct (Lethbridge, AB), 5,327 ft.; Connaught Tunnel/ Mount Macdonald Tunnel (between Calgary, AB, and Revelstoke, BC), 26,517 ft.; Spiral Tunnels (Kicking Horse Pass, BC)

Provinces and states served: NS, NB, QC, ON, MB, SK, AB, BC, WA, ND, MN, WI, IL, IA, MI, IN, NY, PA, VT, ME, MO, SD

Major cities served: Buffalo, Chicago, Detroit, Kansas City, Milwaukee, Minneapolis/ St. Paul, Montreal, New York City, Ottawa, Philadelphia, Quebec, Toronto

To feed its transcon and better serve Canada, CP developed a network of feeder routes and branch lines across Ontario, Manitoba, and Saskatchewan. Improvements over Kicking Horse Pass in the Canadian Rockies resulted in the abandonment of the original 4.4 percent grade for a new line that utilized spiral tunnels that reduced the grade to 2.2 percent (equivalent to the maximum on most American transcon lines). In addition to its railway network, CP was involved in steamships, a hotel chain, and an airline. As with Canadian National, its long-distance passenger services were conveyed to VIA Rail in 1978.

From its early days, CP had important American connections. Over the years it expanded its reach in the United States. It took control of the Minneapolis, St. Paul & Sault Ste. Marie in 1890, and although the "Soo Line" retained its own identity, CP extended its influence through this property and reached Chicago in 1909. In the 1980s, CP Rail (as it was known from 1968 to 1996) took advantages of upheavals in the American railway scene to further extend its influence south of the border. In 1985, Soo Line merged with the scaled-down Milwaukee Road network. In 1990, CP took control of the Delaware & Hudson and negotiated trackage rights between Chicago and Detroit to better link its American network. The Conrail breakup allowed CP to extend D&H's reach into New York City, although this corridor failed to develop. In the early 1990s, CP also divested of most of its lines east of Montreal, selling many routes to short-line and regional operators. Today, CP has survived its American affiliates.

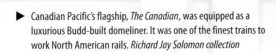

► Canadian Pacific's flagship, *The Canadian*, was equipped as a luxurious Budd-built domeliner. It was one of the finest trains to work North American rails. *Richard Jay Solomon collection*

"dome" route across Canada — via Banff and Lake Louise in the Canadian Rockies

▲ The Spiral Tunnels at Kicking Horse Pass allowed Canadian Pacific a more reasonable crossing of the Canadian Rockies than that provided by its original steeply graded line. *Richard Jay Solomon collection*

► Advertisement, 1961. *Richard Jay Solomon collection*

▲ Detailed view of logo on side of an SD40-2. *Brian Solomon*

Flagship passenger trains: *The Dominion* (Montreal–Vancouver) and *The Canadian* (Montreal–Vancouver)

Other name passenger trains: *The Alouette* (Montreal–Boston) and *The Atlantic Limited* (Montreal–Halifax, jointly run with Canadian National)

Notable freight commodities: Mineral ore, coal, grain

Principal freight yards: Calgary, Montreal, Toronto, Vancouver, Winnipeg; Soo Line yards at Bensenville (Chicago) and Pig's Eye (St. Paul)

CENTRAL OF GEORGIA RAILROAD

Central Rail Road and Banking Company of Georgia began operations in 1835 (the name was later foreshortened to the familiar Central of Georgia Railway). Originally, the railroad embraced the southern standard track gauge of 5 feet (compared with the 4 feet 8 ½ inches that was standard on northern lines), but was converted to the northern standard after the Civil War.

During the nineteenth century, the railroad assembled a strategic network connecting most major cities in Georgia and Alabama along with a line to Chattanooga, Tennessee. In 1888, it was controlled by a precursor of the Southern Railway. While control formally ended prior to J. P. Morgan's formation of the Southern system, CG remained friendly to the Southern until the former was acquired by Edward H. Harriman interests in 1907. Harriman had controlled the Illinois Central, and between 1909 and 1948, CG remained a close affiliate of the IC system. In the 1950s, Frisco looked to control and merge with the CG, but the Interstate Commerce Commission blocked the deal, and instead in 1963 CG became a subsidiary of Southern Railway System. Under the Southern umbrella, CG gradually lost its identity and today is part of the Norfolk Southern network.

The line played an important link in the movement of traffic between midwestern hubs and cities in Georgia and Florida, a role highlighted by its participation in operation of Chicago–Florida passenger trains such as the *City of Miami*.

▼ CG's handsome 4-8-4s, built by Lima in 1943, were similar to Southern Pacific's wartime Class Gs6 4-8-4s. These machines had short careers; displaced by dieselization, they were scrapped in 1953. *Witbeck photo, Solomon collection*

Headquarters: Savannah, GA

Years operated: c. 1835–1963

Disposition: Acquired by Southern Railway in 1963; amalgamated under Southern Railway as Central of Georgia Railroad in 1971; today operated as part of Norfolk Southern

Route mileage: 1,757 (c. 1952)

Locomotives (c. 1952)

    Steam: 129

    Diesel: 78

Reporting mark: CG

Slogan: Serving with Dependable Trains between the North, West and Florida

Primary locomotive shops: Macon and Savannah, GA

States served: Alabama, Florida, Georgia, Tennessee

Major cities served: Atlanta, Augusta, Birmingham, Chattanooga, Macon, Montgomery, Savannah

Name passenger trains: *Nancy Hanks II* (Atlanta–Savannah); *Man o' War* (Atlanta–Columbus, GA); *City of Miami* (Birmingham, AL–Albany, GA, leg of Chicago–Miami route with Atlantic Coast Line, Florida East Coast, and Illinois Central); *Dixie Flyer* (Atlanta–Albany, GA, leg of Chicago–Miami route with Chicago & Eastern Illinois; Louisville & Nashville; Nashville, Chattanooga & St. Louis; and ACL); *Dixie Limited* (Atlanta–Macon, GA, leg of Chicago/St. Louis–Atlanta/Jacksonville route with C&EI, L&B, NC&StL, ACL, and cars to Miami via FEC); *The Seminole* (Birmingham, AL–Albany, GA, leg of Chicago–Jacksonville route with IC and ACL); *The Southland* (Atlanta–Albany, GA, leg of Chicago–Tampa/St. Petersburg route with Pennsylvania Railroad, L&N, ACL, and cars to Miami via FEC)

▼ Public timetable, 1959. *Solomon collection*

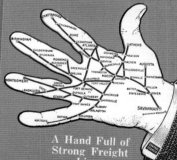

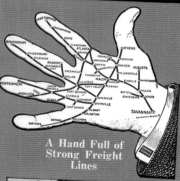

WINTER 1959-60

CENTRAL OF GEORGIA

A Hand Full of Strong Freight Lines

▲ In 1953, Electro-Motive Division issued this ad featuring a watercolor by famed railroad artist Howard Fogg depicting CG Nos. 137 and 138—a pair of RS-3s—working through the pine forests of Georgia. *Voyageur Press collection*

CENTRAL RAILROAD OF NEW JERSEY

Central Railroad of New Jersey was created in 1849 from the union of Elizabethtown & Somerville (chartered in 1831) and Somerville & Easton railroads. By 1852, CNJ reached Phillipsburg at the Jersey side of the Delaware River opposite Easton, Pennsylvania. Here, it met the Lehigh Valley and the Delaware, Lackawanna & Western (and later a branch of the Pennsylvania Railroad) and served as a bridge route to forward coal east toward the New York metro area.

CNJ extended east to Jersey City and built extensive terminal facilities on filled land along the Hudson opposite Manhattan. By the early 1870s, Lehigh Valley and DL&W had extended their own lines east of the Delaware River, which encouraged CNJ to build west into anthracite country. In April 1871, it leased the Lehigh & Susquehanna from the Lehigh Coal & Navigation Company. With this acquisition CNJ reached White Haven, Pennsylvania, via Mauch Chunk, and from there pushed its main line to Wilkes-Barre via the steeply graded Ashley Planes and finally to Scranton. Expansion ran parallel to Lehigh Valley, and in many places their main lines were adjacent to one another.

In 1879, CNJ expanded southward with the purchase of the New Jersey Southern. It connected these lines to the rest of its network via the New York & Long Branch, a railroad it jointly owned and operated with the Pennsylvania Railroad. Philadelphia & Reading took control of CNJ in the 1880s, only to lose it but regain it again after 1900. During that time, B&O controlled the Reading, using both it and CNJ to forward its traffic to the New York City area.

▼ CNJ had a significant fleet of anthracite-burning "Camelback" steam locomotives. While 4-4-2 Atlantic No. 595 was pictured here at Jersey City in the early 1930s, some Camelbacks survived in suburban service until the 1950s. A similar engine, CNJ No. 592, is preserved and displayed at the B&O Railroad Museum in Baltimore. *Robert A. Buck collection*

Headquarters: New York, NY

Years operated: 1849–1976

Disposition: Merged into Conrail in 1976; surviving routes operated by CSX, NJ Transit, Norfolk Southern, and various short lines

Route mileage: 633 (c. 1953)

Locomotives

    Steam: 535 (c. 1929)

    Diesel: 100 (c. 1976)

Reporting mark: CNJ

Emblem: Statue of Liberty

Nickname: The Big Little Railroad

Primary locomotive shop: Elizabethport, NJ

Notable features: Ashley Planes, PA, a cable-worked 14.7 percent grade; Newark Bay Lift Bridge, 7,411 ft.; Jersey City Terminal; car floats

States served: NJ, NY, PA

Major cities served: New York City (via ferries), Newark, Scranton

Flagship Passenger Trains: *The Blue Comet* (Jersey City–Atlantic City) and *Queen of the Valley* (Jersey City–Harrisburg, jointly run with Reading Company)

Notable freight commodities: Coal and merchandise

Principal freight yards: Allentown, PA, and Jersey City, NJ

◀ In 1966, CNJ local passenger trains meet on the New York & Long Branch at Matawan, New Jersey. CNJ and Pennsylvania Railroad jointly served the NY&LB. CNJ's trains served its massive waterfront terminal at Jersey City until 1967, when they were re-routed into Pennsylvania Railroad's Newark Penn Station. *Richard Jay Solomon*

▼ Passenger schedules, 1945. *Richard Jay Solomon collection*

CNJ developed an intensive suburban passenger service and expanded its main line to four tracks to accommodate business. It was one of only a few American lines to operate bi-directional suburban tank engines (similar to British suburban service tanks). In 1925, CNJ was the first railroad to purchase a commercially produced diesel-electric, a 300-horsepower boxcab, which it assigned to New York City waterfront trackage. In the 1940s, it bought a unique fleet of double-ended Baldwin "Babyface" diesels for suburban work.

After World War II, CNJ's traffic declined rapidly with the collapse of anthracite coal and general declines in heavy industry. CNJ consolidated its Pennsylvania trackage with Lehigh Valley in 1965. Then in 1967, it closed its Jersey City passenger terminal, detouring trains via the Aldene Plan to the Pennsylvania Railroad's Newark, New Jersey, Penn Station, and filed for bankruptcy. The line struggled on until 1976, when it was mercifully included in Conrail.

CENTRAL VERMONT RAILWAY

The Central Vermont Railway was created in 1873 from the reorganization of the Vermont Central, a company that began operations between Windsor and Burlington, Vermont, in 1849. This Yankee empire was gradually expanded through construction and line acquisition and included the New London Northern route between Brattleboro, Vermont, and New London, Connecticut (with steamship service to New York City), Rutland Railroad, and lines to Rouse Point and Ogdensburg, New York. Reorganization as result of the Panic of 1893 separated both the Rutland Railroad and Ogdensburg route from CV control.

▶ Central Vermont ran mainline steam until 1957, longer than most railroads in southern New England. CV 2-8-0 No. 464 works State Line Hill at Smiths Bridge, Stafford Hollow Road, Monson, Massachusetts. The steam exhaust from the tender shows that the locomotive's tender-truck booster engine is working. *Robert A. Buck*

The growl of Electro-Motive 16-567 diesels resonates through Palmer, Massachusetts, as three CV GP9s with local 562-B deliver interchange to Conrail. In its last years, CV operations on the south end of its line were based at Palmer, Massachusetts. Today, Palmer is a hub for CV successor New England Central. *Brian Solomon*

Headquarters: St. Albans, VT

Years operated: 1873–1995

Disposition: Sold to RailTex, renamed New England Central

Route mileage: 367 (c. 1972)

Locomotives

    Steam: 53 (c. 1952)

    Diesel: 26 (c. 1991)

    Gas-electric railcars: 2 (c. 1940)

Reporting mark: CV

Emblems: CENTRAL VERMONT RAILWAY on maple leaf or red box; later CV in stylized letters commonly referred to as the "toothpaste" or "wet noodle" logo

Primary locomotive shop: St. Albans, VT

Notable features: Tall Bridge (Georgia, VT); Connecticut River Bridge (East Northfield, MA); Millers River Bridge (Millers Falls, MA)

States served: CT, MA, NH, NY (via rail until 1893), VT

In 1898, Canada's Grand Trunk Railway took control of CV, and for the next 97 years it remained a Canadian-controlled line. In 1923, Canadian National Railways assumed control of GT, yet continued to operate CV as a U.S. subsidiary, granting it considerable autonomy.

Torrential rains in November 1927 caused flash floods that wiped away much of CV's Vermont infrastructure, forcing CN to rebuild these portions to modern standards using high fills and plate-girder viaducts. This was new construction that contrasted with older standards.

The railroad operated freight with 2-8-0s, but in 1928 bought 10 modern 2-10-4s that were the smallest of the Texas types and yet the largest locomotives in New England. These were limited to service north of Brattleboro, where the improved line was capable of accommodating their greater weight. The railroad clung to mainline steam a few years later than other lines in New England, and it wasn't fully dieselized until 1957.

CV and Boston & Maine shared trackage on the Connecticut River route between Windsor and the Massachusetts state line at East Northfield. Beginning in the early 1970s, Amtrak used the B&M/CV/CN route for its Washington–Montreal *Montrealer*. In the mid-1980s, service was suspended when trackage on the B&M-maintained portion was deemed unsuitable for passenger service. This resulted in a complex legal case that wrested the Windsor–Brattleboro section from its then owner and transferred it via Amtrak to CV. The *Montrealer* was restored in 1989, running over the length of the CV route until 1995, when it was discontinued in favor of the daytime *Vermonter* that used only the CV route north of Palmer, Massachusetts, to St. Albans, Vermont. By that time, CN had sold the route to regional rail operator RailTex, which renamed the line New England Central.

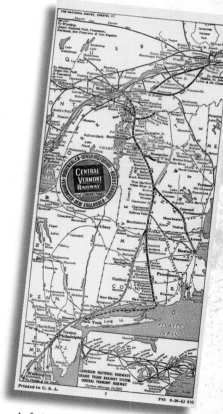

System map, 1942.
Richard Jay Solomon collection

CHESAPEAKE & OHIO RAILROAD

Chesapeake & Ohio was the product of the 1868 merger between Virginia Central and the Covington & Ohio. It grew to become a coal-hauling dynamo of the Pocahontas Region. Key to C&O's early fortunes was Collis P. Huntington—one of the "Big Four," as the men responsible for Central Pacific and Southern Pacific were known—who assumed the presidency of the line on July 15, 1869. He encouraged rapid C&O expansion, and by April 1873, it reached 428 miles from Richmond, Virginia, to the Ohio River port at Huntington, West Virginia. Lines were extended to tap coal-rich central Appalachia, and in 1882, C&O reached the tidewater port of Newport News, Virginia, and developed as a coal conduit.

Through connecting lines, C&O reached the Cincinnati gateway in 1881. Despite Huntington's hopes for C&O to serve as part of a transcontinental transportation scheme, the railroad faltered, and he lost control in 1888 when Vanderbilt interests backed by Drexel, Morgan & Company took over.

▼ A C&O 2-6-6-6 Alleghany works as a helper at the back of a loaded coal train. Between 1941 and 1948, Lima built 60 Alleghenies for C&O, which were among the heaviest steam locomotives ever built. *Photographer unknown, Solomon collection*

Vanderbilt control of C&O brought dynamic financing and more expansion. C&O acquired the Richmond & Alleghany, a low-grade route ideal for moving coal. By 1900, C&O stretched from Newport News and Washington, D.C., to Cincinnati and Louisville. Vanderbilt control ended in 1908, a result of antitrust efforts to separate railroad empires. Yet C&O continued to expand. By 1911, it had taken control of the Hocking Valley, which connected the Ohio River city of Gallipolis, Ohio, to Toledo. In this period C&O also reached Chicago, although, surprisingly this was never a principal C&O gateway.

In 1923, the Van Sweringen brothers bought control of the line, and by the early 1930s controlled C&O, Pere Marquette, Erie Railroad, and a host of other lines, which they hoped to merge into one super system. Their plans were dashed by the ICC, and then the onset of the Great Depression unraveled their financial empire. In 1936, financial wizard Robert Young took control of the Van Sweringens' railroads, emerging as chairman of C&O in 1942. In 1947, he merged C&O and Pere Marquette. In 1954, he left C&O to pursue his ambitions with New York Central, but in the 1950s C&O remained among the most prosperous railroads in the United States. Its merger with B&O in the 1960s resulted in the colorful Chessie System of the 1970s, which in turn became a primary component of the CSX network in the 1980s.

Now I GET A REST

ON this trip I'm an "idler"—working but not carrying a load. It's a break for me. You see, those concrete piles are 75 feet long so it takes three of us to carry a load like this, and the car in the middle is the goat. But, believe me, I *earned* this little rest! In the last few weeks I've covered over 3000 miles, most of the time carrying the heaviest doggone machinery you ever saw . . . from Cincinnati to Lynchburg, Virginia, with a ditch digger large enough to scoop out the Panama Canal . . . on to Richmond to get a pair of transformers for a power plant near Charleston . . . back to Cincinnati to pick up a contractor's outfit for Washington . . . But—that's life!

Right you are, C&O 80293, that's life on a hard-working, fast-working railroad. Part of the Chesapeake and Ohio's success is due to equipment, plant and personnel that are always ready to handle both rush and routine shipments on fast, dependable schedules, with unsurpassed efficiency and care.

Cheaspeake and Ohio representatives, located in principal cities, are ready to swing this efficient organization into action on your shipping problems.

CHESAPEAKE and Ohio LINES
CONTROLLED PERFORMANCE

▲ Freight advertisement, 1938.
Richard Jay Solomon collection

Headquarters: Cleveland, OH

Years operated: 1869–1987

Disposition: Became a component of Chessie System, later part of CSX

Route mileage:
3,092 (c. 1943); 5,116 (c. 1952)

Locomotives

Steam: 818 (c. 1938)

Diesel: 1,056 (c. 1962)

Self-propelled railcars:
6 (c. 1952)

Reporting mark: C&O

Emblems: C&O in a circle; silhouette of a kitten

Nickname: George Washington's Railroad

Primary locomotive shops:
Clifton Forge, VA; Huntington, WV

Notable features: Alleghany Tunnel (near Alleghany, VA), parallel bores 4,741 and 4,743 ft.; Big Bend Tunnels (near Hillsdale, WV), parallel bores 6,168 ft.; Ohio River Bridge (Cincinnati), 4,834 ft.; Ohio River Bridge (Sciotoville, OH), 3,437 ft.; Richmond, (VA) Viaduct, 14,827 ft.

States and province served:
IL, IN, KY, MI, NY, OH, VA, WV, WI (via car ferries), plus ON

Major cities served: Buffalo, Chicago, Cleveland, Cincinnati, Columbus, Detroit, Louisville, Washington, D.C.

Flagship passenger trains:
The George Washington (Cincinnati–Washington, D.C.)

Other name passenger trains:
The Fast Flying Virginian (Washington, D.C.–Cincinnati) and *The Sportsman* (Newport News–Detroit)

Notable freight commodity: Coal

Principal freight yards: Clifton Forge and Newport News, VA; Hinton and Huntington, WV; Presque Isle docks (near Toledo), OH; Russell, KY

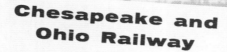

Chesapeake and Ohio Railway

PASSENGER TRAIN SCHEDULES

Along the Chessie Ro[ute]

Issued April 26, 1959

◀ Public timetable, April 1959.
Richard Jay Solomon collection

CHESAPEAKE AND OHIO LINES

Sleep like a Kitten

ROUTE OF

THE GEORGE WASHINGTON

THE SPORTSMAN

THE F. F. V.

OCTOBER 24, 1943

FOR VICTORY BUY UNITED STATES WAR BONDS AND STAMPS

TIME TABLES

▶ October 1943 public timetable featuring the famous Chessie Kitten.
Richard Jay Solomon collection

▲ C&O's train No. 6, the eastward *Fast Flying Virginian*, takes mail during its scheduled station stop at Kenova, West Virginia. *The F.F.V.*, as it was commonly known, operated daily, connecting Cincinnati, Washington, D.C., and New York City (via the Pennsylvania Railroad). *Richard Jay Solomon*

▶ C&O was known as the Chessie Route, a name that was used for the combined C&O/B&O Chessie System in the 1970s and 1980s. *Richard Jay Solomon collection*

79

CHICAGO & EASTERN ILLINOIS RAILROAD

The Chicago & Eastern Illinois was formed in 1877 as a result of reorganization of several midwestern Class 1 railroads. Its simple route structure bridged traffic from gateways at St. Louis, Missouri; Thebes and Joppa, Illinois; and Evansville, Indiana, north to Chicago. During the 1920s, it benefited from a southern Illinois coal boom, but this declined during the Great Depression.

C&EI's western stems served Missouri Pacific, while its eastern routes benefited Louisville & Nashville (L&N). It historically served as a route for passenger trains connecting Chicago with Georgia and Florida, but it operated its own classy passenger trains, as well.

In the diesel era, C&EI acquired Electro-Motive's sole BL1, the prototype for the BL2, an early road switcher design and precursor to EMD's General Purpose types built on a wide scale in the 1950s. In the 1960s, C&EI and L&N operated a joint Chicago–Nashville–Atlanta intermodal train.

▼ An E7A leads a Budd-built streamliner over the 21st Street Bridge at Chicago on August 10, 1947. C&EI not only provided a key link for long-distance passenger trains between Chicago and the Deep South, but it operated several of its own streamliners.
J. R. Quinn collection

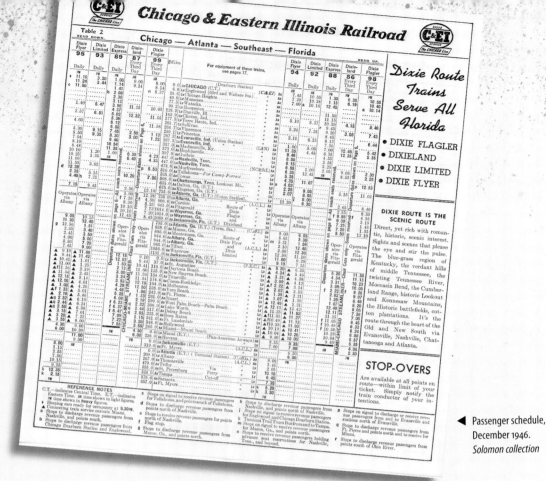

Passenger schedule, December 1946. *Solomon collection*

In the middle years of the twentieth century, C&EI entertained various merger options. In 1960, it courted Missouri Pacific (MP), but failed to make an immediate offer, so C&EI entertained L&N. C&EI continued this coy game, and for several years L&N and MP vied for control, ultimately agreeing to divide C&EI. The Interstate Commerce Commission approved MP's purchase of the C&EI in February 1967, including the provision that the former sell L&N the C&EI's eastern route from Evansville, Indiana, to Danville and Woodland Junction, Illinois, with trackage rights the rest of the way to Chicago. The ICC approved L&N's purchase in October 1968, and L&N introduced through traffic to Chicago in 1969.

Chicago & Eastern Illinois handed out ink blotters featuring company advertising. *Solomon collection*

Headquarters: Chicago, IL

Years operated: 1894–1976

Disposition: Divided between Missouri Pacific and Louisville & Nashville in the 1960s, with former routes today operated by Union Pacific and CSX

Route mileage: 909

Locomotives

   Steam: 357 (1923)

   Diesel: 93 (1959)

Reporting mark: C&EI

Emblem: Oval encircling railroad's initials

Nicknames: Danville Route, Dixie Route, The Boulevard of Steel, The Chicago Route

Primary locomotive shop: Oaklawn (Danville, IL)

States served: IL, IN, MO

Major cities served: Chicago and St. Louis

Name passenger trains:

The Whippoorwill (Chicago–Evansville, IN); *The Meadowlark* (Chicago–Cypress, IL); plus jointly operated services to Florida and Georgia: *Dixie Flagler* (Chicago–Miami); *Dixie Flyer* (Chicago–Jacksonville, FL); *Dixie Limited* (Jacksonville, FL–Chicago); *Hummingbird* and *The Georgian* (Chicago–Atlanta)

Notable freight commodity: Coal

Principal freight yards: Yard Center (Chicago); Brewer (Danville); Mitchell (near East St. Louis), IL

23

CHICAGO, BURLINGTON & QUINCY RAILROAD

▼ Burlington's Class O5-A 4-8-4 No. 5634 crosses the three-way diamond at the tower in Mendota, Illinois, in 1958. Here CB&Q's Chicago–Aurora–Galesburg double-track main line crossed secondary lines operated by Milwaukee Road and Illinois Central. CB&Q was among the last to operate big steam in the Midwest. *John E. Pickett*

Chicago, Burlington & Quincy's earliest component was the Hannibal & St. Joseph, chartered by the Missouri legislature on February 16, 1847; however, the 12-mile Aurora Branch Railroad, chartered in 1849, was the first Chicago, Burlington & Quincy predecessor to lay tracks and operate trains. More importantly, it played a key role in the organization that evolved into the CB&Q.

John Murray Forbes viewed America's vast unsettled prairies and plains as fertile grounds for railroad building, so in 1852 he founded a railroad that was renamed Chicago, Burlington & Quincy in 1855. By 1878, CB&Q had built or acquired approximately 2,700 route miles and numerous branch lines laced across its territory in Illinois and Missouri.

▲ On July 24, 1958, CB&Q SD9 No. 302 works a local freight at Centralia, Illinois. The railroad's slogan, "Everywhere West," described its extensive midwestern network and connections with lines to the Pacific Coast. *Richard Jay Solomon*

Headquarters: Chicago, IL
Years operated: 1855–1970
Disposition: Merged with Great Northern, Northern Pacific, and Spokane, Portland & Seattle to form Burlington Northern; routes now operated by BNSF
Route mileage: 11,000 (c. 1952)
Locomotives
  Steam: 1,575 (c. 1929)
  Diesel: 665 (c. 1970)
  Gas-electric railcars: 3 (c. 1952)
Reporting marks: CBQ; also BREX, RBBQ, RBBX
Emblem: Rectangle around "Burlington Route"
Slogan: Everywhere West
Primary locomotive shop: West Burlington, IA
Notable features: Mississippi River Bridge (Quincy, IL); Wind River Canyon, WY
States served: CO, IL, IA, KA, KY, MN, MO, MT, NE, NM, SD, TX, WI, WY
Major cities served: Chicago, Denver, Dallas/Ft. Worth, Houston, Kansas City, Minneapolis/St. Paul, Omaha, St. Louis

In the 1890s, CB&Q was the strongest of the midwestern "granger lines"—railroads that served, and survived, on agricultural traffic generated in the nation's breadbasket. CB&Q lines connected crucial gateways, which developed as the railroad's most lucrative and valuable routes. It established a hub at Lincoln, Nebraska, and pushed a line to Denver by 1882, offering that city's most direct link to Chicago. In 1886, CB&Q's Chicago, Burlington & Northern affiliate was built along the Mississippi River, connecting Chicago and the Twin Cities and providing a crucial link to the Northern Pacific (and later to James J. Hill's Great Northern). In 1894, a new line was completed across northern Nebraska that created a second gateway to Northern Pacific at Billings, Montana.

By the time Forbes died in 1898, CB&Q's sound management, excellent route structure, and healthy traffic had put it in an enviable position. In 1901, the line became the subject of the titanic struggle when western rail giants Hill and Harriman vied for its control. Ultimately, Hill prevailed and his Great Northern and Northern Pacific lines jointly owned the railroad. This arrangement survived, despite the federal government's forced dissolution of Hill's gigantic Northern Securities holding company, with which he had hoped to merge CB&Q, Northern Pacific, and Great Northern.

Hill encouraged further expansion, including control of the Colorado & Southern and its Texas affiliate, Fort Worth & Denver City, in late 1908. In the early twentieth century, CB&Q began equipping its main lines with automatic block signals and then invested heavily in Centralized Traffic Control after World War II.

CB&Q may be best remembered for its flashy Budd-built diesel streamliners. In 1970, the railroad was finally unified with the other Hill properties to form the Burlington Northern system.

Flagship passenger trains: *Zephyr* fleet (see below)

Named Passenger Trains: *Afternoon Zephyr* (Chicago–Minneapolis/St. Paul); *California Zephyr* (Chicago–Denver–Oakland, joint operation with Rio Grande and Western Pacific); *Denver Zephyr* (Chicago–Denver); *Empire Builder* (Chicago–Seattle and via SP&S to Portland, joint operation with Great Northern); *Morning Zephyr* (Chicago–Minneapolis/St. Paul); *Nebraska/Ak-sar-ben Zephyr* (Chicago–Omaha–Lincoln); *North Coast Limited* (Chicago–Seattle and via SP&S to Portland, joint operation with Southern Pacific)

Notable freight commodities: Coal and grain

Principal freight yards: Billings, MT; Cicero (Chicago) and Galesburg, IL; Denver; Lincoln, NE; Northtown (Minneapolis); North Kansas City, MO

▶ Burlington's July 1946 public timetable features one of its distinctive Budd-built shovel-nose *Zephyrs*. *Richard Jay Solomon collection*

▶ A CB&Q advertisement touts the pioneering role of the railroad's *Zephyr* service. *Richard Jay Solomon collection*

Burlington's
VISTA-DOME **DENVER ZEPHYR**
CHICAGO – DENVER – COLORADO SPRINGS

◀ This photo montage of the *Denver Zephyr* with the Rocky Mountains at Marias Pass ignores the fact that the train terminated before reaching the mountains. *Richard Jay Solomon collection*

▼ Burlington's *Pioneer Zephyr* was America's first diesel-powered streamliner. Its success spurred the railroad to order more trains. One of its Budd-built streamliners pauses at Hannibal, Missouri, on April 12, 1936. *Robert A. Buck collection*

CHICAGO CENTRAL & PACIFIC RAILROAD

24

In the 1980s, Illinois Central Gulf embarked on extensive network pruning and formed regional systems as it trimmed secondary main lines and branches. The first formed was Chicago, Central & Pacific (commonly known simply as Chicago Central), which began operations in December 1985 using the old Illinois Central east–west mainline routes between Sioux City, Iowa, and Omaha, Nebraska, and Chicago. It also operated several Iowa branches, including those to Cedar Rapids, and Ida Grove.

Initially led by Jack Haley, Chicago Central made an aggressive effort to attract business, which included operation of fast short intermodal trains. Haley's efforts failed, and in 1987, the railroad entered bankruptcy to stave off creditors and Haley was forced out. Post-Haley management embraced a more conservative approach to operations and cut costs. For the remainder of its decade-long independence, Chicago Central operated one single daily road freight between Chicago and Council Bluffs, along with local freights and

▼ On October 21, 1995, a CC&P freight in central Iowa rolls westward under stormy skies. This colorful midwestern regional enjoyed a decade of independence before being reabsorbed into the Illinois Central system. Today the line is run by Canadian National. *Brian Solomon*

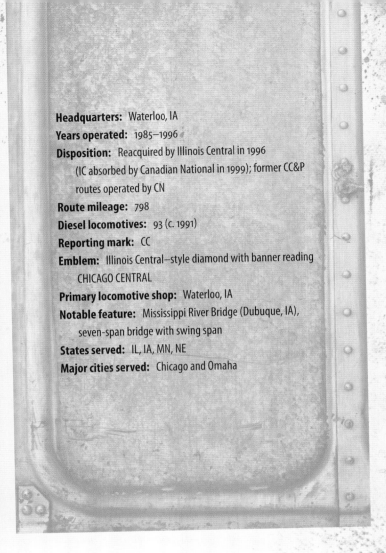

Headquarters: Waterloo, IA

Years operated: 1985–1996

Disposition: Reacquired by Illinois Central in 1996 (IC absorbed by Canadian National in 1999); former CC&P routes operated by CN

Route mileage: 798

Diesel locomotives: 93 (c. 1991)

Reporting mark: CC

Emblem: Illinois Central–style diamond with banner reading CHICAGO CENTRAL

Primary locomotive shop: Waterloo, IA

Notable feature: Mississippi River Bridge (Dubuque, IA), seven-span bridge with swing span

States served: IL, IA, MN, NE

Major cities served: Chicago and Omaha

▲ In 1995, former Illinois Central GP18 No. 9408 was still wearing factory paint while working on CC&P as a B-unit. *Brian Solomon*

unit coal and grain trains as needed. Additionally, it hosted diversions from the parallel Chicago & North Western/Union Pacific main line. In 1996, Illinois Central (which had dropped "Gulf") reacquired Chicago Central partly in response to Union Pacific's merger with Chicago and North Western.

All of Chicago Central's locomotives were acquired second-hand, and many came from Illinois Central Gulf as part of the original purchase. These were largely "Paducah Geeps"— ICG's remanufacture of Electro-Motive GP models at its Paducah, Kentucky, shops in the late 1960s and early 1970s. Many of these locomotives struggled on in faded IC/ICG paint. Chicago Central also operated a fleet of 10 GP38s dressed in the corporate scarlet.

▶ Detailed view of a CC&P locomotive at its Chicago yards. *Brian Solomon*

25

CHICAGO GREAT WESTERN RAILWAY

The name "Chicago Great Western Railway" was adopted in 1893 with the reorganization of the Minnesota & Northwestern. Although the railway had its formative stirrings in an 1854 charter, the classic CGW was really the brainchild of A. B. Stickney, who decided to add more route miles to a Midwest region already blanketed by lines. Through a mix of new construction and line acquisition, he first connected St. Paul and Chicago in 1888 and reached the Kansas City gateway in 1891 and Omaha in 1903. Its main lines crossed at Oelwein, Iowa, which was developed as the railroad's principal hub.

Although CGW connected four principal midwestern gateways, all of the routes were parallel to established carriers that generally offered superior lines, leaving CGW to compete fiercely for traffic (CGW operated a nominal passenger service, but focused primarily on freight). CGW was reorganized in 1908, exchanging *Railway* for *Railroad* in its name; bankrupt again in the Great Depression, another reorganization led to the readoption of *Railway*.

▼ CGW assembled a motley collection of Electro-Motive F-units in a succession of small orders that included F3As F7As, a pair of FP7s, and F3Bs and F7Bs. In its latter days, it operated long freights with as many as 10 Fs roaring away across the Iowa cornfields. *Richard Neumiller*

CGW is remembered for a variety of unusual equipment. In 1910, its Oelwein shops homebuilt some peculiar 2-6-6-2 Mallets, while in the 1930s it was one of only a few midwestern lines to adopt 2-10-4s for heavy freight work. Efforts to economize on passenger services led it to acquire a variety of internal combustion railcars, including aerodynamic McKeen cars. In 1929, it rebuilt some McKeens into a multicar, self-propelled train that foreshadowed the articulated streamliners of the mid-1930s. CGW completed dieselization in 1950 and was bought by C&NW in 1968. Precious little of it survives today.

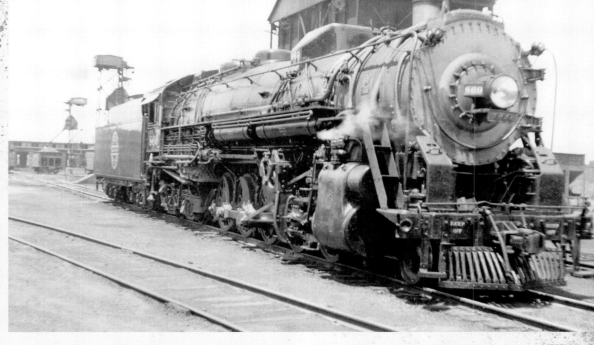

▲ One of CGW's big 2-10-4s. Although Burlington also embraced the Texas type, CGW was unusual among midwestern lines for its adoption of the 2-10-4. *Robert A. Buck collection*

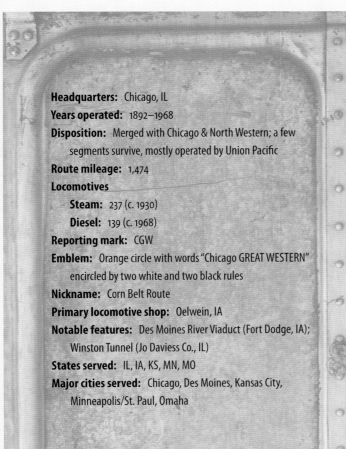

Headquarters: Chicago, IL

Years operated: 1892–1968

Disposition: Merged with Chicago & North Western; a few segments survive, mostly operated by Union Pacific

Route mileage: 1,474

Locomotives

    Steam: 237 (c. 1930)

    Diesel: 139 (c. 1968)

Reporting mark: CGW

Emblem: Orange circle with words "Chicago GREAT WESTERN" encircled by two white and two black rules

Nickname: Corn Belt Route

Primary locomotive shop: Oelwein, IA

Notable features: Des Moines River Viaduct (Fort Dodge, IA); Winston Tunnel (Jo Daviess Co., IL)

States served: IL, IA, KS, MN, MO

Major cities served: Chicago, Des Moines, Kansas City, Minneapolis/St. Paul, Omaha

▲ Public timetable, 1947. *Solomon collection*

26

CHICAGO, INDIANAPOLIS & LOUISVILLE RAILWAY

The Chicago, Indianapolis & Louisville Railway, otherwise known as the Monon, formed a gigantic X across the state of Indiana. Its earliest antecedent, New Albany & Salem, had projected a route between its namesake Indiana towns, the former being located on the Ohio River opposite Louisville. During the middle decades of the nineteenth century, this route evolved into the Louisville, New Albany & Chicago, which in 1883 merged with the Chicago & Indianapolis Air Line Railway. The two routes crossed at the village of Monon, Indiana, from which the railroad took its trade name. The merged railroad retained the name after it was reorganized in 1896 as the Chicago, Indianapolis & Louisville Railway.

Chronic financial problems dogged the line. It trimmed passenger operations to a minimum, but still the company struggled through the 1930s and was reorganized in 1946, with John W. Barriger III as president. Barriger's administration modernized the railroad in postwar fashion with diesels replacing steam, among other improvements, including a trio of named passenger trains. In the mid-1960s, Monon ordered a small fleet of Alco C-628 diesels to handle an anticipated coal boom. Alco delivered the big six-motor diesels in handsome black and gold paint, but the traffic failed to materialize, so Monon traded them back for more versatile C-420 units. Monon served to forward traffic from Chicago to the Louisville & Nashville at Louisville, but was swept up in the 1960s merger-mania. On August 1, 1971, it was merged with L&N.

▼ A pair of Fairbanks-Morse road switchers leads an employee's excursion at Michigan City, Indiana, on July 25, 1948. The 60-mile Monon–Michigan City line was one of the Monon's lightest-used lines. By the time of this excursion, the line no longer had regular passenger services. *Perry Frank Johnson photo, Center for Railroad Photography and Art*

▲ A set of new Monon F3 diesels was seen at the Lafayette, Indiana, servicing facilities on May 16, 1948. Under John W. Barriger III, the Monon rapidly dieselized its operations. *Perry Frank Johnson photo, Center for Railroad Photography and Art*

Headquarters: Chicago, IL

Years operated: 1897–1971

Disposition: Merged with Louisville & Nashville; surviving routes operated by CSX

Route mileage: 541 (c. 1952)

Locomotives

   Steam: 174 (c. 1929)

   Diesel: 44 (c. 1970)

Reporting marks: CIL and MON

Emblem: Circles around a stylized M with stone arrowhead

Nickname: The Hoosier Line

Trade name: Monon

Primary locomotive shop: Lafayette, IN

States served: IL, IN, KY

Major cities served: Chicago, Indianapolis, Louisville

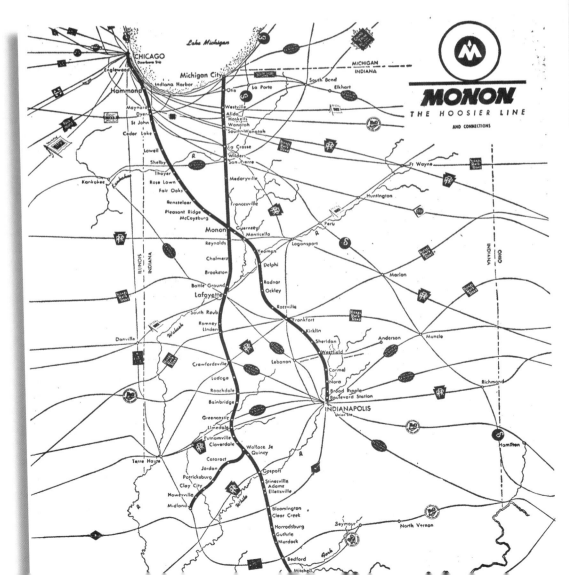

◀ A railroad map from June 1957 shows Monon's various interchange points. Lines toward Chicago offered freight connections to numerous midwestern carriers. *Solomon collection*

27

CHICAGO, MILWAUKEE, ST. PAUL & PACIFIC RAILROAD

By John Gruber

Incorporated in 1847 as the Milwaukee & Waukesha Rail Road Company, the Chicago, Milwaukee, St. Paul & Pacific, better known simply as the Milwaukee Road, grew into a major twentieth-century system that served the Midwest and Northwest. Its tracks connected the Lake Michigan port city of Milwaukee and the Mississippi River in 1857, spanning Wisconsin. Initially, it concentrated its service in the Midwest. Later, feeling competitive pressures, it built west from South Dakota to Puget Sound, Washington. A last-spike ceremony on May 14, 1909, in western Montana commemorated the completion of the extension.

▼ An *Olympian Hiawatha* stop in Deer Lodge, Montana, in 1955, afforded time to photograph electric locomotives near the depot. *John Gruber*

New Hiawathas are rollin'!

SIXTEEN Milwaukee Road Hiawathas are now rolling up nine thousand miles a day of superb service in ten midwestern and northwestern states. Velvety smooth and silent, these orange-maroon-and-silver flyers are as delightful to look at as they are to ride in—close to perfection for day or night rail travel.

With a huge fleet of new cars, the great majority of them built in its own shops, The Milwaukee Road has put new Hiawathas on the road—re-equipped existing Hiawathas—improved many other through trains.

Hiawatha-land is shown on the map below. Anywhere you go in this broad area, you can treat yourself to a zestful, restful ride on a Milwaukee Road Speedliner. H. Sengstacken, Passenger Traffic Manager, 708 Union Station, Chicago 6, Illinois.

Hiawatha Routes

THE *Milwaukee* ROAD
Speedway of the Speedliners

▲ Milwaukee Road advertisements feature its Skytop Lounge observation cars, among the most distinctive cars to work American rails. *Solomon collection*

Headquarters: Chicago, IL

Years operated: 1850–1985

Disposition: Merged into Soo Line (Canadian Pacific), 1985

Route mileage: 10,671 (1950)

Locomotives (1953)
    Steam: 600
    Diesel: 349
    Electric: 54

Reporting mark: MILW

Emblem: Angled red rectangle with italicized *THE MILWAUKEE ROAD* inside

Trade name: The Milwaukee Road

Primary locomotive shop: West Milwaukee, WI

Notable feature: Pacific Coast Extension through Belt, Rocky, Bitterroot, Saddle, and Cascade mountain ranges

States served: ID, IL, IN, IA, KS, KY, MI, MN, MO, MT, NE, ND, SD, WA, WI

Major cities served: Chicago, Milwaukee, Minneapolis/St. Paul, Seattle, Tacoma

Soon after, the railroad decided to electrify 647 miles through western mountains. The 3,000-volt DC project was the longest electrification undertaking in the world. The initial section between Harlowton, Montana, and Avery, Idaho, was completed from 1914 to 1916, and a second section between Othello and Tacoma, Washington, was finished in 1920. In 1950, the Milwaukee Road purchased 12 electric locomotives from General Electric. They were originally intended for sale to the Soviet Union, hence their "Little Joe" nickname, a nod to Joseph Stalin. Electric operations continued until 1974.

High-speed passenger trains, sometimes reaching 120 miles per hour, traveled the Milwaukee Road between Chicago and Minneapolis–St. Paul. The road made a prospectus drawing of a *Zephyr*-like articulated motor train in 1934, but instead turned to fast steam locomotives for its famed *Hiawatha* service, inaugurated in 1935. The Milwaukee Road continually improved this service, calling on famed industrial designer Otto Kuhler for attractive locomotive and even station designs. In the May 1957 issue of *Trains*, Donald M. Steffee listed the *Morning Hiawatha*'s 81-mile-per-hour run from Sparta to Portage, Wisconsin, as the world's only steam-powered run to exceed 80 miles per hour.

After World War II, the railroad shifted its industrial design work to Brooks Stevens, a Milwaukee artist best known for his end-of-the-train Skytop Lounge. The railroad operated the *Olympian Hiawatha* from 1947 to 1961 and, beginning in 1955, the "Western Cities" streamliners with the Union Pacific.

The railroad's Milwaukee Shops, under the leadership of chief mechanical officer Karl Nystrom, performed innovative work. While other railroads purchased passenger and freight cars from established builders, the Milwaukee Road constructed its own cars.

Flagship passenger trains:

Afternoon and *Morning Hiawathas* and *Pioneer Limited* (Chicago– Minneapolis/St. Paul); *Chippewa Hiawatha* (Chicago–Ontonagon, MI); *Midwest Hiawatha* (Chicago–Omaha via Sioux City); *North Woods Hiawatha* (New Lisbon, WI–Minocqua, WI); *Olympian Hiawatha* (Chicago–Seattle/Tacoma)

Other name passenger trains: *Copper County Limited* (Chicago–Calumet, MI); *Marquette* (Chicago– Mason City, IA); *Sioux* (Chicago–Rapid City, SD); *Arrow* (Chicago–Omaha/ Sioux City); *Southwest Limited* (Chicago–Kansas City, MO); *On Wisconsin* (Madison–Milwaukee)

Named freight train: *XL Special*

Notable freight commodities: Grain, coal, automobiles, lumber, paper, pulp

Principal freight yards: Bensenville, IL, and Pig's Eye (St. Paul), MN

▶ Milwaukee Road often touted its Pacific electrification in advertisements. *Solomon collection*

Yellowstone thru new Gallatin Gateway. Mount Rainier National Park, Puget Sound, Olympic Peninsula, Alaska.

Think! Vacations made to order! To fit your own fancy, purse and leisure! You'll like them immensely when you see how completely they embrace your own ideas, how generously they provide of Summer's joys in the enchanted Northwest.

Follow the trail of the new Olympian—The Milwaukee Road's famous roller-bearing de luxe train. 656 *electrified, smokeless, cinderless, mountain* miles. Once in the West, choose action —there's plenty of it. See Yellowstone's mystic land via inspiring new Gallatin Gateway. Try "wrangling" on dude ranches. Visit the Inland Empire's lakes. Then on across the Cascades to

The Romantic Northwest Wonderland

Vacations made to order for you—all-expense tours from Chicago for $145.00 and up. Ask for sample itinerary.

Seattle and Tacoma, wonder cities—vacation capitals.

Close by Mount Rainier's glaciers—Alpine sports all Summer ... Indian guides into the primal regions of the Olympic Peninsula, by dug-out or pack train ... snow-cloaked Mount Baker ... myriad isles of Puget Sound ... quaint Victoria, cosmopolitan Vancouver ... farther on, Alaska.

Leave it to Milwaukee Road travel specialists to fashion your trip. Gladly they'll submit samples, giving you five-fold pleasure for every dollar you spend. Costs are modest—$145 and up, all-expense from Chicago—due to low Summer fares. Mail coupon today.

The MILWAUKEE ROAD
ELECTRIFIED OVER THE ROCKIES TO THE SEA

Geo. B. Haynes, Passenger Traffic Manager, The Milwaukee Road, Room 920, Union Station, Chicago, Ill. Send me full information about: ☐ All-expense tours. ☐ Personally-escorted, all-expense tours. I have a ...... days' vacation and have about $ .... to spend. I would like to include in my itinerary: ☐ Yellowstone via Gallatin Gateway; ☐ Inland Empire (Spokane and Lake Region); ☐ Rainier National Park; ☐ Puget Sound Country; ☐ Olympic Peninsula; ☐ Alaska; ☐ Black Hills.

430-19

Name ....

Address ....

◀ Super Domes built for the *Olympian Hiawatha* were the antithesis of the extra-lightweight cars built for the Milwaukee Road's original *Hiawatha*. Designed for comfort and touring rather than speed, the domes were among the heaviest passenger cars ever built. *Solomon collection*

Notes along the Trail of the Super Dome

THE MILWAUKEE ROAD

Olympian Hiawatha

★

CHICAGO--SEATTLE TACOMA

THE MILWAUKEE ROAD'S FAMOUS SUPER DOME
OLYMPIAN *Hiawatha*

▶ Milwaukee Road advertising for its Super Dome services promised passengers a variety of fetching sights. *Voyageur Press collection*

Nystrom held about 100 patents for car construction and was especially well known for developing and building smooth-riding passenger-car trucks.

In 1963, the Milwaukee Road inaugurated the 55-hour *XL Special* and *Thunderhawk* freights, then the fastest between Chicago and the Pacific Northwest. Its main and branch lines provided regional marketing and distribution systems for many years. Under conditions of the Burlington Northern merger in 1970, the Milwaukee Road received additional gateways and trackage rights into Portland, Oregon. Two years later, as a condition of another merger, its service extended to Louisville, Kentucky.

The railroad survived bankruptcies in 1925 and 1935, but a third in 1977 resulted in its demise. The railroad abandoned or sold two-thirds of its lines, including almost everything west of Terry, Montana. After a bidding war, the courts awarded the Milwaukee Road to the Soo Line; it was fully merged into the Soo on December 31, 1985. Its legacy continues through such organizations as the Friends of Locomotive 261, which operates matching orange-and-maroon passenger cars, including a Super Dome and Skytop Lounge.

▼ A Milwaukee Road freight train carries open automotive racks across the Mississippi River on the Short-Line Bridge in Minneapolis in 1962. *Wallace W. Abbey photo, Center for Railroad Photography and Art Collection*

CHICAGO NORTH SHORE & MILWAUKEE RAILROAD

By John Gruber

The Chicago North Shore & Milwaukee, a high-speed electric interurban known for its *Electroliners* and every-hour-on-the-hour departures between Chicago and Milwaukee, had its beginnings as the Bluff City Electric, which opened in Waukegan, Illinois, in 1896. The company became the Chicago & Milwaukee Electric Railway, which in 1899 built south to Evanston (and connections to Chicago), then north to Milwaukee in 1908.

► Among the North Shore Line's innovations was its pair of streamlined articulated *Electroliners*. These entered service in 1941, with styling in part by Chicago architect James Eppenstein. The tavern-lounge car offered food and beverages, including cleverly named items such as the Electroburger. *John Gruber*

The company entered bankruptcy in 1908. Chicago utilities executive Samuel Insull reorganized it in 1916 and renamed it the Chicago North Shore & Milwaukee, most often referred to simply as the North Shore Line. Insull invested heavily in track and equipment improvements while initiating the use of innovative advertising and art-quality posters. One ad that appeared in 1925 called attention to "The North Shore Style" of architecture in referring to stations and company buildings, describing it as "careful design by a single architect," Arthur Gerber of Chicago.

The original (or shore) line was built through the heart of communities, with tracks running on city streets through downtown areas. A 23-mile, high-speed bypass route through the Skokie Valley opened in 1926 to the west of the shore line, and in 1927 the North Shore won *Electric Traction* magazine's speed trophy. The railway won the trophy five times in nine years and took permanent possession of it in 1933.

The North Shore's freight service included such innovations as the first piggyback (trailer-on-flatcar) service on any U.S. railroad in 1926.

A 14-year bankruptcy began in 1932, yet World War II traffic brought record passenger counts—almost 28 million riders in 1945. But with the establishment of the Chicago Transit Authority that put elevated and streetcar lines under a single municipal corporation in 1947, the joint offices that had been established in 1917 with other Insull railways were abolished.

In 1955, the shore line was shut down. In 1958, the railway asked the Interstate Commerce Commission for permission to abandon all service. Protests by a commuter association prolonged the legal proceedings, but the trains completed their final runs on the morning of January 21, 1963.

Headquarters: Highwood, IL

Years operated: 1896–1963

Disposition: Mostly abandoned; Chicago Transit Authority assumed operation of 5-mile segment from Howard Street Station to Skokie, IL

Route mileage: 122

Locomotives (1952)
  Electric: 8

Electric railcars: 142 single cars and 2 *Electroliner* articulated sets

Reporting mark: CNS&M

Emblem: Shield with outward arrows at ends and NORTH SHORE LINE inside

Trade name: North Shore Line

States served: IL and WI

Major cities served: Chicago and Milwaukee

Flagship passenger train: *Electroliners*

▼ Both of the classic trains in this *Electroliner* brochure have been preserved, one restored to North Shore's livery at the Illinois Railway Museum, the other at the Shade Gap Trolley museum at Orbisonia, Pennsylvania. *Richard Jay Solomon collection*

◄ Public timetable, April 1957. *Richard Jay Solomon collection*

NEVER BEFORE TRAINS LIKE THESE!
THE *Electroliners*
An entirely new kind of luxury travel in the world's most beautiful All-Electric trains

CHICAGO
NORTH SHORE
AND MILWAUKEE
RAILWAY

Schedule of Trains

TIME TABLE 58 · EFFECTIVE APRIL 28, 1957

NORTH SHORE LINE

"the route of the Electroliners"

CHICAGO & NORTH WESTERN RAILWAY

Chicago & North Western Railway was formed in 1859 from the reorganization of the Chicago, St. Paul & Fond du Lac Rail Road. During the second half of the nineteenth century it grew to become one of the largest networks radiating west from Chicago. Among the lines melded into C&NW was the Galena & Chicago Union Railroad (which in 1848 had been the first to operate west of Chicago). Also in the C&NW fold was the Omaha Road (trade name for the Chicago, St. Paul, Minneapolis & Omaha Railway), which retained a degree of independence while connecting Omaha, Minneapolis–St. Paul, and Duluth.

C&NW gobbled up potential competitors during the second half of the twentieth century, acquiring Litchfield & Madison in 1958, Minneapolis & St. Louis in 1960, and Chicago Great Western in 1968. C&NW largely dismembered these acquisitions, leaving only fragments to augment its own lines. In the 1960s, C&NW and the Milwaukee Road seriously considered merger but couldn't agree on the details. In 1980, C&NW acquired Rock Island's Twin Cities–Kansas City "Spine Line," eventually enabling it to abandon most of the parallel CGW route.

▼ One of C&NW's most famous landmarks was the massive 2,685-foot-long Kate Shelley Bridge on its Chicago–Omaha main line west of Boone, Iowa. On the stormy night of July 6, 1881, 15-year-old Kate Shelley heroically braved the weather to warn a C&NW passenger express of a washout on the line. *Brian Solomon*

▲ C&NW controlled the Chicago, St. Paul, Minneapolis & Omaha Railway. Locomotives assigned to "the Omaha Road" were sub-lettered for the line. This 4-6-2 Pacific was photographed at Minneapolis in the early 1930s and features the C&NW logo on the tender, with "CStPM&O" on the sides of its cab. *S. W. Henderson photo, Robert A. Buck collection*

Significantly, in 1984, C&NW expanded into Wyoming's Power River Basin coal fields with help from Union Pacific. In its last decades, C&NW became increasingly focused on forwarding Powder River coal and UP's east–west traffic between Fremont and Omaha and Chicago. It gradually paired back its network, selling and abandoning branches and secondary routes. In its final years, C&NW had several "island operations"—lines orphaned from its core that gave its system map a patchy disconnected appearance. Following the announcement of the Burlington Northern Santa Fe merger, and UP's failed bid to woo Santa Fe from BN, UP acquired C&NW, merging the properties in spring 1995.

Among C&NW's distinctive qualities were left-hand running on directional double-track lines, use of an unusual short-blade semaphore, and its "pink lady" quartz ballast quarried at Rock Springs, Wisconsin. C&NW's massive Proviso Yard in the Chicago suburbs was the largest of its kind for many years. C&NW also operated an intensive Chicago-area suburban passenger service that in the 1950s was one of the first to make use of modern bi-level push-pull equipment. C&NW's 400-mile route between Chicago and the Twin Cities resulted in C&NW cleverly naming its crack 1930s passenger trains *The 400s*.

Headquarters: Chicago, IL

Years operated: 1859–1995

Disposition: Merged with Union Pacific, by which time many routes had been truncated or abandoned; surviving lines largely part of UP system

Route mileage (incl. affiliates): 9,539 (c. 1948); 4,991 (c. 1995)

Locomotives
  Steam: 699 (c. 1952)
  Diesel: 707 (c. 1995)

Reporting mark: CNW

Emblem: Circle bisected by oversized diagonal banner reading CHICAGO AND NORTH WESTERN SYSTEM

Primary locomotive shops: Marshalltown and Oelwein, IA (former CGW)

Notable feature: Kate Shelly Bridge over Des Moines River (near Boone, IA), double-track deck-plate, tower-supported trestle, 2,685 ft. long, 184 ft. tall

States served: IL, IA, MI, MN, MO, NE, ND, SD, WI, WY

Major cities served: Chicago, Milwaukee, Minneapolis/ St. Paul, Omaha, Peoria, St. Louis

▶ In 1945, C&NW was keen to mark its history on the back cover of the public timetable. *Solomon collection*

▼ Timetable, December 1945. *Solomon collection*

YESTERDAY and TOMORROW . . . . a story of Transportation FIRSTS

GRAND-DADDY OF 'EM ALL !

and a magnificent thing to behold

October 10, 1848, was a great day in Chicago, for it was then that the brig "Buffalo" came into port with Chicago's first railway locomotive, the "Pioneer," on board.

True, it was a second-hand locomotive, though in excellent condition. Its one pair of driving wheels were directly under the cab; and its 10″-diameter cylinders tilted slightly rearward—the fashion of the day.

It was a magnificent thing to behold! And less than a month later, on its official run, many of Chicago's "Who's Who" made a short run west. There were directors, stockholders, business men and editors—the west's first passengers—who sat on seats fitted hastily into a couple of work cars to experience a new speed thrill.

Thus it was that Chicago and North Western became a living, moving reality.

The old "Pioneer" is now on display at the Museum of Science and Industry, Jackson Park, Chicago.

Many years have passed since that first locomotive—the old "Pioneer"—went into honorable retirement, to be succeeded by ever larger and more powerful locomotives. Today's mighty power plants are busy "keeping 'em rollin'" toward final victory. When you travel only when it is absolutely essential you help in this vital work. In the peace days to come, with its postwar plans finding expression in new and even finer equipment, "North Western" will continue to serve—*and serve well*—the shippers and travelers of America.

CHICAGO and NORTH WESTERN SYSTEM
SERVING AMERICA IN WAR AND PEACE FOR ALMOST A CENTURY

DECEMBER 15, 1946

CHICAGO AND NORTH WESTERN SYSTEM

SF-1   400   400   SF-1

Serves the

WEST, NORTHWEST PACIFIC COAST

CHICAGO AND NORTH WESTERN
RAILWAY

Route of the 400's, The *Streamliners* and the *Challengers*

Serves the

WEST, NORTHWEST PACIFIC COAST

NORTH WESTERN UNION PACIFIC

The Overland Route

Flagship passenger trains: *400s* (see below); premier trains operated with Southern Pacific and Union Pacific, including *Overland Limited* (Chicago–Oakland) and *City of San Francisco* (Chicago–Oakland)

Other name passenger trains: *Arrowhead Limited* (Duluth–Chicago); *Capitol 400* (Chicago–Madison); *City of Denver* (Chicago–Denver, operated with Union Pacific); *City of Los Angeles* (Chicago–Los Angeles, operated with Union Pacific); *City of Milwaukee 400* (Chicago–Milwaukee); *City of Portland* (Chicago–Portland, operated with Union Pacific); *North Western Limited* (Chicago–Minneapolis/St. Paul and Duluth); *Peninsula 400* (Chicago–Ishpeming, MI); *Shoreland 400* (Chicago–Green Bay); *The Nightingale* (Minneapolis/St. Paul–Omaha); *The North American* (Minneapolis/St. Paul–Los Angeles, operated with Union Pacific); *The Viking* (Chicago–Minneapolis/St. Paul); *Valley 400* (Chicago–Green Bay)

Notable freight commodities: General freight, grain, coal

Principal freight yards: Marshalltown, IA, and Proviso (Chicago)

An eastward C&NW piggyback train approaches the diamond crossing with Burlington Northern at Rochelle, Illinois, on April 2, 1995—less than two months before C&NW was absorbed into the Union Pacific system. *Brian Solomon*

▼ Pocket calendar, 1908. *Voyageur Press collection*

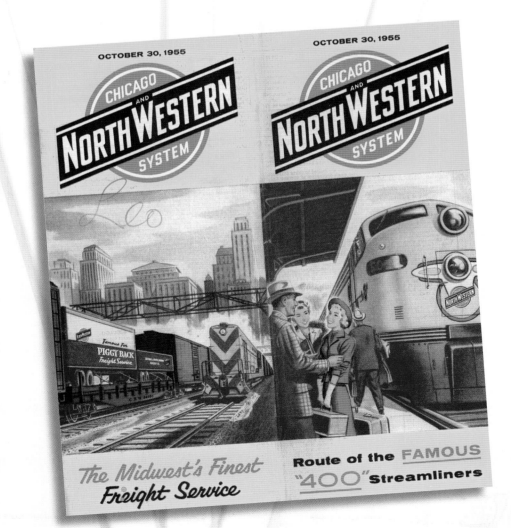

◀ Public timetable, October 1955. Many railroads used passenger timetables as a general promotion for their routes and services. *Solomon collection*

CHICAGO, ROCK ISLAND & PACIFIC RAILROAD

The Rock Island & LaSalle Railroad was conceived in 1847 as a line running west of Chicago. Renamed the Chicago & Rock Island, construction began in 1851. By 1852, it reached from Chicago to Joliet and connected its namesakes by 1854. A consolidation resulted in the railroad changing its name to Chicago, Rock Island & Pacific in 1866.

In the late nineteenth century, it expanded rapidly between Chicago and the Rockies and continued to grow into the early decades of the twentieth century. Ultimately, it connected most important gateways in the region, reaching the Twin Cities to the north, Denver and Colorado Springs to the west, Dallas to the south, and Chicago, St. Louis, and Memphis to the east. Unfortunately for "the Rock," just about everywhere it went it faced stiff competition from stronger railroads with superior routes. One of its few distinctive corridors was its line connecting Memphis, Oklahoma City, and Tucumcari, New Mexico.

▼ Several months after Amtrak assumed operation of most American long-distance passenger trains, Rock Island's *Peoria Rocket* departs Chicago's LaSalle Street Station. Although Rock Island didn't join Amtrak in 1971, and continued to operated its own trains, both the train and the railroad only survived a few more years.
George W. Kowanski

▲ The Rock commissioned this stunning artwork for the cover of their 1960 annual report. *Voyageur Press collection*

Suffering from chronically inadequate finances, the Rock struggled into the motor age thanks partly to an influx of heavy traffic during World War II. In the early 1960s, Rock considered merging with Southern Pacific, but was wooed by Union Pacific. Other railroads protested a merger, and the case carried on for more than a decade. In the meantime, Rock Island withered. By the mid-1970s, it suffered from years of underinvestment and deferred maintenance. The railroad was too broke to join Amtrak in 1971 and continued operating its own limited passenger services. The Interstate Commerce Commission approved the Union Pacific–Rock merger in 1974, but the Union Pacific declined when the Rock declared bankruptcy in 1975. Despite this, the Rock struggled on for a few more years, with new management introducing a modern image. Sadly, there was no helping the dying carrier, and the Rock gave up the ghost in March 1980.

The Rock Island shield. *Brian Solomon*

Headquarters: Chicago, IL

Years operated: 1866–1980

Disposition: Property liquidated and sold off piecemeal with some routes abandoned; Chicago–Joliet operated by Metra; Joliet–Council Bluffs operated by Iowa Interstate; Belleville, KS–Limon, CO, operated by Kyle Railroad; numerous other surviving segments operated by Union Pacific, BNSF, and various short lines

Route mileage: 7,649 (c. 1952)

Locomotives

   Steam: 1,453 (c. 1929)

   Diesel: 602 (c. 1980)

Reporting marks:

   RI and ROCK

Emblem: Unusually shaped shield with "Rock Island"

Nickname: Route of the Rockets

Trade name: Rock Island Lines

Primary locomotive shops:

   Silvis, IL, and Horton, KS

Notable features: Cimarron River Bridge (near Liberal, KS), 1,269 ft.; Harahan Bridge over Mississippi River (Memphis), 4,909 ft.; Truman Bridge over Missouri River (Randolph, MO), 2,634 ft.

States served: AR, CO, IL, IA, KS, LA, MN, MO, NE, NM, OK, SD, TN, TX

Major cities served: Chicago, Dallas/Ft. Worth, Des Moines, Denver, Houston, Kansas City, Little Rock, Memphis, Minneapolis, St. Louis

Lines and locomotives were sold off, with many of the Rock's routes surviving. The Tucumcari–Kansas City line went to Southern Pacific; the "Spine Line" went to Chicago & North Western; the Joliet–Omaha line emerged as the Iowa Interstate; Union Pacific and Katy picked up other sections; and portions of the main line across Kansas and Colorado were operated by the Kyle Railroad. Chicago suburban services were retained by the Regional Transportation Authority (later operated by METRA). Ironically, the strategic Memphis–Tucumcari route was largely abandoned.

▶ A Rock Island advertisement for its Chicago–Denver and Colorado Springs *Rocky Mountain Rocket*. *Solomon collection*

▶ Rock Island and Southern Pacific jointly ran the Chicago–Los Angeles *Golden State*. *Solomon collection*

▲ In the Rock's last years it adopted a new sky-blue livery. The railroad was in its final days when freight No. 216 worked eastbound past the station at Ottawa, Illinois, on March 15, 1980. *John Leopard*

CHICAGO SOUTH SHORE & SOUTH BEND RAILROAD

During the 1890s, the electrically powered street railway concept was expanded into lightly constructed interurban electric railways running between cities and towns and typically in competition with traditional steam railways. Within a few decades, interurban electric lines had blanketed the United States, with the greatest concentration of lines in the Midwest. Many interurbans suffered from precarious finances and faired poorly when paved highways allowed motorized transport to erode their traffic bases rapidly. By the end of World War I, many electric interurban lines were in trouble, and most vanished from the scene during the 1920s and 1930s. The Chicago South Shore & South Bend was the exception to the rule and has survived as an interurban electric operation to the present day, earning the moniker "America's Last Interurban."

The South Shore, as it's known colloquially, originated with a street car line in East Chicago, and by 1904 had been expanded into the Chicago Lake Shore & South Bend, which built eastward largely parallel to New York Central's main line. Connection with Illinois Central, and electrification of Illinois Central's suburban lines, ultimately allowed the South Shore to serve Chicago directly. Key to its survival was the reorganization in 1925 as the Chicago South Shore & South Bend Railroad by Chicago Public Utilities mogul, Samuel Insull, who had already revitalized the Chicago North Shore & Milwaukee

▼ The South Shore's Michigan City shops display a variety of equipment on July 14, 1958. From left to right: GE "Little Joe" electric No. 802, Electro-Motive SW1 No. 602, and a typical modernized all-steel electric multiple-unit. *Richard Jay Solomon*

Contemporary freight diesels are dressed in South Shore's classic colors. GP38-2 No. 2005 was photographed in February 1995. *Brian Solomon*

Headquarters: Michigan City, IN

Years operated: 1903–present

Route mileage: 88 (c. 1971)

Locomotives (c. 1971)

　Diesel: 1

　Electric: 10

　Electric railcars: 48 motorcars and 9 trailers

Reporting mark: CSS

Emblems: Historically a "Tootsie Roll"–shaped emblem with burgundy outline and SOUTH SHORE LINE; currently with reversed colors and words SOUTHSHORE FREIGHT

Nickname: America's Last Interurban

Trade name: South Shore Line

Primary locomotive shop: Michigan City, IN

States served: IN and IL

Major cities served: Chicago

interurban. Insull set about modernizing and improving the South Shore, including re-electrification with a 1,500-volt direct-current system and an all-new fleet of large steel interurban cars.

South Shore benefited from healthy freight business as well as robust passenger traffic. Although the line was in bankruptcy during the Depression, it was one of a few interurbans to survive after World War II. In the early 1950s, it acquired three streamlined electric locomotives from General Electric that had been intended for the Soviet Union, and were thus known as "Little Joes" after Soviet dictator Joseph Stalin. Chesapeake & Ohio acquired the line in 1967, and beginning in 1973, public finances were committed to subsidize passenger services, ultimately resulting in formation of the Northern Indiana Commuter Transportation District (NICTD). C&O successor CSX sold the South Shore to Vernango River Corporation in 1984, but by 1990 Vernango was forced to sell South Shore, allowing NICTD to take over passenger services. In recent years, a private company has handled freight under the Chicago South Shore & South Bend name and under the trade name Southshore Freight.

▼ Eastward schedules, 1945. *Richard Jay Solomon collection*

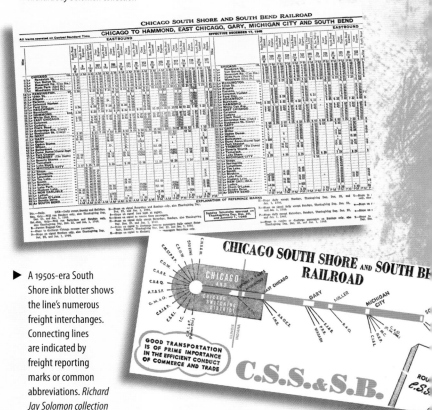

▶ A 1950s-era South Shore ink blotter shows the line's numerous freight interchanges. Connecting lines are indicated by freight reporting marks or common abbreviations. *Richard Jay Solomon collection*

107

CLINCHFIELD RAILROAD

The Clinchfield was a modern north–south line built to exceptionally high standards. The line traced its origins to 1886, when myriad schemes were conceived to tap coal fields in Virginia and eastern Kentucky. George L. Carter picked up where others had failed and in 1908 consolidated existing lines as the Carolina, Clinchfield & Ohio. Within a year his railroad connected Dante, Virginia, with Spartanburg, South Carolina.

Where Clinchfield's precursors suffered from poorly engineered lines, Carter funded line relocations to bring the railroad to modern standards. To navigate difficult terrain, the railroad employed numerous bridges and tunnels to maintain reasonable gradients. A connection with Chesapeake & Ohio at Elkhorn City, Kentucky, required a 35-mile extension northward from Dante that opened in February 1915 and featured some of the most spectacular engineering on the whole railroad, including 20 tunnels that combined measured nearly 4 miles. In total, the Clinchfield had four mountain crossings; the most spectacular, at Alta Pass, North Carolina, used a series of reverse curves to ascend a summit of 2,620 feet above sea level.

Clinchfield's strategic route and lucrative coal traffic made it a desirable property. In 1924, the Atlantic Coast Line and Louisville & Nashville signed a joint 999-year lease on the Clinchfield. Yet, the Clinchfield maintained a distinctly independent appearance into the 1970s before becoming a component of Seaboard Coast Line's and L&N's "Family Lines" marketing scheme. It was melded into CSX's Seaboard System at the end of 1982.

▼ In October 1978, Clinchfield senior engineer J. D. Davis eases his loaded coal train to a stop as he approaches a meet near Sevier, North Carolina. Clinchfield was partial to Electro-Motive 20-cylinder models, ordering SD45s and SD45-2s, both rated at 3,600 horsepower. Clinchfield No. 3619 is an SD45-2; trailing is SD45 No. 3628. *Lewis Raby photo, Tom Kline collection*

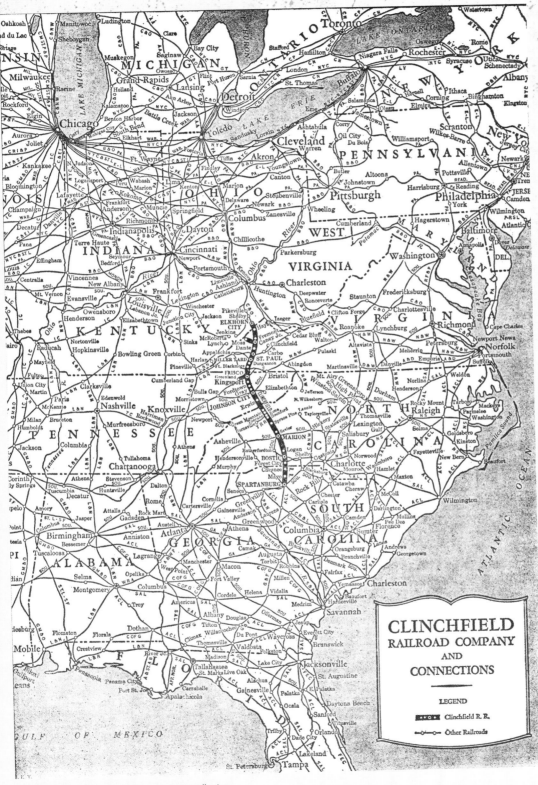

▲ A Clinchfield route map, circa 1949. *Solomon collection*

Headquarters: Erwin, TN
Years operated: 1924–1982
Disposition: Melded into Seaboard System; now operated by CSX
Route mileage: 317 (c. 1952)
Locomotives
  Steam: 86 (c. 1950)
  Diesel: 98 (c. 1982)
Reporting mark: CRR
Primary locomotive shop: Erwin, TN
Notable features: Altapass (NC) Loops, featuring 18 tunnels; 36 additional tunnels and numerous tall bridges; Nolichucky River Gorge (near Erwin, TN)
States served: KY, NC, SC, TN, VA
Notable freight commodity: Coal

33

CONRAIL

Consolidated Rail Corporation was the government-designed rescue for a half-dozen bankrupt eastern lines, including Central Railroad of New Jersey, Erie Lackawanna, Lehigh & Hudson River, Lehigh Valley, Reading Company, and most of all, Penn Central.

Better known by its trade name, Conrail, and colloquially as "Big Blue," this massive network struggled into life on April Fool's Day 1976. Some in the industry feared it was the first step toward total nationalization of America's railroad network, a dreaded prospect contrary to capitalistic principles during the height of the Cold War. Yet, while the new railroad was wholly owned by the government, it still functioned as a private company. It was, by far, the largest railroad in the United States. Conrail's 1976 annual report noted that it encompassed more than 34,000 track miles (roughly 17,000 route miles), employed

▼ One of Conrail's prime assets was the former New York Central "Water Level Route," which it used as a major east–west freight corridor. On August 30, 1988, piggyback train, symbol TV-79, races west at Tifft Street, Buffalo, New York. *Brian Solomon*

▲ Conrail operations executive Richard Hassleman was once quoted in *Trains* as saying, "The Delaware Division is lovely. But what the hell is down there?" Nonetheless, in the mid-1980s, the former Erie Railroad division across New York and eastern Pennsylvania saw a resurgence as a choice Conrail route for double-stack container trains. Conrail GP40s with train symbol TV-300 (Chicago–Kearny, New Jersey) work east along the Delaware River near Long Eddy, New York, in June 1988. *Brian Solomon*

nearly 96,000 employees, and moved more than 1,500 freight trains and 1,864 commuter trains daily. Yet, Conrail, by design, was intended to slim down railroading operations in the East. Numerous lines deemed surplus, redundant, or otherwise unworthy of continued operation were excluded from the network at its start. The western reaches of the Erie Lackawanna and Lehigh Valley systems were left to rot. Other key routes, such as the former Penn Central Northeast Corridor, were conveyed to Amtrak, with Conrail operating on them only via trackage rights.

Once Conrail began operations it spent the next 23 years thinning its route map. Numerous once-important routes withered. The old Delaware, Lackawanna & Western route was truncated, bits of it were sold, and much of it was downgraded or abandoned. Former Penn Central lines were largely favored over the other component railroads, and former New York Central lines were favored west of the Pennsylvania-Ohio state line, leaving large portions of the old Pennsylvania Railroad to be downgraded. Some

Headquarters: Philadelphia, PA

Years operated: 1976–1999

Disposition: Acquired and divided by CSX and Norfolk Southern

Route mileage: 17,000 (c. 1977)

Locomotives (c. 1977)

   Diesel: 4,500

   Electric: 148

Reporting mark: CR

Emblem: Stylized steel wheels on rails

Primary locomotive shops:
   Altoona, PA; Collinwood (Cleveland); DeWitt (Syracuse) and Harmon, NY

Notable features: Horseshoe Curve (near Altoona, PA); Portage Bridge over Letchworth Gorge (near Castile, NY); Rockville Bridge over Susquehanna River (Rockville–Marysville, PA), 3,820 ft.; Smith Memorial Bridge over Hudson River (Castleton-on-Hudson–Selkirk, NY); Starrucca Viaduct (Lanesboro, PA), 1,040 ft. long, 100 ft. high

States and provinces served:
   CT, DE, IN, IL, MD, MA, MI, MO, NJ, NY, OH, PA, VA, WV, plus ON and QC

Major cities served:
   Baltimore, Boston, Buffalo, Chicago, Cincinnati, Cleveland, Columbus, Detroit, Indianapolis, Montreal, New York, Philadelphia, Pittsburgh, Rochester, St. Louis, Syracuse, Toledo, Washington D.C.

Notable freight commodities: Chemicals, coal, general merchandise, intermodal, vehicular traffic (autos and auto parts)

Principal freight yards: Allentown, Conway (near Pittsburgh), and Enola (near Harrisburg), PA; Avon (Indianapolis) and Elkhart, IN; Collinwood (near Cleveland); DeWitt (Syracuse), Frontier (Buffalo), and Selkirk (near Albany), NY; East St. Louis and Rose Lake (Washington Park), IL; Oak Island (near Newark), NJ; Potomac (near Washington D.C.)

electrified Pennsy routes were conveyed to Amtrak, but the portions built for freight didn't fit into Conrail's operating scheme and were de-energized (a seemingly bizarre move in retrospect, given the late-1970s energy crisis). It took years for Conrail to establish its own distinctive identity. Billions of federal dollars were injected to improve its physical plant, and deregulation turned the tide of decay, so that by the early 1980s Conrail was earning a profit. It was freed from government ownership in 1987. A decade later, CSX and Norfolk Southern agreed to purchase and divide the property. Conrail's independent operations ended in the spring of 1999.

▲ In 1995–1996, Conrail took delivery of its first diesels to feature a state-of-the-art three-phase alternating current traction system. The SD80MACs, 30 in all, were rated at 5,000 horsepower each and painted in this distinctive scheme. *Brian Solomon*

▲ On December 15, 1992, Conrail's westward intermodal train symbol TV9 (Boston to Chicago) ascends Washington Hill on the former Boston & Albany Railroad. The train has reached Washington Cut, the deepest of many rock cuts on the line that was completed in 1841. The B&A route is considered to be the oldest mountain main line in the world, and much of the original alignment remains in use today by CSX. *Brian Solomon*

34

CSX

▼ Of America's six largest railroads, CSX has the most complex modern history. Not only does it encompass Chessie System and Seaboard Coast Line railroads, but it involves large portions of the former Conrail system, including the old Boston & Albany route. A westward freight ascends Washington Hill near Middlefield, Massachusetts, on October 19, 2009. *Brian Solomon*

CSX was created in 1978 as a holding company to merge Seaboard Coast Line and its affiliated railroads (Louisville & Nashville, Clinchfield, and so on) with the Chessie System (Baltimore & Ohio, Chesapeake & Ohio, and Western Maryland). Though the railroads were grouped under this new banner in 1980, initially they continued to function as before. In 1983, the SCL components were consolidated to form the Seaboard System as a result of the formal merger between SCL and Louisville & Nashville, which together already owned Clinchfield.

For a few years it appeared as if the individual CSX railroads would retain a degree of their independent identities. However, in 1986, CSX Transportation was created as

Headquarters: Jacksonville, FL

Years operated: 1980–present

Route mileage: 21,190 (2009)

Diesel locomotives: 4,071 (2009)

Reporting mark: CSXT

Primary locomotive shops: Waycross, GA; Corbin, KY; Cumberland, MD; Huntington, WV

Notable features: Former Chesapeake & Ohio Alleghany Tunnel (Alleghany, Virginia); Altapass (NC) Loops, featuring 18 tunnels (former Clinchfield); Howard Street Tunnel (Baltimore; former Baltimore & Ohio), 7,341 ft.; former C&O Big Bend Tunnels (near Hillsdale, WV), parallel bores 6,168 ft.; James River Bridge and viaducts (Richmond, VA), former C&O; Ohio River bridges (Cincinnati and Sciotoville, OH); Sand Patch Tunnel (near Meyersdale, PA; former Baltimore & Ohio); Smith Memorial Bridge over Hudson River (Castleton-on-Hudson–Selkirk, NY); former B&O Susquehanna River Bridge (Havre de Grace, MD); former B&O Tray Run Viaduct (WV)

States and provinces served: AL, CT, DE, GA, FL, IL, IN, KY, LA, MD, MA, MS, MO, NJ, NY, NC, OH, PA, SC, TN, VA, WV, plus ON and QC

Major cities served: Atlanta, Baltimore, Boston, Buffalo, Chicago, Chattanooga, Cincinnati, Cleveland, Columbus, Detroit, Indianapolis, Jacksonville, Louisville, Memphis, Miami, Mobile, Montreal, Nashville, New Orleans, New York, Philadelphia, Pittsburgh, Rochester, St. Louis, Toledo

Notable freight commodities: Automobiles, coal, general freight, intermodal, perishables, phosphates

Principal freight yards: Avon (Indianapolis); Barr (Chicago); Boyles (Birmingham); Cumberland, MD; DeWitt (Syracuse), Frontier (Buffalo), Selkirk (near Albany), NY; Hamlet, NC; Osborn (Louisville); Queensgate (Cincinnati), Stanley (Toledo), Willard, OH; Radnor (Nashville); Rice (Waycross) and Tilford (Atlanta), GA

part of a larger corporate restructuring, which ultimately ended the Chessie System and Seaboard System images. Now CSXT, the railroad painted its first locomotives in April 1986, and on July 1, Seaboard System became CSX, while Baltimore & Ohio was officially merged with Chesapeake & Ohio on April 30, 1987. When the C&O was finally merged into CSXT on September 2, 1987, CSX was left as the dominant corporate image. In 1990, CSXT merged with Richmond, Fredericksburg & Potomac and absorbed the assets of Pittsburgh & Lake Erie in 1992.

The most significant expansion occurred in the late 1990s, when, along with Norfolk Southern, CSXT agreed to acquire and divide the slimmed-down Conrail network. Under the plan, CSX would primarily acquire former New York Central lines east of Cleveland, along with joint ownership and operation of key routes in the New Jersey and Detroit terminal areas. The Surface Transportation Board granted formal approval for the acquisition on July 23, 1998, and CSX and NS took control of Conrail in August. CSX assumed its operation of Conrail lines at the end of May 1999. In a roundabout way, this satisfied the plan considered 40 years earlier for a three-way merger among B&O, C&O, and New York Central.

▲ Entrance sign to CSX's former Baltimore & Ohio yard at New Castle, Pennsylvania. *Brian Solomon*

▲ On October 5, 2005, a pair of AC6000CWs leads a southward CSX freight at Weldon, North Carolina, on the former Atlantic Coast Line. CSX concentrated traffic south of Richmond on the old ACL route while abandoning through services on the former Seaboard Air Line. *Brian Solomon*

◀ The lightning bolt under the unit number on this General Electric ES44AH signifies the locomotive has a three-phase alternating current traction system. *Brian Solomon*

◀ One of the steepest double-track lines in the United States—and one of the most difficult sections of main line in the East—is the Cranberry Grade on the old Baltimore & Ohio "Westend" (Cumberland, Maryland, to Grafton, West Virginia), today operated as CSX's Mountain Subdivision. On October 24, 1992, a trio of CSX SD50s shoves at the back of a loaded coal train ascending Cranberry Grade at McMillan, West Virginia. The grade crests at Terra Alta, but the helpers will stay on at least as far as Altamont, Maryland. *Brian Solomon*

35

DAKOTA, MINNESOTA & EASTERN RAILROAD

Dakota, Minnesota & Eastern was among the longer of the 1980s-era regional spin-off lines, and like many of these medium-size carriers carved out of the Class 1 systems, its independence was relatively short-lived. Its traffic and potential was too valuable to remain outside the Class 1 fold.

DM&E began operations on former Chicago & North Western (C&NW) trackage in September 1986. Originally it reached west from Winona, Minnesota, to Rapid City, South Dakota, with branches reaching Aberdeen and Watertown, South Dakota, and Mason City, Iowa. It expanded in 1995, with acquisition of the former C&NW Colony Line between Crawford, Nebraska, and Colony and Rapid City, South Dakota (formerly an isolated C&NW operation that had little value for Union Pacific after its merger with C&NW). DM&E shook the industry in 1997 when it unveiled a controversial proposal for an

▼ This DM&E business car train is running empty as it passes Elkton, South Dakota, on October 21, 2007. *John Leopard*

▲ DM&E Nos. 6612 and 6614—a pair of ex–Chicago & North Western SD9s—are bracketed by two ex–Milwaukee Road SD10s—Nos. 549 and 559—while working eastbound at Minnesota City, Minnesota. *John Leopard*

extension to Wyoming's Powder River Basin to compete for lucrative low-sulfur coal traffic. While DM&E's proposal was ultimately approved by the Surface Transportation Board, the 280-mile extension to Wyoming remained unbuilt.

In 2002, DM&E bought the I&M Rail Link (former Milwaukee Road lines connecting Chicago, Kansas City, and the Twin Cities via Sabula, Iowa), renaming it the Iowa, Chicago & Eastern. DM&E and Iowa, Chicago & Eastern were bought by Canadian Pacific in autumn 2008 and now function as CP subsidiaries, using the same blue-and-yellow livery and sharing motive power.

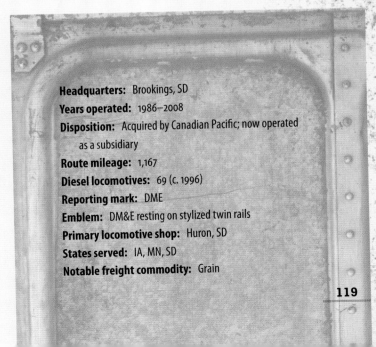

Headquarters: Brookings, SD

Years operated: 1986–2008

Disposition: Acquired by Canadian Pacific; now operated as a subsidiary

Route mileage: 1,167

Diesel locomotives: 69 (c. 1996)

Reporting mark: DME

Emblem: DM&E resting on stylized twin rails

Primary locomotive shop: Huron, SD

States served: IA, MN, SD

Notable freight commodity: Grain

36

DELAWARE & HUDSON RAILWAY

▼ A northward milk train on D&H's Washington Branch crosses the Hoosick River at Eagle Bridge, New York. D&H's pastoral branches in upstate New York were a contrast to its heavy coal lines farther south. Today, a portion of this D&H branch survives as New York's Battenkill Railroad. *Jim Shaughnessy*

Delaware & Hudson Canal Company was chartered in 1823 as a waterway to move anthracite coal from underground mines at Carbondale, Pennsylvania, to the New York City market. In conjunction with its 108-mile canal, during 1828–1829 D&H constructed a 17-mile tram/gravity railway with inclined planes to transport coal from mines to the canal head at Honesdale, Pennsylvania. It was the first U.S. line to import and test British-made locomotives, but it found the engines too heavy for practical operation.

In a classic pose, D&H freights meet on its line over Ararat Summit beneath a westward freight on Erie Lackawanna's famed Starrucca Viaduct. At the time, D&H and Erie Lackawanna were controlled by Norfolk & Western through its Dereco subsidiary. In 1980, D&H shifted traffic away from its Ararat Line to the parallel former Lackawanna line between Binghamton and Scranton acquired from Conrail. *Jim Shaughnessy*

Successful transport of coal allowed D&H to expand its operations, and it evolved from a coal canal into a conventional common carrier steam railroad. Its lines reached south to Scranton and Wilkes-Barre to tap mines and interchange with other lines, and northward into New York State. Through the leases of the Albany & Susquehanna (built as a 6-foot gauge feeder to the Erie Railroad) and Rensselaer & Saratoga, as well as new construction northward along the west shore of Lake Champlain, D&H reached Montreal in 1875. As its conventional lines prospered, however, the original canal and tram railway suffered from obsolescence and were closed in 1898.

Coal remained important to D&H in the first half of the twentieth century, with the railroad moving significant quantities of anthracite and bituminous varieties. To augment this staple, it developed as a bridge route for traffic to New England and Quebec;

Headquarters: New York, NY

Years operated: 1829–1990

Disposition: Operated by Guilford Transportation 1984–1988, by New York, Susquehanna & Western 1988–1990; acquired by Canadian Pacific in 1990; melded into CPR's U.S. operations

Route mileage: 794 (c. 1952) and 1,699 (c. 1977, incl. trackage rights on Conrail)

Locomotives

    Steam: 369 (1940)

    Diesel: 137 (1981)

Reporting marks: DH and DHNY

Emblem: Classic shield with initials D&H

Primary locomotive shop: Colonie, NY

Notable features: Belden Hill (NY) Tunnel and Ararat Summit, PA

States and province served: NY, PA, VT, plus QC (1952); MD, NJ, NY, PA, VT, plus QC (after 1976)

▶ Centerfold of D&H passenger service brochure, 1950s. *Voyageur Press collection*

from connections with Erie Railroad, Lackawanna, Central Railroad of New Jersey, Lehigh Valley, and Pennsylvania Railroad, D&H forwarded traffic to Boston & Maine in the Albany area, Rutland Railroad at that line's Vermont namesake, and Canadian roads at its northern end.

D&H was among the few eastern railroads to buy 4-6-6-4 Challengers. It was relatively late to dieselize, and instead of following the typical pattern of acquiring Electro-Motive E and F units, it bought Alco road-switchers and, in the 1960s, secondhand Alco PA passenger units from Santa Fe Railway.

In 1976, D&H was greatly expanded to provide the guise of competition for Conrail by using trackage rights over Conrail to Buffalo, Harrisburg, Philadelphia, Baltimore, and Washington, D.C. The railroad was briefly part of the Guilford network between 1984 and 1988, but following a bankruptcy and a period of designated operation by New York, Susquehanna & Western between 1988 and 1990, it was sold to Canadian Pacific. Since that time it has functioned as an arm of CP, with trackage south of Albany also hosting Norfolk Southern traffic.

▲ The D&H *Laurentian*, operated in conjunction with New York Central and Canadian Pacific, connected Grand Central Terminal in New York City with Albany, and Montreal via the western shore of Lake Champlain. *Solomon collection*

This detailed view of D&H RS-11 No. 5003 was made at East Binghamton, New York, in 1986. D&H's famous shield and characteristic script were used for advertising its coal, also appearing on the sides of its locomotives and rolling stock. While former D&H main lines remain important freight routes, the old D&H shield has largely given way to Canadian Pacific's corporate image. *Brian Solomon*

▼ D&H 0-8-8-0 No. 1607 and 4-6-6-4 No. 1534 work as helpers at the back of a coal train passing Sink Hole Siding, Pennsylvania, on June 17, 1948. D&H operated some of the largest steam locomotives in the Northeast and was one of only a few railroads in the region to order 4-6-6-4 Challengers—40 of the type were built by Alco's Schenectady Works between 1940 and 1946. The big locomotives had very short life spans; all were replaced by Alco diesels in the early 1950s. *Photographer unknown, author collection*

DELAWARE, LACKAWANNA & WESTERN RAILROAD

I n 1849, the Liggett's Gap Railroad was chartered as a broad gauge feeder to the Erie Railroad. It was reorganized in 1851 as the Lackawanna & Western, then in 1853 merged with its affiliate, Delaware & Cobb's Gap Railroad, to form the Delaware, Lackawanna & Western—commonly known simply as the Lackawanna.

In its early years, it connected Scranton to the Erie Railroad at Great Bend, Pennsylvania. East of Scranton, the Lackawanna pushed its line along Roaring Brook to Moscow, then over Pocono Summit and through the scenic Delaware Water Gap. It continued from there, crossing the Delaware into New Jersey, where it initially linked with Central Railroad of New Jersey (CNJ), which forwarded its coal traffic toward New York City. Because the Lackawanna was built to 6-foot gauge and CNJ to standard gauge, CNJ required dual-gauge track to accommodate Lackawanna interchange. In 1869, the Lackawanna bypassed CNJ by leasing the Morris & Erie, a move that brought it to the Hudson River at Hoboken, New Jersey, opposite Manhattan. There it established a major freight and passenger terminal. Not only was New York City a primary market for its coal, but coal was shipped from there to New England.

▼ The Lackawanna was among 25 railroads to buy Electro-Motive's pioneering model FT road freight diesel. It followed up after World War II with orders for F3s. Lackawanna FTs (with rows of four porthole windows) and F3s congregate at Scranton, Pennsylvania, on June 20, 1948. *John E. Pickett*

▲ At the time it was introduced in 1953, the Fairbanks-Morse H-24-66 Train Master was the most powerful commercially built diesel locomotive. Lackawanna bought 12 (Nos. 850–861) and worked them in both freight and passenger service. *Sirman collection*

In the 1870s, the Lackawanna built north and west into New York State, acquiring routes to Syracuse, Oswego, and Utica. In 1876, it converted operations from broad to standard gauge. Jay Gould exerted his influence on the Lackawanna, encouraging it in 1880 to construct a route between Binghamton and Buffalo, largely new and parallel with the Erie Railroad through the Chemung Valley.

The Lackawanna's operational focal point was in Scranton where its yards and shops were based. Situated in a valley, however, meant grades to the east and west for its coal trains. In 1899, William H. Truesdale took control of the Lackawanna and transformed it into a modern railroad by skillfully managing the line and infusing massive investment in some of the most impressive railroad infrastructure in the East. Truesdale made the Lackawanna into a showcase for reinforced concrete construction in modern passenger stations, in signal towers, and on massive bridges. By lowering grades, reducing curvature, and shortening main lines, the Lackawanna improved its efficiency and lowered its operating costs to make its route more competitive. Its Lackawanna Cutoff in western New Jersey opened in 1908, followed a few years later by Summit Cutoff over Clarks Summit between Scranton and Binghamton, featuring the massive Tunkhannock and Martin Creek viaducts.

DL&W's fortunes waned with the decline of anthracite business, and in 1960 it merged with Erie Railroad to form the Erie-Lackawanna Railway.

Headquarters: New York, NY

Years operated: 1853–1960

Disposition: Merged with Erie Railroad; routes melded into Conrail in 1976. Mergers fragmented DL&W's route structure and key sections were abandoned, especially west of Binghamton, NY; surviving portions operated by NJ Transit and Norfolk Southern in NJ; Canadian Pacific between Scranton, PA, and Binghamton; and short lines elsewhere

Route mileage: 968

Locomotives
   Steam: 680 (1929)
   Diesel: 156 (c. 1952)
   Electric railcars: 141 (c. 1952)

Reporting mark: DLW

Emblem: Rectangle with "Lackawanna Railroad"

Nickname: Route of the Phoebe Snow

Primary locomotive shop: Scranton, PA

Notable features: Bergen Hill Tunnel (Jersey City), 4,280 ft.; concrete viaducts crossing Paulins Kill (NJ), 1,100 ft. long, 117 ft. high; Delaware River, 1,450 ft. long, 64 ft. high; Tunkhannock Creek (PA), 2,375 ft. long, 242 ft. high; and Martins Creek (PA), 1,600 ft. long, 150 ft. tall; Hoboken (NJ) Terminal

States served: NJ, NY, PA

Major cities served: New York, Newark, Scranton, Buffalo

Flagship passenger trains: *The Lackawanna Limited* (Hoboken–Buffalo, with through Chicago cars via Nickel Plate Road) and *Phoebe Snow* (Hoboken–Buffalo, with through Chicago cars via NKP)

Other name passenger trains: *The Twilight* (Hoboken–Buffalo, with through Chicago cars via New York Central) and *Westerner Limited* (Hoboken–Buffalo, with through Chicago cars via NKP)

Notable freight commodities: Coal, general freight, milk

Principal freight yards: Buffalo and East Binghamton, NY; Hoboken and Port Morris, NJ; Scranton, PA

◄ Phoebe Snow was a mythical female passenger created to advertise the clean-running qualities of the *Lackawanna Limited*. After World War II the train was reequipped as a diesel streamliner and named *The Phoebe Snow. Richard Jay Solomon collection*

38

DENVER & RIO GRANDE WESTERN RAILROAD

▼ On August 16, 1952, Rio Grande Class K-37 No. 492 works as a midtrain helper on an eastward freight working east of Chama, New Mexico, on its ascent of Cumbres Pass. Between 1928 and 1930, Rio Grande rebuilt its narrow gauge K-37 2-8-2s from older standard gauge locomotives. Today, the run from Chama to Antonito, Colorado, is operated by the Cumbres & Toltec Scenic Railroad. *John E. Pickett*

In 1870, the Denver & Rio Grande was formed to realize General William Jackson Palmer's dream of putting Denver on the railroad map by building south to Mexico City, hence the hopeful reference to the river between the United States and Mexico. A trip to Wales, where he inspected narrow gauge slate-hauling lines, inspired Palmer to build D&RG using 3-foot gauge, thus making it the first significant U.S. line to adopt a narrow standard.

Although it opened 76 miles to Lake Divide, Colorado, by October 1871, D&RG was slow to fulfill its goals. In the late 1870s, D&RG vied with the Santa Fe Railway for territory

D. & R. G. TRAIN CROSSING SOLDIER SUMMIT,
90 MILES EAST OF SALT LAKE CITY, UTAH.

▲ The Rio Grande's original crossing of Soldier Summit required a stiff 4 percent climb on its western slope. Operational difficulties were displayed in this staged photo depicting a quadruple-headed passenger train with a helper at the back. This line was replaced by a more circuitous, but gentler, crossing using the famed Gilluly loops. *Solomon collection*

Headquarters: Denver, CO

Years operated: 1870–1988

Disposition: Melded into Southern Pacific after 1988; with SP, merged into Union Pacific in 1996

Route mileage: 2,248 (c. 1952, incl. 407 mi. of 3 ft. gauge)

Locomotives (1959)

    Steam: 22 (narrow gauge)

    Diesel: 254

Reporting mark: DRGW

Emblem: Circle with legend MAIN LINE THRU THE ROCKIES around silhouette of snow-crested mountains and crossed with banner reading RIO GRANDE

Slogans: Through the Rockies, Not around Them and Main Line thru the Rockies

Trade name: Rio Grande

Primary locomotive shop: Burnham (Denver)

Notable features: Moffat Tunnel (CO), 32,799 ft.; Royal Gorge Hanging Bridge over Arkansas River (near Cañon City, CO); Soldier Summit crossing of Wasatch Mountains, incl. Kyune tunnels and Gilluly loops; Tennessee Pass (CO) Tunnel

States served: CO, KS (after 1981 UP–Missouri Pacific–Western Pacific merger), NM, UT

Major cities served: Denver and Salt Lake City

as it shifted construction westward to tap the developing Rocky Mountain mining trade. As a condition of a truce with the Santa Fe, D&RG gave up on dreams of reaching Mexico and instead focused on lines into the mountains. One crossed Le Veta Pass, reaching Alamosa, Colorado, by 1878; via its San Juan extension, it crossed Cumbres Pass to Chama, New Mexico, and beyond to Durango, Colorado, with branches north to Silverton, Colorado, and south from Antonito to Santa Fe, New Mexico. Another route (initially shared with standard gauge Santa Fe) traversed the Royal Gorge and reached the Leadville mining district in 1881. This was eventually extended over Tennessee Pass. Another route reached west from Salida over Marshall Pass to Grand Junction. By 1883, D&RG's affiliate, Denver & Rio Grande Western, had built west to Salt Lake City. Although for a time there was animosity between the two narrow gauge lines, they settled differences, but would not formally merge until 1908, while retaining the name Denver & Rio Grande. After a period of receivership, the railroad reorganized and reemerged as the Denver & Rio Grande Western in 1921.

To meet the requirements of transcontinental interchange, the Rio Grande, as the railroad became more commonly known, finally conceded to the advantages of standard gauge and built its own standard gauge route between Denver to Salt Lake using a mix of new construction and conversion of older narrow gauge lines, with some dual gauge track where necessary. Gradually, the Rio Grande converted many of its older routes to standard gauge, yet key portions of its network survived for decades. Declines in the railroad's traditional business, combined with government-built highways, doomed the Rio Grande's narrow gauge and the network was gradually abandoned. Remarkably, a few lines survived

Flagship passenger trains:

California Zephyr and *Exposition Flyer* (Chicago–Denver–Oakland, operated with Chicago, Burlington & Quincy and WP) and *Royal Gorge* (St. Louis–Kansas City–Denver–Oakland, operated with WP and MP)

Other name passenger trains: *The Mountaineer* (Denver–Grand Junction, CO), *The Prospector* (Denver–Salt Lake City); *The Scenic Limited* (Denver–Ogden, UT), *Yampa Valley Mail* (Denver–Craig, CO)

Notable freight commodities: Coal, general freight, intermodal

Principal freight yards: Denver North, Grand Junction, Pueblo, CO; Roper (Salt Lake City)

until the late 1960s, at which time they were among the last steam-hauled common carrier routes in the United States. Two portions of the San Juan extension survive as tourist railways: Durango & Silverton and Cumbres & Toltec Scenic.

In the early twentieth century, railroad visionary David Moffat had set about building a transcontinental link west of Denver through the Colorado Front Range. He died in 1911, and his road was renamed the Denver & Salt Lake. A 6-mile tunnel under the Continental bearing Moffat's name was completed in 1928 to replace the original sinuous crossing of Rollins Pass that crested at 11,660 feet above sea level. In 1934, the Dotsero Cutoff linked the D&SL route with the Rio Grande, finally allowing the Moffat line to serve as a through route. D&SL and Rio Grande were formally merged in 1947. Rio Grande and Southern Pacific came under common management in 1988, and Southern Pacific merged with Union Pacific in 1996. A year later Union Pacific shut down Rio Grande's steeply graded Tennessee Pass crossing in favor of the Moffat route, while diverting most through traffic to its Wyoming transcontinental route. The Moffat route remains a busy coal line and hosts Amtrak's *California Zephyr*.

▼ Like many other roads, the Rio Grande encouraged industrial development along its lines. Railroads benefited more from originating and terminating traffic than from "overhead" business. *Solomon collection*

▶ A Rio Grande agent's coupon for the *Rio Grande Zephyr*, which the railroad operated on its own from 1970 to 1983, when the company finally joined Amtrak. *Solomon collection*

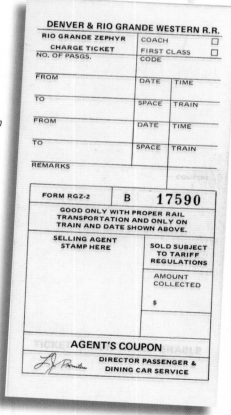

▶ Rio Grande SD40T-2 Tunnel Motors roar upgrade with a loaded coal train, having just met a priority piggyback train in the siding at Troublesome, Colorado, in September 1989. The coal train is climbing toward the western portal of the Moffat Tunnel on the old Denver & Salt Lake route. *Brian Solomon*

39

DULUTH, MISSABE & IRON RANGE RAILWAY

▼ The Missabe Road's 18 Class M-3 2-8-8-4 Yellowstones were built by Baldwin and were among the last big mainline steam to work in the United States. No. 227 leads a train of loaded ore jennies late in its career.
John E. Pickett

In 1901, U.S. Steel acquired the Duluth & Iron Range Rail Road and the Duluth, Missabe & Northern Railway, both of which tapped iron-rich areas of Minnesota north of Lake Superior. D&IR dated from 1874, having built northward into the Vermillion Range from Two Harbors, while the DM&N was a more recent development. Over the previous decade it extended its lines from Duluth into the Mesabi Range. (*Missabe* and *Mesabi* are derived from the Ojibwa word meaning "giant.")

▲ The Missabe arrowhead (a reference to the "Arrowhead" region of Minnesota, which it serves) on the side of a freshly painted former Southern Pacific Tunnel Motor. *Brian Solomon*

For three decades, the two lines operated independently, each delivering large volumes of iron ore to their respective docks at Duluth and Two Harbors, where it was transferred to lake boats for shipment to steel-producing centers in the Midwest. Consolidation began in 1930, when D&IR leased the DM&N. In 1937, the properties were formally merged as the Duluth, Missabe & Iron Range Railway.

Between 1941 and 1943, DM&IR acquired 18 massive 2-8-8-4 Yellowstone locomotives to move exceptionally heavy ore trains in road service. Also significant were nine unusual switchers using the 0-10-2 arrangement acquired secondhand from Union Railroad, another U.S. Steel property. DM&IR completed dieselization relatively late, with its 2-8-8-4s working until 1959 and some steam locomotives remaining on the roster into the early 1960s.

DM&IR remained a U.S. Steel property until 1988 (by then the steelmaker was known as USX), when the railroad, along with Chicago-based Elgin, Joliet & Eastern and Pittsburgh-based Bessemer, were sold to Transtar. All three lines were later acquired by Canadian National, with DM&IR entering the CN fold in 2004.

Headquarters: Duluth, MN

Years operated: 1937–present

Disposition: Subsidiary of CN since 2004

Route mileage: 522 (c. 1939)

Locomotives

   Steam: 120 (c. 1939)

   Diesel: 69 (c. 1966)

Reporting mark: DMIR

Emblems: Railroad name in red circle surrounded by green circle with legend SAFETY FIRST; yellow script "Missabe" in maroon arrowhead

Trade name: Missabe Road

Primary locomotive shop: Proctor, MN

Notable features: Ore docks at Duluth and Two Harbors, MN

States served: MN and WI

Major city served: Duluth

Notable freight commodities: Iron ore and taconite pellets

▲ Although DM&IR was primarily a heavy-freight hauler, it also operated a nominal passenger service into the 1950s. Its lone RDC passes the yards at Proctor, Minnesota, probably in 1952 or 1953. Budd's RDCs were well-suited to light passenger services such as DM&IR's, as they lowered costs and improved passenger accommodations. Today, the DM&IR route is freight only. *John E. Pickett*

▲ The Missabe's logo on the side of a well-worn ore jenny. *Brian Solomon*

◀ A trio of DM&IR SD9s leads empty ore jennies up Proctor Hill, a twisting 7 miles of 2.2 percent grade running from the Lake Superior docks in Duluth to sorting yards at Proctor, Minnesota. The western extremity of Lake Superior can be seen in the distance. *John Leopard*

DURANGO & SILVERTON RAILROAD

▼ The Rio Grande began promoting its Silverton Branch as an attraction in the 1950s.
Robert A. Buck

The former silver-mining hub of Silverton is located high in Colorado's Rockies. Founded in 1876, it remained an isolated outpost until the arrival of the Denver & Rio Grande in 1882. In its heyday, it served as railway hub with three lines winding down steep mountain passes to feed traffic to the D&RG and later the Rio Grande.

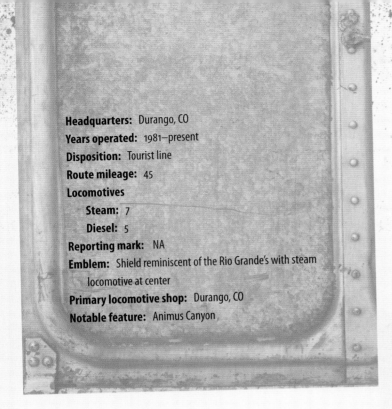

Headquarters: Durango, CO

Years operated: 1981–present

Disposition: Tourist line

Route mileage: 45

Locomotives

    Steam: 7

    Diesel: 5

Reporting mark: NA

Emblem: Shield reminiscent of the Rio Grande's with steam locomotive at center

Primary locomotive shop: Durango, CO

Notable feature: Animus Canyon

▼ The former Rio Grande Silverton Branch is among the most scenic lines in the United States. In season, several daily trains ply the line between Durango and Silverton hauled by historic Rio Grande 2-8-2 Mikados. *Brian Solomon*

The Silverton branch handled considerable freight in its first decade, but traffic declined after 1893 following the repeal of the Sherman Silver Purchase Act, which curtailed the output of local mines. By the late 1940s, a three-times-weekly mixed train was sufficient to handle remaining traffic. But the ancient-looking steam locomotive hauling narrow gauge cars, combined with the natural scenic splendor and remoteness of the Animas Canyon, proved so compelling that visitors came to Durango simply to ride the Rio Grande's quaint Silverton mixed. By the 1950s, the growing tourist interest encouraged the Rio Grande to promote the train as an attraction. As a result, the Silverton branch evolved into one of America's first tourist railways, and the Durango & Silverton line survived when the remaining narrow gauge lines were abandoned in 1969.

Rio Grande last operated the branch in 1980, and in 1981 it conveyed to private operation as the Durango & Silverton Narrow Gauge Railroad. While the railroad has since changed hands several times, it remains one of the most successful tourist trains in the United States. The locomotives on the line are former Rio Grande K28 and K36 Mikados, lending a degree of authenticity to the line, which otherwise tends to feel like an Old West theme park.

EAST BROAD TOP RAILROAD

On May 3, 1936, EBT 2-8-2 No. 12 leads an excursion near Joller, Pennsylvania. In its last decades, the railroad relied on its fleet of Baldwin-built Mikados (Nos. 12–18), of which No. 12 was the first and smallest. On today's preserved EBT, No. 12 is affectionately known as Millie. *Solomon collection*

In the 1870s, the narrow gauge movement swept the United States. The ability to negotiate tighter curves with less grading and lighter cars and locomotives lowered construction and operational costs. Over the next two decades dozens of narrow gauge railways were built, often to locations previously deemed uneconomical to connect by rail. Among the first was East Broad Top, a railroad chartered in the 1850s to tap the Broad Top coal fields, but remained dormant until 1872 when 3-foot gauge was adopted.

The line pushed south from a connection with Pennsylvania Railroad at Mt. Union, working along Aughwick Creek to Rockhill Furnace, near Orbisonia, where it built its shops near preexisting iron furnaces. To reach the coal fields it ascended a 2.7 percent ruling grade

through tunnels at Sideling Hill and Wray's Hill to Robertsdale, 30 miles south of Mt. Union. Branches were built to mines, and in the 1880s it began an extension to connect with New York Central's aborted South Pennsylvania Railroad.

Coal traffic peaked in 1926. Although the railroad moved other commodities, including ganister stone for use in steel-making, the line's freight-hauling fate was sealed as the coal tapped out. Scheduled passenger service ended in 1954, and the railroad ceased functioning as a common carrier in 1956. Kovalchick Salvage Company acquired the property, but rather than scrap the line, in 1960 the company opted to develop a short section near Orbisonia as a tourist attraction. Seasonal excursions using authentic EBT equipment have entertained visitors for more than 50 years.

Headquarters: Philadelphia, PA

Years operated: 1872–1956 (common carrier) and 1960–present (tourist line)

Disposition: Sold to Kovalchick Salvage Company, which has operated 3.5-mile Orbisonia–Colgate Grove segment as a tourist line since 1960

Route mileage: 45 (c. 1952)

Locomotives (1952)

   Steam: 8

   Gas-electric railcars: 1

Reporting mark: EBT

Emblem: EAST BROAD in wide banner across shield, with TOP on lower half of shield

Primary locomotive shop: Rockhill Furnace (Orbisonia), PA

Notable features: Wray's Hill Tunnel, 1,235 ft. long, and Sideling Hill Tunnel, 830 ft. long

Notable freight commodities: Coal, iron, ganister stone

▼ In the foggy gloom of a cool October 1997 morning, East Broad Top No. 15, a Baldwin 2-8-2, begins its day at Rockhill Furnace, Pennsylvania. *Brian Solomon*

ERIE LACKAWANNA RAILWAY

American railroad consolidation was discussed at length in the early decades of the twentieth century, yet little was accomplished before World War II. Postwar, as numerous lines began to suffer from declining traffic, consolidation was viewed with renewed interest. Merger talks between Erie Railroad and Delaware, Lackawanna & Western began in 1954, with the two railroads viewing their underutilized parallel main lines across the southern tier of New York as ripe for consolidation. Initially, a three-way merger was planned with Delaware & Hudson, but D&H chose to remain independent. The two lines began integrating some operations prior to formal merger.

▼ Erie Lackawanna acquired a variety of high-horsepower second-generation diesels designed for moving heavy freight. On October 16, 1975, a westward freight roars through New York's Canisteo Valley behind an SDP45 and two other 20-cylinder EMDs. *Bill Dechau photo, Doug Eisele collection*

▲ EL melded its predecessors' routes into a stronger line. An eastward EL freight led by a GE U36C and EMD SD45 roars passed the former Lackawanna tower at Alford, Pennsylvania, on March 27, 1976, while making its way between Binghamton, New York, and Scranton, Pennsylvania. In the early twentieth century, Lackawanna was an enthusiastic user of reinforced concrete and used it to build many structures, including towers, stations, and bridges.
George W. Kowanski

Erie-Lackawanna was approved by the ICC on September 13, 1960, and became effective on October 17. EL concentrated traffic on the best of its combined route structure allowing some redundant lines to be downgraded and ultimately abandoned, notably most of DL&W's main line west of Binghamton. While consolidation provided some financial relief, more serious issues regarding growing passenger deficits, declining freight traffic, and high labor costs, along with exceptionally high taxes in New Jersey and New York, continued to plague EL. In response to the proposed Penn Central merger, Erie-Lackawanna sought inclusion into the Norfolk & Western–Nickel Plate–Wabash combination of 1964. ICC agreed, and as a condition of merger urged Norfolk & Western to support both EL and Delaware & Hudson. To address concerns regarding EL's high debt and poor finances, N&W formed a holding company called Dereco to shield it from EL's (and D&H's) financial liabilities. While N&W assumed control of EL in April 1968 (at which point the hyphen was dropped from the name), its influence was short-lived. The bottom fell out of EL in June 1972, when Hurricane Agnes devastated its main lines across New

Headquarters: Cleveland, OH

Years operated: 1960–1976

Disposition: Melded into Conrail; remaining portions operated by Norfolk Southern, Metro-North/New Jersey Transit, Western New York & Pennsylvania, and various short lines

Route mileage: 3,029 (c. 1971)

Locomotives (c. 1971)

   Diesel: 523

   Electric railcars: 120 cars plus trailers

Reporting mark: EL

Emblem: Diamond and circle around a combined stencil-like E and L

Primary locomotive shops: Hornell, NY; Marion, OH; Scranton, PA

Notable features: Bergen Hill Tunnel (Jersey City), 4,280 ft.; Belfast (NY) Viaduct; concrete viaducts crossing Paulins Kill (NJ), 1,100 ft. long, 117 ft. tall; Delaware River, 1,450 ft. long, 64 ft. tall; Tunkhannock Creek (PA), 2,375 ft. long, 242 ft. tall; and Martins Creek (PA), 1,600 ft. long, 150 ft. tall; Hoboken (NJ) Terminal; Otisville (NY) Tunnel, 5,314 ft. long; Portage Viaduct over Genesee River (Portageville, NY); Starrucca Viaduct (Lanesboro, PA), 1,040 ft. long, 100 ft. tall

States served: IL, IN, NJ, NY, PA, OH

Major cities served: Buffalo, Chicago, Cincinnati, Cleveland, New York, Scranton

139

York's southern tier. The route was rebuilt, but the blow to EL was irreversible. Although it was hoped that EL would stay out of Conrail, in the end it was included. Ironically, EL lines west of Youngstown, Ohio, which had carried its heaviest traffic and were unscathed by the hurricane, suffered the most under Conrail's rationalization plan and were mostly abandoned. By contrast, the lines hit by Agnes were rebuilt and have largely survived.

Today, the former Erie Railroad route between Binghamton and Buffalo serves as a Norfolk Southern main line, while the DL&W route between Binghamton and Scranton is operated by Canadian Pacific and carries both NS and Canadian Pacific traffic. Former DL&W lines radiating from Hoboken remain important commuter lines operated by New Jersey Transit. Other portions of the former EL are operated as successful short lines and regionals.

▼ Erie Railroad and Lackawanna began consolidation of facilities several years prior to the merger. This April 1957 advertisement explains that Erie's trains would be using Lackawanna's Hoboken Terminal instead of Erie's Jersey City station. *Solomon collection*

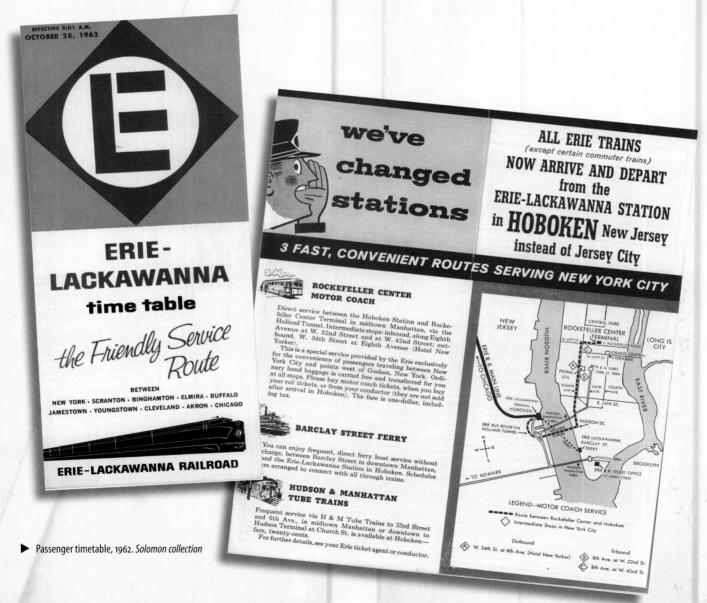

▶ Passenger timetable, 1962. *Solomon collection*

▲ The distinctive bass throb of EMD's 20-cylinder 645E3 engine fills New York's rural Canisteo River Valley west of Rathbone, New York, on October 5, 1974, as a westward EL freight races toward Hornell. In the lead is SD45 No. 3620, followed by an SDP45 and another SD45, which together provide 10,800 horsepower. Much of the trackage along the Canisteo River had been badly damaged by Hurricane Agnes in June 1972. Although reduced to single-track, today this portion of the former Erie Railroad handles 10 to 12 Norfolk Southern trains daily. *Doug Eisele*

◀ A former Delaware, Lackawanna & Western caboose brings up the back of an eastward EL freight at Newburgh Junction, New York, in October 1970. *George W. Kowanski*

ERIE RAILROAD

The New York & Erie Railroad was perhaps the most unusual major nineteenth-century American railroad. From its inception in 1832, the Erie was conceived as a trunk route (i.e., a through link to connecting gateways in long-distance transport). In 1851, when it finally reached its first western terminus at the Lake Erie port of Dunkirk, New York, it was the longest railway in the world under unified operation.

Erie was built to 6-foot gauge, by far the widest in general use in North America. But the efficiencies of broad gauge proved illusory, and any advantages offered by wider tracks and larger equipment were soon obviated by inconvenient interchange. In 1880, Erie re-gauged its entire line, including the conversion of locomotives and cars. Among Erie's other peculiarities was the ill-founded decision to build several miles of its original line through central New York State on wooden piles instead of conventional grade. Most piles were replaced even before the route opened to traffic. In the 1850s, Erie claimed to be the first line to use telegraphic transmissions to amend operation by timetable, which set an important precedent. By the late nineteenth century, this practice was an American standard.

Erie's early prominence attracted financial manipulators in the 1860s, and the railroad made world headlines when, through dubious stock shenanigans, Daniel Drew, Jay Gould, and Jim Fisk foiled Cornelius Vanderbilt's attempts to take control of the line, an incident

▼ Looking east at Marion, Ohio, in 1948, a set of new Erie Railroad Alco FA/FB diesels reverse back onto their train. Although it was the weakest financially of the four big trunk lines, the Erie moved a lot of freight.
J. William Vigrass

◀ The cover of Erie's 1953 system map featured a set of the railroad's Alco FA/FB diesel locomotives. *Voyageur Press collection*

Headquarters: Cleveland, OH

Years operated: 1833–1960

Disposition: Merged with DL&W; routes melded into Conrail in 1976, most lines west of the Pennsylvania-Ohio state line downgraded or abandoned; surviving routes operated by NJ Transit, Norfolk Southern, CSX, and various regional and short lines.

Route mileage: 2,231 (c. 1953)

Locomotives

   Steam: 1,396 (1926)

   Diesel: 371 (1954)

Reporting mark: ERIE

Emblem: Square diamond with a circle around ERIE

Primary locomotive shops: Hornell, NY; Dunmore and Susquehanna, PA, Marion, OH

Notable features: Belfast (NY) Viaduct; Portage Viaduct over Genesee River (Portageville, NY); Otisville (NY) Tunnel, 5,314 ft. long; Starrucca Viaduct (Lanesboro, PA), 1,040 ft. long, 100 ft. tall

States served: IL, IN, NJ, NY, OH, PA

Major cities served: Buffalo, Chicago, Cincinnati, Cleveland, New York

Flagship passenger train: *Erie Limited* (Jersey City–Chicago)

Other name passenger trains: *Atlantic Express/Pacific Express* (Jersey City–Chicago); *Southern Tier Express* (Jersey City–Buffalo); *The Lake Cities* (Jersey City–Cleveland and Chicago)

Notable freight commodities: Coal, steel, general merchandise

Principal freight yards: Croxton (Secaucus), NJ; East Hornell, NY; Meadville, PA; Marion, OH

that tarnished the railroad's reputation among investors. By the 1870s, Erie was outflanked by the New York Central and Pennsylvania Railroad systems. Despite these problems, Erie reached west by leasing the Atlantic & Great Western, which brought it to key Ohio gateways. West of Marion, Ohio, it constructed additional lines to reach Chicago. Branches to Rochester, Buffalo, Cleveland, and Scranton helped it tap lucrative industrial centers and traffic gateways, yet Erie's main line missed virtually every major city between New York and Chicago.

In the twentieth century, Erie benefited from progressive management that built low-grade cutoffs and modern yards, installed automatic block signalling, and purchased high-output locomotives. By the 1920s, Erie continued to operate intensive New York–area suburban services, as well as electrified Rochester-area passenger service, but elsewhere passenger services were deemphasized as the railroad focused on freight business. Its flagship *Erie Limited* lacked the prominence, and swift schedules of long-distance trains operated by its competitors. Yet, Erie maintained a basic long-distance service until its merger with Delaware, Lackawanna & Western in 1960.

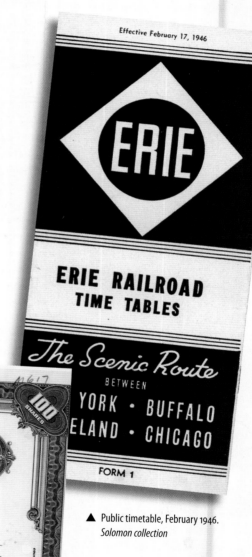

An advertisement from March 1894 boasts of the Erie Railroad's scenery, undoubtedly some of the finest in the eastern United States. *Solomon collection*

Public timetable, February 1946. *Solomon collection*

Erie Railroad stock certificate. *Solomon collection*

Esso Standard Oil Company Salutes the Erie Railroad...

in Partnership with Service and Progress for 100 Years

This month the Erie Railroad passes an outstanding milepost...its 100th Anniversary. This century of service is a truly great accomplishment...a record of constant enterprise and continuing development...a history of progress and public service. Congratulations to the Erie on a job well done!

The Esso Standard Oil Company is proud that dependable, high-quality Esso Railroad Fuels and Lubricants are being used by the Erie. Our continuing aim is to serve the needs of railroading with products that are "tailor made" to railroad specifications.

The Sign of QUALITY **ESSO** *The Sym... SERV...*

RAILROAD PRODUC...

SOLD IN: Maine, N. H., Vt., Mass., R. I., Conn., N. Y., N. J...
Del., Md., D. C. Va., W. Va., N. C. S. C. Tenn., Ark., La...
ESSO STANDARD OIL COMPANY — Boston, Mass. — New Yo...
N. Y. — Elizabeth, N. J. — Philadelphia, Pa. — Baltimore, Md...
Richmond, Va. — Charleston, W. Va. — Charlotte, N. C. — Columbia, S...
Memphis, Tenn. — New Orleans, La.

Esso Railroad Products are backed by constant research and follow-u...

May 14, 1951

◀ This 1951 advertisement for the centennial of Erie reaching Dunkirk, New York, depicts F3 diesels working west across the Starrucca Viaduct at Lanesboro, Pennsylvania. *Solomon collection*

"Sleuth"... FOR YOUR NEW PLANT LOCATION

WHEN you are seeking a new plant location, you usually don't want to advertise your plans. Yet, there's much information you need before you can make a decision.

Here is where Erie's Industrial Development Department can help you. Its services are yours and your identity and the information you seek will be confidential.

Erie has essential data on numerous advantageous industrial locations throughout the "Erie Area"—The Heart of Industrial America—which embraces the six states . . . Illinois, Indiana, Ohio, Pennsylvania, New Jersey, New York . . shown in the map above.

Write George F. Weston, Industrial Commissioner, Erie Railroad, Midland Building, Cleveland 15, Ohio.

Erie Railroad

▶ Erie actively encouraged industry to locate along its lines, a focus that caused Erie and its successors to suffer from the gradual decline of heavy industry after World War II. *Solomon collection*

FLORIDA EAST COAST RAILWAY

Railroad visionary and Florida developer Henry M. Flagler bought a budding Florida narrow gauge line in 1885 and renamed it the Florida East Coast. Over the next decade he converted it to standard gauge and extended it along the length of its namesake to connect Jacksonville and Miami. In the early twentieth century, Flagler hoped to tap the lucrative Cuban trade and anticipated a trade boom as result of the completion of the Panama Canal. Between 1905 and 1912, he pushed an extreme railroad to a new deepwater port at Key West by island-hopping west from Miami. Approximately 30 of this extension's 128 miles were on bridges. Flagler died soon after the line opened, and his dream proved illusory. Yet, the extension remained in operation until 1935, when much of it was swept away by a hurricane. The railroad line was abandoned, but in 1938, parts were incorporated into a highway.

▼ An FEC freight rolls across a trestle at Stuart, Florida, in 2011. *Joe Posik*

FEC continued to operate its Jacksonville–Miami trunk, doing brisk business by forwarding other railroads' long-distance passenger trains to popular tourist destinations and moving freight, especially perishables. The line was reorganized in 1960, but then became involved in a prolonged series of strikes between 1963 and 1976. This precipitated the introduction of two-man crews and caboose-less operations, which set precedents for the rest of the industry. Despite waves of mega-mergers, as of 2011 FEC has remained independent of major North American carriers, but since 2007 has been controlled by Fortress Investment Group, which also owns short line conglomerate Rail America.

Headquarters: St. Augustine, FL

Years operated: c. 1885–present

Route mileage: 853 (c 1928) and 571 (c. 1952)

Locomotives

    Steam: 249 (1928)

    Diesel: 74 (2005)

Reporting marks: FEC and FECR

Emblem: Circle with image of palm-covered beach

Nickname: The St. Augustine Route

Primary locomotive shop:

    New Smyrna Beach, FL

Notable features: Key West Extension (completed 1912, abandoned 1938) featured numerous long bridges, including the Long Key Viaduct, nearly 2 mi. long and comprising 180 50-ft. concrete arches, and the Spanish Harbor Bridge, 3,312 ft. long

Major cities served: Jacksonville, Miami, West Palm Beach

Name passenger trains: Forwarded a variety of named trains between Jacksonville and Miami. New York–Miami trains operated with Atlantic Coast Line, Richmond, Fredericksburg & Potomac, and Pennsylvania Railroad included *Champion*, *Havana Special*, and *Miamian*; Chicago–Miami trains operated with numerous connecting carriers included *South Wind*, *City of Miami*, and *Dixie Flagler*; also operated *Royal Palm* (Miami–Detroit and Chicago) with Louisville & Nashville and New York Central, and its own *Daylight Special* (Miami–Jacksonville)

Notable freight commodities: Automobiles, intermodal, perishables

Principal freight yards: Bowden (Jacksonville) and Hialeah (Miami)

▼ FEC forwarded passenger trains originating in New York; Washington, D.C.; Chicago; and other northern cities. *Solomon collection*

▶ FEC offered steamship services from the port of West Palm Beach to Cuba through the 1950s. *Solomon collection*

THE FLORIDA ALL-RAIL ROUTE
TO CUBA

Florida East Coast Railway to Port of Palm Beach
Thence West India Fruit & Steamship Co. Car Ferries

Over this ALL-RAIL route to Cuba shipments move in the same car from point of origin to destination, eliminating the need for costly export packing, and time-consuming transfers of cargo enroute. Damage and pilferage

45

GENESEE & WYOMING RAILROAD

The Genesee & Wyoming Railroad was formed in 1899 to assume operation of the 14-mile line connecting the massive Retsof, New York, salt mines with P&L Junction near Caledonia, New York (P&L referred to Pittsburgh and Lehigh). This five-way junction connected the G&W with the Buffalo, Rochester & Pittsburgh Railway, Erie Railroad, Lehigh Valley, and the New York Central.

As a prelude to diversification, G&W Industries was formed in 1977. G&W worked with the New York State Department of Transportation, Conrail, CSX, and Delaware & Hudson to revitalize underutilized railways in western New York and improve the flow of salt from Retsof. As a result, G&W acquired former Delaware, Lackawanna & Western trackage in 1982 and extended its reach via trackage rights largely on former BR&P lines in the mid-1980s. These extensions led to the creation of several new subsidiaries.

▼ On October 23, 1987, a southward G&W local carrying empty hoppers for the Retsof Salt Mine—one of the world's largest—crosses the former New York Central "Peanut Line" at P&L Junction near Caledonia, New York. *Brian Solomon*

▲ G&W began expanding its reach in 1986 with the purchase from CSX of Baltimore & Ohio's former Fourth Subdivision running from Rochester to Ashford Junction, New York, with trackage rights to East Salamanca. On April 9, 1988, R&S's southward road freight RS-1 is seen near Machias, New York. *Brian Solomon*

G&W's Rochester & Southern began operations in 1986 over the former Baltimore & Ohio (ex–BR&P) Fourth Subdivision between Rochester and Ashford Junction, New York, with trackage rights to East Salamanca. In 1988, the Buffalo & Pittsburgh Railroad began operations on approximately 400 miles of former BR&P trackage. Its main line ran from Buffalo, New York, to Eidenau, Pennsylvania, with trackage rights to New Castle, Pennsylvania. B&P connected with R&S at Ashford Junction.

Expansion outside G&W's western New York core began in the mid-1980s and has continued ever since. In 2011, G&W encompassed some 63 different railroad operations in the United States, Canada, Europe, and Australia. Operations of the original Genesee & Wyoming Railroad have largely been melded into those of R&S.

Headquarters: Retsof, NY, and Greenwich, CT
Years operated: 1898–present
Route mileage: 14 (original G&W) and approx. 8,800 (2011 global holdings)
Reporting mark: GNWR
Primary locomotive shop: Retsof, NY (original G&W)

149

46

GENESEE VALLEY TRANSPORTATION

▼ Delaware-Lackawanna freight PT98 works at Cresco, Pennsylvania, on the former Delaware, Lackawanna & Western main line. In the lead is a former Canadian Pacific M-630, painted in GVT's corporate colors and lettered for D-L. *Brian Solomon*

Genesee Valley Transportation is a New York State–based railroad operator established in 1985. In its early years GVT initially functioned as a transportation logistics and railroad equipment–leasing company. In the late 1980s, as Conrail looked to shed surplus lines and secondary trackage, GVT developed into a railroad operator and bid for operation on potentially lucrative track segments. As a locally managed short line, GVT offered operating advantages not afforded by massive interstate Class 1 railroads. Unrestricted by complex labor arrangements, GVT was also in a better position to focus on small customers.

In 1989, GVT began its first railway operation on a short stretch of former Lackawanna main line in Buffalo that it called Depew, Lancaster & Western—a name that harkened back to the historic Delaware, Lackawanna & Western that merged with the Erie Railroad in 1960. Over the next seven years, GVT acquired operations on a variety of disconnected line segments and clusters, including Scranton, Pennsylvania–based Delaware-Lackawanna, and New York State operations such as the Mohawk, Adirondack & Northern. GVT's most recent acquisition was the 45-mile Falls Road Railroad in 1996, which serves the former New York Central line between Lockport and Brockport and is named for the Central's predecessor on that route.

GVT has largely operated its lines with a fleet of historic Alco diesels, ranging from 1950s-era RS-3s to large six-motor types, including those built by onetime Alco Canadian affiliate Montreal Locomotive Works. GVT is among the few railroads in the United States that remain dedicated to Alco-designed locomotives.

▲ Depew, Lancaster & Western is one of several railroads to carry the GVT flag. *Brian Solomon*

Headquarters: Batavia, NY

Years operated: 1989–present

Route mileage: Approx. 300

Diesel locomotives: 34 (2011)

Reporting marks: FRR, MHWA, DL, DLWR, LBR

Emblem: Golden wreath encircling flying flag similar to Lehigh Valley's with GV enclosed in black diamond with gold trim

Railroads and subsidiaries: Batavia Transload Warehouse; Delaware-Lackawanna (1993–present); Depew, Lancaster & Western (1989–present); Falls Road (1996–present); Lowville & Beaver River (1990–present); Mohawk, Adirondack & Northern (1991–present)

Primary locomotive shop: Scranton, PA

States served: NY and PA

Major cities served: Buffalo and Scranton

GRAND TRUNK WESTERN RAILROAD

Grand Trunk Western (GTW) had its origins in the old Grand Trunk Railway (GTR), a broad gauge scheme devised in the 1850s to connect Portland, Maine, with Montreal and Chicago, the latter of which it reached in 1880. It was hoped this plan would reduce transit time between Europe, Quebec, and the American Midwest.

GTR was largely financed by British investors in London, and although it had American terminals, it was designed to keep Canadian traffic on Canadian corridors. In 1923, GTR was absorbed by Canadian National Railways, and in 1928, CN created the Grand Trunk Western to operate former GTR lines in the Midwest, while GTR's Canadian lines were melded into Canadian National's network, The Portland–Montreal segment was operated as the Grand Trunk on the U.S. side of the border. GTW continued to operate big steam on its Pontiac–Detroit suburban services until 1960—later than most other North American railroads.

In 1970, CN consolidated its various U.S. properties under the newly formed Grand Trunk Corporation, which included GTW, Central Vermont Railway, and Duluth, Winnipeg & Pacific, although the latter two retained a degree of independence from GTW. GTW expanded its network with the 1980 acquisition of Detroit, Toledo & Ironton and in 1981 with the Detroit & Toledo Shore Line, as well as some surplus Conrail trackage. In the mid-1980s, GTW shed many of its Michigan branch lines. While GTW's routes remain important parts of the Canadian National network, in recent years its image has been largely replaced with that of its parent company.

▼ A stylized version of the GTW route map.
Solomon collection

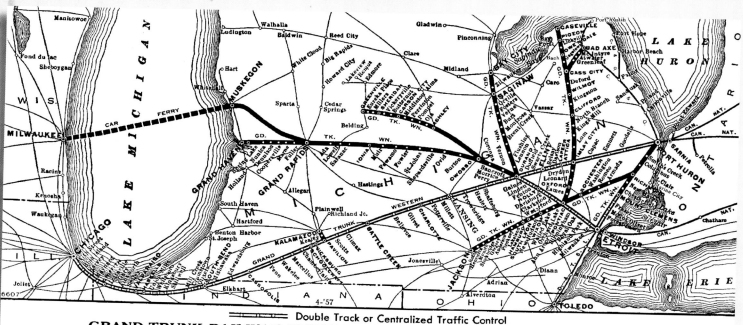

GRAND TRUNK RAILWAY SYSTEM Lines West of Detroit and St. Clair Rivers

Double Track or Centralized Traffic Control

Headquarters: Detroit, MI

Years operated: 1928–present

Disposition: Operated as part of Canadian National

Route mileage: 1,071 (c. 1949) and 925 (1995)

Locomotives
  Steam: 250 (1938)
  Diesel: 258 (1984)

Reporting marks: GTW, DTS, DTI

Emblems: Historically maple leaf around the words GRAND TRUNK WESTERN; since 1960, GT in stylized letters commonly referred to as the "toothpaste" or "wet noodle" logo

Slogan: The Good Track Road

Primary locomotive shop: Battle Creek, MI

Notable feature: Sarnia (MI) Tunnel

States served: IL, IN, MI, OH, WI (via car ferries)

Major cities served: Chicago, Detroit, Toledo

time table   april 29, 1962

GT

Grand
Trunk

◀ A GTW 4-8-4 leads a freight on a bleak winter day. GTW's locomotive roster mimicked that of Canadian National's and featured large numbers of moderately proportioned 4-8-2s and 4-8-4s. *John E. Pickett*

◀ GTW adopted the modern Canadian National image in the late 1950s. "Toothpaste" lettering and bold colors took the place of the ornate Canadian maple leaf logo and subtle greens and mustard. *Solomon collection*

GREAT NORTHERN RAILWAY

GN originally electrified its operation in the Washington Cascades using an unusual three-phase system supplied by General Electric. The railroad replaced this system with an alternating current single-phase overhead system when it completed its second Cascade Tunnel in the late 1920s. Here, single-phase electrics lead a freight. GN discontinued electric operation altogether in the early 1950s. *John E. Pickett*

America's Great Northern Railway was the vision of James J. Hill, one of America's most dynamic railroad builders. In 1878, Hill and his partners bought control of the St. Paul & Pacific. Through clever management and careful investment, Hill built up the "St. Paul Road," which he used as a stepping stone for a new transcontinental route.

In 1889, Hill created the Great Northern Railway, which assumed control the St. Paul Road, and hired engineering talent John F. Stevens to survey a low-grade route to the Pacific. Stevens located both a low crossing of the Continental Divide at Marias Pass, as well as the crossing of the Washington Cascades that bears his name. The GN route was

Headquarters: St. Paul, MN

Years operated: 1889–1970

Disposition: Merged into Burlington Northern; surviving routes operated by BNSF

Route mileage: 8,300 (c. 1952)

Locomotives (1952)

    Steam: 433

    Diesel: 509

    Electrics: 20

    Self-propelled railcars: 27

Reporting mark: GN

Emblem: Silhouette of mountain goat in circle surrounded by railroad name

Primary locomotive shops: Dale Street (St. Paul) and St. Cloud, MN; Havre, MT; Hillyard (Spokane), WA

Notable features: Cascade Tunnel (WA), 7.8 mi.; Crooked River Gorge Bridge (OR), 350 ft. long, 320 ft. high; Sheyenne River Bridge (Karnak, ND), 2,742 ft. long, 160 ft. high; Hill Bridge over Mississippi River (Minneapolis), 2,100 ft.

States served: CA, ID, IA, MN, MT, ND, SD, OR, WA, WI

Major cities served: Duluth, Minneapolis/St. Paul, Seattle

completed between St. Paul and Seattle on January 6, 1893. Yet, Stevens reengineered the Cascade crossing three times, with the ultimate execution requiring the 7.8-mile Cascade Tunnel, completed in 1929.

Hill carefully managed GN to ensure adequate traffic. Numerous branches were added to feed the main line. Hill also developed a trans-Pacific steamship trade and tapped mineral wealth in the Minnesota Iron Range. In the 1890s, Hill bought control of GN's rival Northern Pacific, and in 1901, GN and NP jointly bought control of Chicago, Burlington & Quincy. But Hill wasn't alone in his empire-building schemes, and he was nearly outflanked by Edward H. Harriman, who controlled Union Pacific and Southern Pacific. When Harriman tried to seize control of NP, Hill moved to secure his railroads from future attacks. In November 1901, he established Northern Securities, a holding company that put GN, NP, and CB&Q under common management. It was the largest railroad consolidation in the United States and, as such, alarmed the federal government. In 1904, the U.S. Supreme Court ruled that Northern Securities was in violation of the Sherman Antitrust Act. True consolidation finally occurred in 1970 with the Burlington Northern merger.

▲ After World War II, GN streamlined its flagship *Empire Builder* and then in the 1950s introduced full-length dome cars. The *Empire Builder* was among the great American streamlined trains. In 1971, the route was assumed by Amtrak and today is one of the last surviving trains to retain its traditional name and routing. *Solomon collection*

▶ GN's mountain goat mascot, "Rocky," serves up a tray of cocktails on a period drink coaster. *Voyageur Press collection*

In the meantime, GN and NP jointly built and operated the Spokane, Portland & Seattle, an exceptionally engineered, modern low-grade line that followed the northern bank of the Columbia River. Begun in 1906, this railroad connected its namesakes by 1909. SP&S enabled GN to penetrate deep into the old Harriman empire, and in 1931 GN and Western Pacific opened the Inside Gateway. This route was a cobbled-together patchwork arrangement of trackage rights on SP&S, Union Pacific, and Southern Pacific lines, along with some highly engineered new construction reaching Western Pacific at the remote northern California town of Bieber.

...lling ...ugh the Rockies

...R uniformed sons and daughters, ...veling over America on the Great ...rn Railway, cross the Continen- ...ide almost without knowing it. ...ain follows a natural route—easy ...ame trail—through the scenic ...ur of the Montana Rockies. That ...ias Pass!

...he top of the pass—at Summit, ...na—they see a statue of its discov- ...ohn F. Stevens, who still is living. ...ecember, 1889, Stevens found a ..., natural corridor through the ...es, which provided the lowest (5,213 ...nd easiest railway pass in the north- ...nited States.

...vens' discovery not only gave Great ...hern its low-altitude pass through ...mountains, it also led to establish- ...of Glacier National Park—the only ...nal park on the main line of an ...rican railway.

...anpower, firepower and supplies for ...rica and her Allies are rolling through ...Rockies faster and on time because ...ias Pass affords swifter, safer han- ...g of trains.

...arias Pass helps make Great North- ...dependable—a vital artery to Victory.

GREAT NORTHERN
RAILWAY
ROUTE OF THE EMPIRE BUILDER
...WEEN THE GREAT LAKES AND THE PACIFIC

▲ This July 1942 advertisement honors John F. Stevens, who engineered much of the GN route. Today, a statue at Montana's Marias Pass commemorates his achievements. *Solomon collection*

EMPIRE BUILDER
Fastest and Finest between Chicago and Seattle

GREAT DOMES
on Great Northern's Greatest Train

OTHER FINE GREAT NORTHERN TRAINS
STREAMLINED WESTERN STAR
Sleek companion streamliner to the Empire Builder. Daily each way between Chicago and Seattle-Portland via St. Paul, Minneapolis, Grand Forks, Great Falls and Spokane. Western Star stops at Glacier National Park daily June 15-September 10.
STREAMLINED INTERNATIONALS
Three departures each way every day from Seattle, Washington, and Vancouver, B.C.
STREAMLINED RED RIVER
Daily round trip between Grand Forks-Fargo, North Dakota, and Minneapolis-St. Paul.
WINNIPEG LIMITED
Daily overnight in both directions between St. Paul, Minneapolis and Winnipeg, Manitoba.
THE GOPHER — THE BADGER
Fast daily afternoon and morning trains each way between St. Paul-Minneapolis and Superior-Duluth.
THE CASCADIAN
Daily each way between Seattle, Wenatchee and Spokane, Washington.

For information or reservations call or write Great Northern representatives located in principal cities of the U.S. and Canada—or write:—

P. G. Holmes
Passenger Traffic Manager
Great Northern Railway, St. Paul 1, Minn.

Form 6024-A-9-57 Printed in U.S.A.

▲ GN was one of only four lines in the United States to buy large "super domes," the other three being Milwaukee Road, Santa Fe, and Southern Pacific. *Solomon collection*

▲ This Class S2 4-8-4 was only two years old when it was photographed at Spokane, Washington, in 1932. It was among the "high-stepping" Northern types equipped with 80-inch driving wheels. *Robert A. Buck collection*

Flagship passenger train: *Empire Builder* (Chicago–Minneapolis/St. Paul–Seattle–Portland, operated with Chicago, Burlington & Quincy and Spokane, Portland & Seattle)

Other name passenger trains: *Western Star* (Chicago–Minneapolis/St. Paul–Seattle, operated with CB&Q), *Oriental Limited* (Chicago–Minneapolis/St. Paul–Seattle and Portland, operated with CB&Q and SP&S)

Notable freight commodities: Grain, iron ore, timber products

Principal freight yards: Havre, MT; Hillyard (Spokane) and Interbay (Seattle), WA; Northtown (Minneapolis); Superior ore docks, WI

GREEN BAY & WESTERN RAILROAD

By John Gruber

The Green Bay & Western Railroad, which touted the advantages of its "fast straight-way route between east and west" across central Wisconsin, connected Lake Michigan and the Mississippi River for 120 years. For most of its life, its investors were the same men who invested in the Delaware, Lackawanna & Western Railroad. The Lackawanna never realized its goal of a through freight route to the Missouri River, but the GB&W maintained an important route that bypassed Chicago for many years.

Completed in 1873 as the Green Bay & Minnesota, through foreclosures it became the Green Bay, Winona & St. Paul in 1881, and the GB&W in 1896. It operated 262 miles in 1900.

▼ Alco FA-diesels rest at night at the Norwood Yard of the Green Bay & Western in Green Bay, Wisconsin, in 1961. These diesels replaced the GB&W/Kewaunee, Green Bay & Western steam locomotives. *John Gruber*

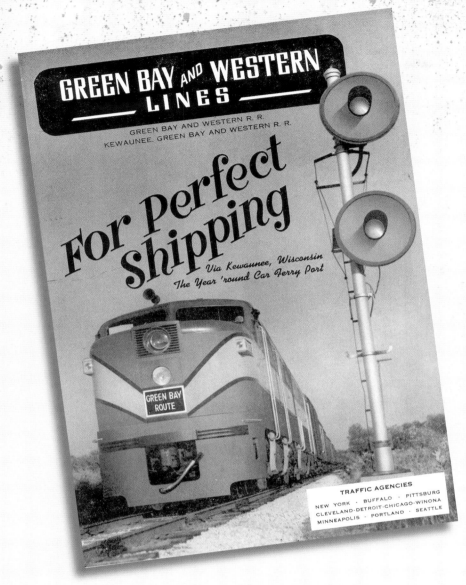

Headquarters: Green Bay, WI
Years operated: 1873–1993
Route mileage: 255 (1993)
Diesel locomotives: 19 (1993)
Reporting mark: GBW
Emblem: GREEN BAY ROUTE in a rectangle
Primary locomotive shop: Norwood (Green Bay), WI
Notable feature: Mississippi River Bridge (Winona, MN)
States served: WI and MN
Major city served: Green Bay

◄ GB&W was known for its allegiance to Alco locomotives, as evident by this 1950s advertising piece. *John Gruber collection*

Car ferry service across Lake Michigan started in 1892 at Kewaunee, Wisconsin. In 1925, GB&W initiated a fast freight for auto parts going from the Ford Motor Company in Dearborn, Michigan, to its assembly plant in St. Paul. Eventually, the Ford traffic shifted to a Conrail–Milwaukee Road unit train to take advantage of volume rates permitted by the Transportation Act of 1958. Itel assumed control of GB&W in 1978.

GB&W was known for its longtime allegiance to Alco locomotives. Since 1907, Alco built all of its new steam and diesel power. The railroad also has a rich family history. During World War II, the railroad added a women's track crew in the Trempealeau River Valley. Many of the women came from families who had men employed at the railroad. Of 137 hourly employees on the summer 1993 payroll, 45 had a father, son, or brother also working for the GB&W.

In 1992, Wisconsin Central announced its intention to acquire GB&W. While implementing agreements were being negotiated with six labor unions, trains continued and business increased. The last agreement was reached on August 27, 1993, and early the next morning the final freight train, still carrying a caboose, rolled into Wisconsin Rapids.

GULF, MOBILE & OHIO RAILROAD

Gulf, Mobile & Ohio was the twentieth-century vision of late-era empire builder Isaac B. Tigrett. Late to coalesce and short-lived, this colorful railroad boasts a more complex history than many older and larger systems in the region.

During the 1930s, Tigrett merged the parallel Mobile & Ohio and Gulf, Mobile & Northern systems, which functioned as the GM&O following formal merger in 1940. Mobile & Ohio was an old system with origins in the 1850s, while GM&N was a late creation that came into being in 1917 from the reorganization of the New Orleans, Mobile & Chicago. During the 1920s and early 1930s, GM&N gobbled up various smaller southern railroads while enjoying an affiliation with Chicago, Burlington & Quincy. M&O, for its part, was closely affiliated with Southern Railway, but ties were broken during the Great Depression.

▼ A pair of well-used Electro-Motive F3As lead a GM&O freight working from Bloomington to Peoria, Illinois, on the old Alton Route. *Terry Norton*

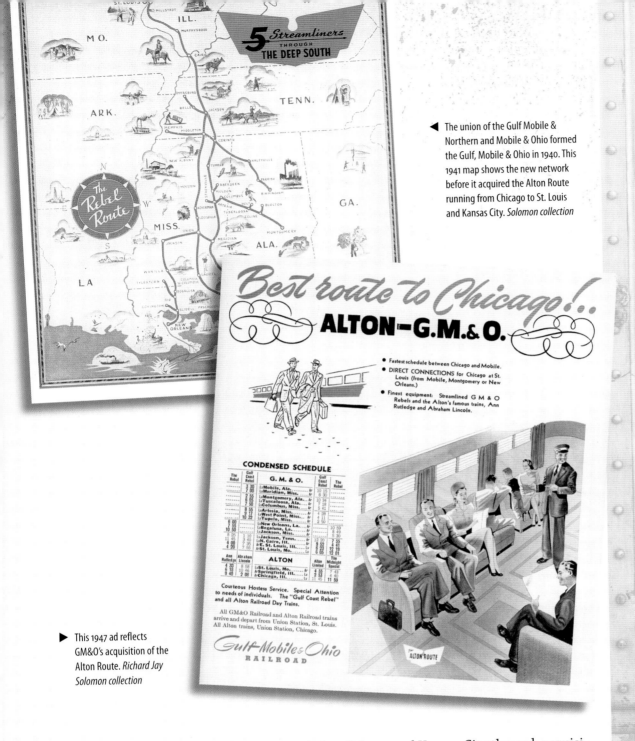

The union of the Gulf Mobile & Northern and Mobile & Ohio formed the Gulf, Mobile & Ohio in 1940. This 1941 map shows the new network before it acquired the Alton Route running from Chicago to St. Louis and Kansas City. *Solomon collection*

This 1947 ad reflects GM&O's acquisition of the Alton Route. *Richard Jay Solomon collection*

Headquarters: Mobile, AL
Years operated: 1940–1972
Disposition: Merged with Illinois Central to form Illinois Central Gulf; ICG abandoned and sold off key routes in 1980s; surviving GM&O routes operated by IC/ICG successor Canadian National, as well as Kansas City Southern, Union Pacific, and various short lines
Route mileage: 2,704 (c. 1970)
Locomotives
   Steam: 136 (1947)
   Diesel: 252 (c. 1970)
Reporting mark: GM&O
Emblem: Red wings emblazoned with letters GM&O
Primary locomotive shops: Bloomington, IL, and Iselin (Jackson), TN
Nicknames: The Rebel Route and The Alton Route
States served: AL, IL, KY, LA, MS, MO, TN
Major cities served: Chicago, Kansas City, Memphis, Mobile, New Orleans, St. Louis

Between 1945 and 1947, GM&O expanded to Chicago and Kansas City through acquisition and merger with the Alton Route. The old Chicago & Alton had been variously affiliated with other major systems, and in the 1920s was acquired by Baltimore & Ohio as part of a larger effort to consolidate the American railroad network. B&O renamed it the Alton, operated it until 1943, and then spun it off, finally selling it to GM&O.

GM&N had been among the smallest operators of diesel streamliners: a pair of sleekly styled Alco-powered trains built by American Car & Foundry in 1935 and controversially named the *Rebels*. After World War II, GM&O was the first large system to dieselize completely, retiring all of its steam by 1950. In 1972, it merged with the largely parallel Illinois Central to form Illinois Central Gulf.

ILLINOIS CENTRAL RAILROAD

▼ IC provided one of the most frequent suburban passenger services in North America. Prior to Chicago's demand for electrification (wired between 1921 and 1926), IC commuter trains were powered by a variety of specialized steam locomotives, such as this 2-4-4T bi-directional tank engine pictured at Chicago. *Solomon collection*

Chartered in 1851, Illinois Central (IC) featured several anomalies in American railroading: (1) Where the majority of large railroads tended to develop around the movement of east–west traffic, IC created America's premier north–south route; (2) it was the only steam railroad in Chicago to develop an intensive multiple-track, electrified suburban service; (3) it was one of just a few twentieth-century railroads to manufacture its own locomotives; and (4) it was among a handful of operations to maintain 100-mile-per-hour operations after 1947. IC is also remembered for both Abraham Lincoln—who lent the railroad his legal services before he became president of the United States—and legendary engineer John Luther "Casey" Jones, who famously crashed one of their trains at Vaughn, Mississippi, on April 30, 1900.

Headquarters: Chicago, IL

Years operated: 1851–1998 (merged with GM&O in 1972 to become Illinois Central Gulf; reassumed Illinois Central name in 1988)

Disposition: Merged with Canadian National in 1998; surviving routes, including Chicago–Omaha/Sioux City lines, operated by CN; routes trimmed from network during 1980s now operated by Union Pacific, Kansas City Southern, Paducah & Louisville, Indiana Railroad, and various short lines

Route mileage: 6,539 (c. 1952), 9,159 (c. 1977), 2,665 (c. 1995)

Locomotives

    Steam: 1,657 (1929)

    Diesel: 365 (1997)

    Electric railcars: 140 two-unit sets (c. 1952)

Reporting marks: IC, ICG, GMO

Emblems: ILLINOIS CENTRAL on yellow bar atop green diamond; stylized "i" that looks like a rail profile within a circle

Nickname: Main Line of Mid-America

Primary locomotive shops: Centralia and Woodcrest (Homewood), IL; Iselin (Jackson), TN; McComb, MS; Paducah, KY

Notable features: Albert (IL) Tunnel, 6,994 ft.; Ohio River Bridge (Cairo, IL), originally 20,461 ft. long, 104 ft. tall; Tulip Trestle (Solsberry–Tulip, IN), 2,306 ft. long, 157 ft. tall

States served: AL, IL, IN, IA, KY, LA, MN, MS, NE, SD

Major cities served: Birmingham, Chicago, Indianapolis, Louisville, Memphis, New Orleans, Peoria, St. Louis

ILLINOIS CENTRAL RAILROAD

Fast and all-freight!

You won't find many stretches of railroad like this. Here the fast freight train is king. No passenger trains move along this unique, high-speed track. None ever has. For this is the famous Edgewood cut-off through the hills of southern Illinois. It was built to cut many hours off the running time of north-south freight trains. Fast track like this for the exclusive use of freight trains helps the Illinois Central provide the shortest, fastest rail service between the Great Lakes and the Gulf of Mexico.

ERNEST J. CARR
Vice President–Traffic

MAIN LINE OF MID-AMERICA

▲ IC was proud of its freight-only 63-mile Edgeworth Cutoff, built in the 1920s in southern Illinois. *Solomon collection*

IC's main north–south trunk connected Chicago and New Orleans in 1883. In addition to this line, there were a number of east–west feeders, including some that predated the north–south route. IC built west to Sioux City, Iowa, in 1870 (eventually extending a line to Council Bluffs, Iowa, and Omaha, Nebraska); in 1900, it reached east to Louisville, Kentucky, and west to St. Louis; while a connection to Birmingham, Alabama, in 1908 came about as a result to its affiliation with Central of Georgia (which concluded in 1948). In 1972, IC merged with its primary post–World War II competitor, Gulf, Mobile & Ohio, to form Illinois Central Gulf.

Where IC had grown its network though a mix of new construction and line acquisition in its first 120 years, in its final years the railroad took a schizophrenic approach, first by aggressively paring back its network, then reversing this trend by reacquiring some previously spun-off routes. Branch-line spin-offs were common in the 1980s, and ICG spin-offs largely involved secondary main lines. Among the more notable were a cluster of former GM&O lines sold to become Gulf & Mississippi in 1985 and its Chicago–Sioux City/Omaha route, which was sold to Chicago Central & Pacific that same year (and reacquired in 1996). In 1986, the Paducah & Louisville was carved out of IC's route between those points, while the Chicago, Missouri & Western was created in 1987 from the bulk of the old Alton Railroad (which had merged with GM&O in 1947).

Having cut much of the GM&O from its route map, IC shortened its name back to Illinois Central in 1988. Ten years later, it made for an incongruous merger partner with Canadian National. Today, CN operates former IC main lines, while Chicago's Metra operates its former electrified suburban services.

▶ IC's public long-distance passenger timetable on the eve of Amtrak. *Solomon collection*

▲ The cover of IC's 1966 public timetable features a simplified system map and rows of E-units that were among the fastest diesels in the United States at the time. *Solomon collection*

▲ In December 1994, an IC local working east on the former GM&O Alton Route clatters across the diamond crossing at Brighton Park, Chicago. *Brian Solomon*

▲ An Illinois Central road switcher catches the winter evening sun at Homewood, Illinois, in December 1994. *Brian Solomon*

52

IOWA, CHICAGO & EASTERN RAILROAD

Milwaukee Road's 1980 bankruptcy resulted in a dramatic paring back of its network. Among the lines retained were its Chicago–Kansas City route and the Mississippi River line to the Twin Cities via Sabula, Iowa. Canadian Pacific's Soo Line affiliate merged with Milwaukee in 1985, and over the next decade its image was phased out in favor of CP's.

In April 1997, CP spun off 1,385 miles of former Milwaukee Road lines centered on the Chicago–Kansas City route and aforementioned Mississippi River line, both to Montana Rail Link's parent company, Washington Corporation, which operates the routes as the I&M RailLink. After five years of operation, Washington deemed the lines unprofitable and sold the railroad in 2002 to Dakota, Minnesota & Eastern, which renamed the line Iowa, Chicago & Eastern. Both railroads used the same blue-and-yellow livery on locomotives, with motive power mixing between the two carriers.

▼ On July 5, 2007, an eastward freight running from Huron, South Dakota, to Chicago's Clearing Yard crosses the Mississippi River Bridge and causeway between Sabula, Iowa, and Savanna, Illinois. IC&E was the fourth railroad to serve this former Milwaukee Road property following Milwaukee Road's merger with Soo Line in 1985. *John Leopard*

▲ At 4:55 p.m. on June 26, 2010, an IC&E local eases across Wisconsin Highway 11 south of Janesville, having completed its interchange with Wisconsin & Southern. Working on former Milwaukee Road trackage, this train will amble at 5 to 10 miles per hour toward its terminal at Davis Junction, Illinois, where this secondary line connects with IC&E's main line running west from Chicago to the Mississippi crossing at Savanna, Illinois. *Brian Solomon*

Both DM&E and IC&E merged with Canadian Pacific in autumn 2008 and now function as CP subsidiaries. Among the changes implemented by CP was the diversion of some DM&E/IC&E freight bound for Chicago off an all-IC&E routing in favor of CP's primary Twin Cities–Milwaukee–Chicago main line. IC&E's roster of all Electro-Motive Division diesels consisted largely of SD40/SD40-2s for use on road freights, with a few EMD four-motor models for locals and switching. IC&E locomotives have continued to work trains for several years after the merger.

Headquarters: Davenport, IA

Years operated: 2002–2008

Disposition: Operated as subsidiary of Canadian Pacific since 2008

Route mileage: 1,385

Diesel Locomotives: 110

Reporting mark: ICE

Primary locomotive shop: Nahant, IA

Notable feature: Mississippi River Bridge (Sabula, IA)

States served: IL, IA, MN, MO

Major cities served: Chicago, Kansas City, Minneapolis

53

IOWA INTERSTATE RAILROAD

Iowa Interstate—abbreviated IAIS—is a successful regional railroad created from the ashes of the old Rock Island. Not only has IAIS flourished in the modern era, it has retained independence from other major carriers. This is in contrast with most 1980s Midwest regional spin-offs, many of which were later reabsorbed into the Class 1 network.

IAIS was formed in 1984 by three former Rock Island men and designed to provide service on 489 miles of former Rock Island main line east from Council Bluffs, Iowa, via Rock Island, Illinois, to Blue Island in the Chicago suburbs. In addition, it has branches from Bureau to Peoria, Illinois; Altoona to Pella, Iowa; and Rock Island to Milan, Illinois. To reach the Chicago area it uses trackage rights on the former Rock Island between Bureau and Joliet (maintained by CSX) and Joliet and Blue Island (maintained by Chicago Metra).

▼ In June 2005, Iowa Interstate's eastward CBBI (Council Bluffs–Blue Island) road freight plies the former Rock Island main line, passing the old passenger station at Ottawa, Illinois. This section of old Rock Island is now owned and operated by CSX, with IAIS using the line via trackage rights. *John Leopard*

Headquarters: Cedar Rapids
and Iowa City, IA

Years operated: 1984–present

Route mileage: 567

Diesel locomotives: 58 (2005)

Reporting mark: IAIS

Emblem: The Rock Island Lines
shield displaying IOWA IAIS
INTERSTATE

Primary locomotive shop:
Homestead, IA

Notable feature: Mississippi
River Bridge at Davenport, IA

States served: IL and IA

Major cities served: Chicago
(Blue Island) and Peoria

◄ On June 9, 1996, IAIS's Iowa City Yard was
packed with carload traffic. Like many
regionals, IAIS has thrived on serving carload
customers, but in recent years has also
benefited from the movement of unit ethanol
trains. *Brian Solomon*

In the last decade, traffic has grown as result of new intermodal business and the rise of ethanol traffic. IAIS boasts connections with all seven of the nation's principal Class 1 freight railroads. During its first two decades, the railroad relied on secondhand diesels, but in 2008 and 2009, IAIS bought a fleet of 14 new General Electric ES44AC diesels to better handle its growing freight business. Locomotive No. 513 was painted in a retro Rock Island livery to commemorate the line's heritage. In addition to its regular freight moves, it has hosted high-profile steam excursions using imported Chinese locomotives.

54

KANSAS CITY SOUTHERN RAILWAY

Arthur Stillwell began his ambitious railway plan in 1887. His Kansas City Suburban Belt Railroad opened in 1890, and during the following decade he built the Kansas City Pittsburg & Gulf Railroad, which reached a new port at the Gulf of Mexico named Port Arthur, Texas, in honor of Stillwell. His railroad was renamed Kansas City Southern in 1900, and soon after Arthur was forced out. (He later went on to pursue another vision called the Kansas City, Mexico & Orient.) In 1939, KCS acquired control of the Louisiana & Arkansas, which connected the New Orleans and Dallas gateways and crossed KCS's system at Shreveport, Louisiana.

KCS survived the wave of mergers that began in the 1960s, but by the 1990s, threatened by merging lines on all sides, KCS took an offensive role by greatly expanding its territory. In 1994, it acquired Illinois Central Gulf spin-off lines operated by MidSouth Rail. Most significant of these was the former Illinois Central Meridian, Mississippi–Shreveport line, which neatly linked with its Louisiana & Arkansas route to Dallas. KCS

▼ A southward KCS unit grain train G-KCMS-27, led by a freshly painted SD70ACe and a GE ES44AC, passes DeQuincy, Louisiana, on April 29, 2008. KCS has readopted the livery originally used on E-units painted for the classy *Southern Belle* passenger train that captured the public imagination between 1940 and 1969. *Chris Guss*

developed the Dallas–Meridian route in partnership with Norfolk Southern as a fast east–west link between cities in the Southeast and the Southwest. It has since emerged as an important intermodal corridor.

Passage of the North American Free Trade Agreement of 1994 spurred additional opportunities for KCS, which positioned itself as a key cross-border carrier between the United States and Mexico. That year, it acquired control of the Texas Mexican Railway. Although isolated from the "Tex-Mex" in 1996, KCS negotiated trackage rights over Union Pacific to link its lines. Later, it negotiated a long-term operating concession with recently privatized Mexican railroad Transportación Ferroviaria Mexicana, and in 2005 completed this expansion by taking complete control of its Mexican affiliate, now known as Kansas City Southern de México. Its Mexican routes extend from the border crossing at Laredo (connection with Tex-Mex route) to myriad markets in Mexico, including Mexico City, Monterrey, Tampico, and Veracruz.

KCS also expanded in the Midwest by acquiring the Gateway Western, a former Alton Railroad (later Gulf Mobile & Ohio) route spun off by Illinois Central Gulf in the mid-1980s. The merger was completed in 2001, giving KCS a Kansas City–East St. Louis route. In more recent years, KCS has made a large investment in modern locomotives, including the latest ES44ACs from General Electric and SD70ACes from Electro-Motive.

▲ SD40-2s lead coal loads destined for Gulf States Utilities over Rich Mountain in the Arkansas Ozarks on October 19, 1986. KCS has survived waves of mergers and today operates lines in Mexico and Panama, as well as the United States. *John Leopard*

Headquarters: Kansas City, MO

Years operated: 1900–present

Route mileage: 1,648 (c. 1952) and approx. 3,200 (2008, U.S. only)

Locomotives
  Steam: 130 (1937)
  Diesel: 627 (2008)

Reporting marks: KCS, KCSR, KCSM

Emblem: Octagon shield emblazoned with "KANSAS CITY SOUTHERN Lines"

Primary locomotive shop: Shreveport, LA

Notable feature: Mississippi River Bridge (Baton Route, LA)

States served: AR, IL, KS, LA, MS, MO, OK, TN, TX, plus Mexico

Major cities served: Dallas, Houston, Kansas City, Mexico City, Monterrey, New Orleans, San Luis Potosí, Veracruz

Flagship passenger train: *Southern Belle* (Kansas City–New Orleans and Port Arthur, TX)

Other name passenger trains: *The Flying Crow* Shreveport–New Orleans); *The Shreveporter* (St. Louis–Shreveport)

Notable freight commodities: Chemicals, coal, intermodal

Principal freight yards: Shreveport, LA, and Knoche (Kansas City), MO

▶ This nose view of brand-new KCS Electro-Motive SD70ACe No. 4025 was made at Page, Oklahoma, on the railroad's crossing of Rich Mountain on June 8, 2006. In recent years KCS has bought large numbers of new locomotives from both EMD and GE. *Tom Kline*

▲ KCS entered the diesel era with a colorful splash. This General Motors builder's card displays an A-B-B-A set of KCS F3s. *Electro-Motive Division, Solomon collection*

◀ Passenger timetable, 1953. *Voyageur Press collection*

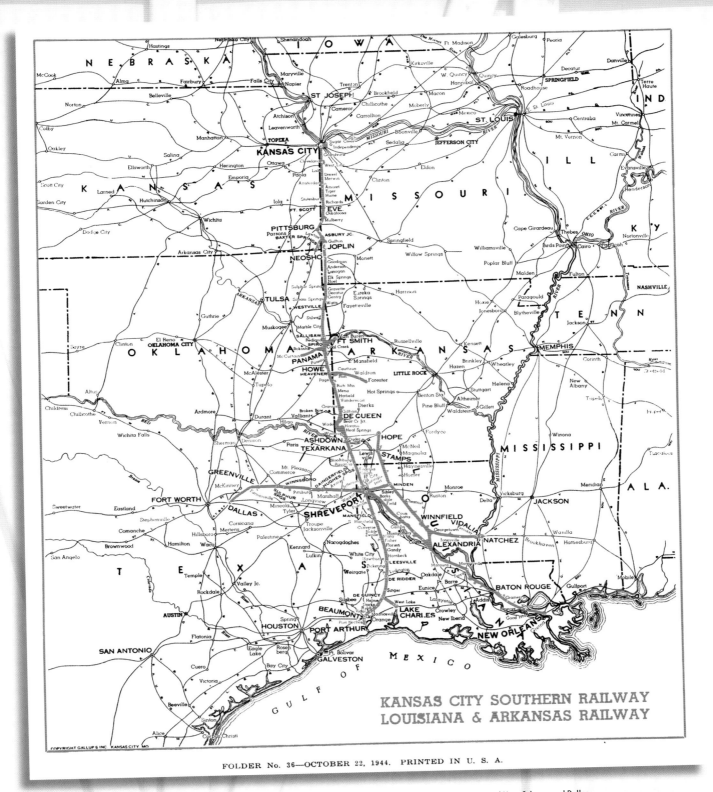

▲ The KCS 1944 system map shows both the north–south KCS main line and its Louisiana & Arkansas subsidiary that connected New Orleans and Dallas.
Richard Jay Solomon collection

55

LEHIGH VALLEY RAILROAD

▼ An eastbound freight led by an A-B-A set of Alco FA/FB diesels pauses at Sayre, Pennsylvania, the location of the Lehigh Valley's shops and yards. Although Sayre's importance diminished when the LV became part of Conrail, the old station survives as home of the local historical society.
Jim Shaughnessy

The Delaware, Lehigh, Schuylkill & Susquehanna Railroad was chartered in April 1846 to compete with Lehigh & Navigation Company's canal in Pennsylvania's Lehigh River Valley. Coal mogul Asa Packer bought control in 1851 and renamed the property the Lehigh Valley Railroad in 1853. It expanded rapidly under Packer's administration, with his chief engineer, Robert H. Sayre, extending lines eastward along the Lehigh River to reach Easton by 1855, where it connected with both the Delaware Canal and Central Railroad of New Jersey.

LV built northwesterly through Lehigh Gorge to White Haven. In 1864, it reached into Wyoming Valley coal fields by merging with Beaver Meadows Railroad, and then with Lehigh & Mahanoy in 1865 and Hazelton Railroad in 1868. North of White Haven,

Headquarters: New York, NY, and Bethlehem, PA

Years operated: 1853–1976

Disposition: Merged into Conrail; most New York State lines abandoned; surviving routes operated by Norfolk Southern, Reading & Northern, and various short lines

Route mileage: 1,254 (c. 1949)

Locomotives

    Steam: 725 (c. 1929)

    Diesel: 156 (c. 1971)

Reporting mark: LV

Emblem: Diamond around LV

Nickname: The Route of the Black Diamond

Primary locomotive shop: Sayre, PA

Notable feature: Pattenburg (NJ) Tunnel

States served: NJ, NY, PA

Major cities served: New York and Buffalo

Flagship passenger train: *Black Diamond* (New York–Buffalo, operated over Pennsylvania Railroad to New York Penn Station)

Other name passenger trains: Through trains operated over PRR to New York Penn Station included *The Asa Packer* (New York–Wilkes-Barre, PA); *The John Wilkes* (New York–Wilkes-Barre–Pittston, PA); *The Maple Leaf* (New York–Buffalo–Toronto, via Canadian National); *The Star* (New York–Ithaca, NY)

Notable freight commodities: Coal and general freight

Principal freight yards: Oak Island, NJ; Manchester, NY; Coxton (Pittston) and Sayre, PA

LV extended its main line to the Susquehanna River's North Branch, which it followed northwesterly to the New York state line, initially to a connection with the Erie Railroad at Waverly. LV built shops and a large yard immediately south of Waverly in Sayre, Pennsylvania, named in honor of the line's engineer. When Central Railroad of New Jersey (CNJ) expanded west into anthracite country, LV responded by building eastward, parallel to CNJ, and reaching the Hudson River at Jersey City (opposite Manhattan) in 1889. As a result, CNJ and LV largely overlapped.

LV built additional branches in the Wyoming Valley and continued west into New York State, extending to Buffalo and Niagara Falls in 1892. Reaching these crucial gateways allowed it to interchange coal traffic and merchandise freight, as well as form a passenger link as a through route to Chicago. To promote its New York–Buffalo route, it operated the famed *Black Diamond Express*, which it deemed "the most beautiful train in the world." LV also built branches across the Finger Lakes region of central New York to provide markets and outlets for anthracite and to serve the dairy business. Control under the U.S. Railroad Administration during World War I allowed LV passenger trains to reach New York City directly over a connection with the Pennsylvania Railroad.

As its anthracite business declined during the middle twentieth century, Lehigh Valley focused on becoming a bridge line. It gave up on passenger service in 1961, and in the 1960s began consolidating its redundant Pennsylvania trackage with CNJ. Pennsylvania Railroad bought controlling interest in LV, and when Penn Central collapsed in 1970, LV quickly followed suit. It was melded into Conrail in 1976.

▲ On May 10, 1972, an LV freight works at Cayuta, New York. LV was among the last major railroads to span western New York to reach important gateways at Buffalo and Niagara Falls. With the creation of Conrail in 1976, most of its New York State routes were abandoned or downgraded. *R. R. Richardson photo, Doug Eisele collection*

▶ This 1946 advertisement promotes industrial development along LV's lines. *Solomon collection*

56

LIVONIA, AVON & LAKEVILLE RAILROAD

Consolidation afforded by the Erie Lackawanna merger of 1960 included the rationalization of Erie Railroad's Rochester Division. In 1964, Livonia, Avon & Lakeville assumed operation of former Erie Railroad trackage between its namesake points. LA&L reached Lakeville by a short branch running south from Conesus Lake Junction. Between 1965 and 1977, LA&L augmented freight operations with steam excursion service and in 1981 abandoned its little-used line segment between Conesus Lake Junction and Livonia.

Development of corn syrup traffic at Lakeville has been the railroad's lifeblood for many years. In the 1990s, as Conrail trimmed its network, LA&L expanded by picking up more trackage and trackage rights. LA&L assumed operation of the "Rochester Cluster" of branch lines, which extended its operations northward on the Erie to Mortimer near

▼ LA&L C425 No. 425 leads a 38-car train at Lakeville, New York, on October 26, 1987. LA&L has developed substantial local traffic moving corn syrup. *Brian Solomon*

Headquarters: Lakeville, NY

Years operated: 1964–present

Route mileage: 8.5 (c. 1986) and 404 (2011, incl. Bath & Hammondsport and Western New York & Pennsylvania)

Diesel locomotives: 3 (c. 1986) and 20 (2011)

Reporting mark: LAL

Primary locomotive shops: Lakeville, NY; Alleghany (Olean), NY (WNY&PA)

States served: NY and PA (via WNY&PA)

Major cities served: Rochester

◀ LA&L's local freight arrives at Avon, New York, on September 24, 1986. This train came up to meet Conrail local WBRO-15, which originated at Rochester's Goodman Street Yard and worked the former Erie Rochester Division to Avon. A decade after this photo was made, LA&L acquired the former Erie line from Avon to the junction with the former West Shore route at Mortimer (south of downtown Rochester). Today, LA&L freights work all the way to the former West Shore Yard at Genesee Junction to interchange with CSX. *Brian Solomon*

Rochester and included a short section of former Lehigh Valley trackage. In 1998, LA&L negotiated additional trackage rights on Conrail to reach the former West Shore Yard at Genesee Junction and over Rochester & Southern to reach Brooks Avenue Yard (near the Rochester airport). During the 1990s, LA&L also acquired the Bath & Hammondsport (a short line dating to the 1870s that had been affiliated with the Erie between 1903 and 1935), as well as former Lackawanna trackage north of Horseheads, New York. Between 2001 and 2007, LA&L's sister railroad, Western New York & Pennsylvania, put together a network in its namesake region, operating on former Conrail trackage largely of Erie Railroad and Pennsylvania Railroad heritage (see Chapter 97). The line operates a colorful fleet of well-maintained Alco diesels.

57

LONG ISLAND RAIL ROAD

Long Island Rail Road ranks as one of America's oldest and most operationally atypical lines. Thanks to its proximity to New York City and that metropolis' rapid growth into America's greatest urban conurbation, LIRR developed as the nation's premier suburban railway. Today, with its state ownership, multiple parallel lines, and intensive electrified passenger operations, it more closely resembles railways of Europe and Japan than typical American lines.

LIRR was conceived as part of a long-distance transport scheme. Originally, its line running east toward Greenport, Long Island, was envisioned as a rail link in a New York–Boston route. It served in this capacity for just six years, ending in 1850, when a coastal Connecticut railway route was opened between New York and Boston. LIRR's longest

▼ A special train for LIRR officials pauses at Ronkonkoma in 1903. Under Pennsylvania Railroad influence, the LIRR would develop as a busy suburban line directly serving New York City via the East River tunnels to Pennsylvania Station at 34th Street. *Solomon collection*

line, the route to Montauk in far eastern Long Island, was completed in 1895 as part of an illusory effort to develop the Montauk terminal as a deep-water Atlantic port. Key to LIRR's success as a major passenger carrier was Pennsylvania Railroad's acquisition of the line in 1900, needed for the development of that railroad's Pennsylvania Station project in Manhattan. New multi-track East River Tunnels brought LIRR directly into Manhattan, while establishing 600-volt DC third-rail operation that was gradually extended over LIRR's busiest routes. Pennsylvania Railroad control further benefited LIRR through the adoption of the Pennsy's standardized locomotive designs and all-steel passenger cars (making it among the earliest railroads in the world to use all-steel equipment) and the Pennsy's safety practices, including distinctive position-light signals.

By the late 1940s LIRR was bankrupt, and over the next two decades, Pennsylvania Railroad worked with New York State in LIRR's transition from private to public ownership. In 1968, New York established the Metropolitan Transportation Authority to operate LIRR's network, making it one of the first state-run passenger networks in the United States. In May 1997, LIRR spun off freight operations to short-line operator New York & Atlantic Railway.

Headquarters: Jamaica Station, NY

Years operated: 1834–present

Disposition: Freight operations conveyed to the New York & Atlantic in 1997; LIRR continues to provide passenger service

Route mileage: 397 (c. 1949)

Locomotives (c. 1952)

   Steam: 18

   Electric: 15

   Diesel: 66

   Multiple-units: 750

Reporting mark: LI

Emblems: Keystone with letters RR impaled on letters LI; letters MTA in blue circle alongside "Long Island Rail Road"

Nickname: Route of the Dashing Commuter

Primary locomotive shop:
   Sunnyside (Queens), NY

Notable features: East River Tunnels

Major city served: New York

◀ LIRR operates the most intensive third-rail electric suburban passenger network in North America. Budd-built M1 third-rail multiple-units became a familiar sight beginning in 1968. The last of these once-common cars was withdrawn in 2007. *Brian Solomon*

MAP OF THE LONG ISLAND RAIL ROAD

AND LIST OF PRINCIPAL POINTS ON LONG ISLAND

The Route of the DASHING COMMUTER

THE LONG ISLAND RAIL ROAD

◄ This LIRR map cover features "Dashing Dan," the railroad's cartoon mascot. *Solomon collection*

One notable characteristic of LIRR is its electrified passenger operation. While in the early years of third-rail operation, it used Pennsy-design electrics, largely in the form of DD1 side-rod types and B class boxcabs, most of its fleet has comprised electric multiple-units (MUs). During the Pennsy era, owl-eyed cars prowled the line. Among the most unusual were squat double-deck cars (really a deck and a half). The MTA era ushered in a modern fleet of Metropolitan-series stainless-steel MUs. Some trains are powered with diesels, and LIRR has operated dual-mode diesel-electric/electrics to Penn Station since 1999.

▲ For many years LIRR's electric operations were characterized by fleets of "owl-eyed" multiple-units derived from those built for parent Pennsylvania Railroad. At 2:15 p.m. on August 11, 1958, train 165 departs the yard at Babylon, New York. *Richard Jay Solomon*

On March 23, 1958, an LIRR fan trip with two Budd RDCs pauses at the Hunterspoint Avenue Station in Queens, New York, immediately west of the sprawling Sunnyside Yard that served New York City's Penn Station. The Interborough Rapid Transit line to Flushing can be seen in the background. *Richard Jay Solomon*

LIRR Metropolitan-series multiple-units navigate the railroad's busiest junction at Jamaica Queens under a March sunset in 2003. *Brian Solomon*

LOUISVILLE & NASHVILLE RAILROAD

Louisville & Nashville's initial survey dated to 1851, and in 1853 its first rails were laid down to 5-foot gauge—the common track width in Kentucky at the time. By 1859, L&N connected its namesakes on a 185-mile line, but its north–south alignment put it in an unusually precarious situation during the American Civil War, which erupted in April 1861. L&N played a significant part in the war; it attempted to maintain a position of neutrality, but provided valued transport to both the Confederacy and the Union. Ultimately, it aided the Union more and suffered extensive damage from Confederate raiders as a result. Despite this, the railroad prospered from war traffic, which paved the way for later success.

After the war, L&N expanded southward through acquisition and new construction and ultimately emerged as one of the foremost southern carriers. It reached Montgomery, Alabama, in 1872, then in the 1880s connected strategic gulf ports at Pensacola, Florida, Mobile, Alabama, and New Orleans, while also establishing connections at the Evansville, Indiana, St. Louis, and Cincinnati gateways. In 1883, it connected Louisville and Knoxville.

Atlantic Coast Line bought majority interest in the L&N in 1902, yet L&N retained a high degree of independence while continuing to expand. Between 1902 and 1907, it built a second north–south main line between Cincinnati and Atlanta via Knoxville.

▼ A variety of Electro-Motive and General Electric road-switchers await assignment at the former Chicago & Eastern Illinois Wansford Yard in Evansville, Indiana, on February 17, 1979. Although steam had finished two decades earlier, C&EI's massive concrete coaling tower survived. In the 1980s, L&N consolidated Evansville operations at its Howell Yard and abandoned Wansford.
Scott Muskopf

Headquarters: Louisville, KY

Years operated: c. 1861–1982

Disposition: Melded into Seaboard System, a component of CSX; surviving routes largely operated by CSX

Route mileage: 4,778 (c. 1952) and 6,574 (c. 1977)

Locomotives

    Steam: 994 (1930)

    Diesel: 1,041 (c. 1977)

Reporting mark: L&N

Emblem: Rectangle with ornate L&N

Nicknames: The Old Reliable and later the Dixie Line

Primary locomotive shop: Corbin, KY

States served: AL, FL, GA, IL, IN, KY, MO, NC, OH, TN

Major cities served: Atlanta, Chicago, Cincinnati, Indianapolis, Memphis, Mobile, Montgomery, Nashville, St. Louis

Flagship passenger trains: *The Humming Bird* (Cincinnati–New Orleans) and *The Pan American* (New York–Cincinnati–New Orleans, operated with Pennsylvania Railroad)

Other name passenger trains: *The Azalean* (operated with PRR, New York-Cincinnati-New Orleans)

Notable freight commodity: Coal

Principal freight yards: Corbin, DeCoursey (South Covington), Loyall, Osborn (South Louisville), KY; Radnor (Nashville) TN

Atypically, after World War II, L&N continued to prefer steam for road freights and didn't commit to total dieselization until 1949, which it completed within a decade. Postwar, L&N implemented Centralized Traffic Control on a wide scale and also built large, modern classification yards.

In 1957, L&N merged with its longtime affiliate, the Nashville, Chattanooga & St. Louis (NC&StL)—a one-time rival it had controlled since 1879—which added 1,043 miles to L&N's map. Significantly, this provided a direct Chattanooga–Atlanta link over the old Western & Atlantic route. (Oddly L&N dropped its long-held "Old Reliable" moniker in favor of the NC&StL's "Dixie Line.") In the 1960s, L&N vied with Missouri Pacific for control the strategic Chicago & Eastern Illinois, but ultimately the two lines opted to divide C&EI. Missouri Pacific purchased C&EI in February 1967 and sold eastern routes to L&N with trackage rights to Chicago that provided L&N access to America's premier railroad gateway. If that wasn't enough, L&N further secured Chicago access with its 1971 acquisition of Indiana-based Monon Route. Today a CSX component, L&N's historic route structure is the most intact of CSX's major constituents.

▲ Louisville & Nashville GP7 No. 395 leads a coal train at Nortonville, Kentucky, in April 1975. L&N was one of a few eastern railroads to equip diesels routinely with oscillating headlights in addition to twin sealed-beam lights. *Terry Norton*

SUMMER — 1957

Choice

L&N

Service

To the SOUTH and FLORIDA

route of . . .

THE SOUTH WIND
THE DIXIELAND
DIXIE FLYER
THE GEORGIAN
THE SOUTHLAND
THE FLAMINGO
THE GULF WIND

TO NEW ORLEANS AND
THE MISSISSIPPI GULF COAST . .

route of

◄ Timetable, 1957. *Solomon collection*

MAINE CENTRAL RAILROAD

▼ MEC GP38 No. 252 leads freight YR-1 upgrade out of a sag at Intervale, New Hampshire. MEC operated its Portland & Ogdensburg route over Crawford Notch as its Mountain Division. In its later years, this typically consisted of a daily freight in each direction between Rigby Yard and St. Johnsbury, Vermont. Changes resulting from the 1980 Staggers Act and the 1981 acquisition of MEC by Guilford Transportation doomed the Mountain Divisions as a through freight route. *George S. Pitarys*

Maine Central Railroad, routinely referred to by its reporting marks MEC, grew to dominate transportation in its namesake territory by the latter nineteenth century. The railroad's earliest antecedent was the Kennebec & Portland, formed in 1836 as a feeder to the broad gauge Atlantic & St. Lawrence (a precursor to the Grand Trunk Railway). As a result, a mix of broad and standard gauge lines were constructed in central Maine during in the mid-nineteenth century. In 1862, MEC was formed to consolidate two established lines. Operations were expanded and then in 1871 converted to standard gauge.

From 1884, MEC was controlled by Boston & Maine as result of B&M's acquisition of Eastern Railroad, B&M's chief competitor that had controlled MEC since the mid-1870s. Although MEC regained independence in 1914, B&M and MEC remained closely affiliated and between 1933 and 1952 worked together under common management. B&M

◀ MEC's Rockland Branch has been considered among the most picturesque lines in the East. In August 1960, a pair of switchers lead a westward freight past ruined schooners *Hesper* and *Luther Little* in the Wiscasset, Maine, harbor on Sheepscot Bay. The largest customer on the branch was Dragon Cement at Thomaston. Today, Maine Eastern operates seasonal passenger trains on the route. *Jim Shaughnessy*

and MEC shared terminal facilities at Portland, including the important Rigby Yard at South Portland. MEC's Portland Terminal subsidiary handled switching for both roads in the Portland area and was noted for running along commercial streets. Both lines benefited from the joint operation of passenger services. In 1935, the railroads operated New England's first diesel streamliner, a Budd-built near copy of Burlington's famous *Zephyr*.

While MEC operations focused on central and coastal Maine, nineteenth-century acquisitions included lease of the Portland & Ogdensburg, which extended its territory over New Hampshire's White Mountains via Crawford Notch to St. Johnsbury, Vermont. Eastward acquisitions resulted in a short extension into New Brunswick and a line reaching more than 50 miles over the U.S. border to Lime Ridge, Quebec.

Maine's timber and paper industries represented MEC's most important freight traffic. Seasonal passenger traffic to vacation destinations, including coast cities such as Rockland, also provided thriving traffic, but by the mid-1950s, MEC was moving only a half-million passengers annually. Passenger services ceased altogether in 1960, and demolition of Portland Union Station a year later symbolized the dramatic decline of the American passenger train.

In 1981, MEC was acquired by Timothy Mellon's Guilford Transportation Industries, which in 1983 acquired B&M. MEC's network was paired back in the 1980s with the abandonment of its Mountain Division to St. Johnsbury, the truncation of its Lower Road via Augusta, and the curtailing of branch-line services. Key portions are still operated by the renamed Guilford system, now known as Pan Am Railways.

▶ Maine Central's 1933 timetable promoted the railroad's freight and passenger services, as well as its scheduled motorcoaches. However, the artist's perception of the railroad looks more like a scene on New York Central than anything found in Maine. *Richard Jay Solomon collection*

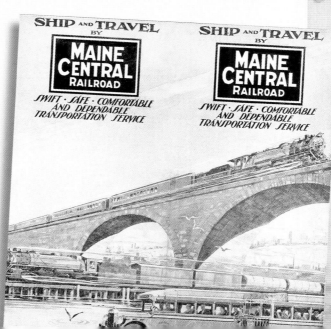

Headquarters: Portland, ME
Years operated: 1862–1981
Disposition: Acquired by Guilford Transportation Industries in 1981; operated since then as part of GTI/Guilford Rail System (today known as Pan Am Railways)
Route mileage: 1,300+ (c. 1917) and 945 (c. 1952)
Locomotives
  Steam: 233 (1923)
  Diesel: 78 (c. 1981)
Reporting mark: MEC
Emblem: Pine tree on circle with MAINE CENTRAL
Primary locomotive shop: Waterville, ME
Notable feature: Lift bridge (Bath, ME)
States served: ME, NH, VT
Major city served: Portland, ME
Flagship passenger train: *Flying Yankee* (Boston–Bangor, operated with Boston & Maine)
Other name passenger trains: *Bar Harbor Express* (Washington, D.C.–Mount Desert Ferry until 1931, to Ellsworth, ME, until 1957, to Bangor until 1960, all operated with Pennsylvania Railroad, New Haven Railroad, and B&M); *Pine Tree* (Boston–Bangor, operated with B&M); *Gull* (Boston–Portland–Halifax, operated with B&M, Canadian National, and Canadian Pacific)
Notable freight commodities: Paper and timber
Principal freight yards: Rigby (Portland) and Waterville, ME

MINNEAPOLIS, ST. PAUL & SAULT STE. MARIE RAILROAD

The history of the Minneapolis, St. Paul & Sault Ste. Marie is atypical and at times confusing because of its unusual growth pattern, the peculiarities of its name, and its close affiliation with the Canadian Pacific Railway. It is easiest to view the railroad through its various developmental phases.

In 1888, the Minneapolis, St. Paul & Sault Ste. Marie Railway (MStP&SSM) was formed from the union of two earlier companies that principally connected its namesake cities. Key to this line was its connection with CP at Sault Ste. Marie, which is actually two gateway communities on both sides of the border between Ontario and Michigan's Upper Peninsula. CP acquired control of the railroad in the 1890s, and expansion over the next couple of decades resulted in lines running west to CP gateways at Noyes, Minnesota, and Portal, North Dakota, as well as the dead-end extension to Whitetail, Montana. Soo's control of Wisconsin Central (WC) in 1909 gave it a route to Chicago. The line was also closely affiliated with Duluth, South Shore & Atlantic (DSS&A).

▼ Soo Line freights meet at Lake Villa, Illinois, in April 1966. Soo adopted its modern red-and-white livery in 1961 when it consolidated its various properties as the Soo Line.
Terry Norton

The next phase occurred in 1961, when MStP&SSM, WC, and DSS&A were merged into a company officially called the Soo Line Railroad, "Soo" being the anglicized phonetic pronunciation of Sault (French for *rapids*). The name change brought about a new simplified SOO LINE logo and a modern red-and-white livery. Among its through freight traffic, Soo Line continued to operate mixed trains on lines in the Upper Peninsula years after these types of services had been discontinued from most other American lines.

In 1985, Soo Line acquired the much trimmed-down Milwaukee Road network, which after its 1980 reorganization had shed its Pacific Extension and numerous secondary routes via line sales and abandonment. Combined with the Milwaukee Road, Soo Line now reached to Chicago, via the old Hiawatha Route that was much superior to Soo's old hill-and-dale line, as well as both the Louisville and Kansas City gateways. In 1986, Soo Line established the Lake States Transportation Division, largely carved out from its old Soo/WC network across Wisconsin and Michigan. This was spun off in 1987 to create Wisconsin Central Limited, effectively a modern reincarnation of the historic WC but with no corporate lineage to the old railroad. Although Soo Line continued to exist within the Canadian Pacific corporate structure, in the 1990s, CP melded its operations with the Soo, and the Canadian railroad's image replaced vestiges of the independent Soo Line.

▲ The latter-day Soo Line was a blend of its historic properties with those of the Milwaukee Road, which it acquired in 1985, minus routes spun off to Wisconsin Central in 1987. Soo freight No. 940 passes Soo Line Junction at St. Paul, where this line passed below the old Soo passenger main to St. Paul Union Station. *John Leopard*

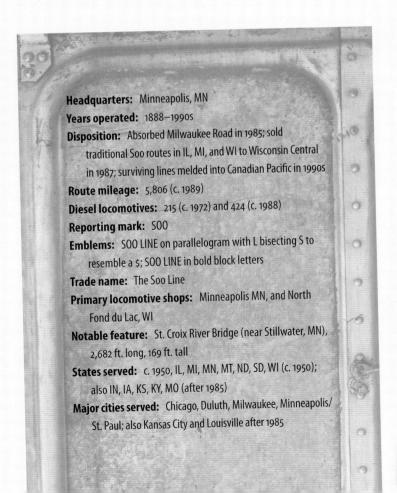

Headquarters: Minneapolis, MN

Years operated: 1888–1990s

Disposition: Absorbed Milwaukee Road in 1985; sold traditional Soo routes in IL, MI, and WI to Wisconsin Central in 1987; surviving lines melded into Canadian Pacific in 1990s

Route mileage: 5,806 (c. 1989)

Diesel locomotives: 215 (c. 1972) and 424 (c. 1988)

Reporting mark: SOO

Emblems: SOO LINE on parallelogram with L bisecting S to resemble a $; SOO LINE in bold block letters

Trade name: The Soo Line

Primary locomotive shops: Minneapolis MN, and North Fond du Lac, WI

Notable feature: St. Croix River Bridge (near Stillwater, MN), 2,682 ft. long, 169 ft. tall

States served: c. 1950, IL, MI, MN, MT, ND, SD, WI (c. 1950); also IN, IA, KS, KY, MO (after 1985)

Major cities served: Chicago, Duluth, Milwaukee, Minneapolis/ St. Paul; also Kansas City and Louisville after 1985

◀ Public timetable, 1963. *Solomon collection*

187

▲ F7A No. 212A works a southbound freight at Byron, Wisconsin, on October 10, 1978. *Terry Norton*

▶ July 2, 1990, finds a pair of Soo Line's ubiquitous EMD GPs hauling a transfer run from Soo's Humboldt Yard in Minneapolis to Chicago & North Western's East Minneapolis Yard. Such scenes were a daily event necessary in the interchange of carload freight. *John Leopard*

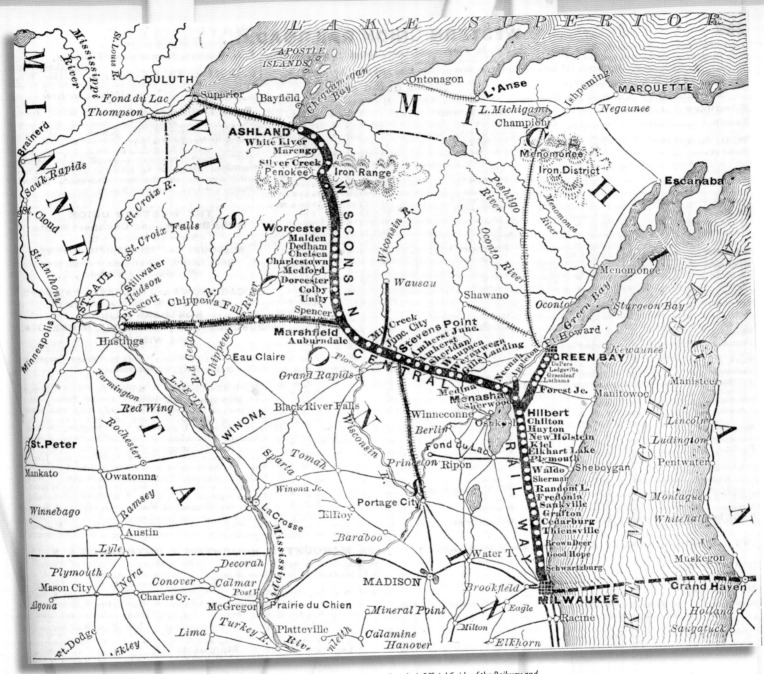

▲ The historic Wisconsin Central was among the Soo Line's components. This map from the *1880 Traveler's Official Guide of the Railway and Steam Navigation Lines in the United States and Canada* shows WC as it existed in 1880, prior to being absorbed by the Soo. More than a century after this map was drawn, Soo Line would spin off a variety of lines, including the historic WC, to a regional startup called Wisconsin Central Limited. Today these WC lines are largely part of the Canadian National, while the Soo Line primarily consists of the old Milwaukee Road network east of the Twin Cities. *Robert A. Buck collection*

MISSOURI-KANSAS-TEXAS RAILROAD

The Missouri, Kansas & Texas Railway was formed in 1870 and throughout most of its existence was universally known as the Katy, a phonetic play on its initials. Almost from the moment of incorporation, the Katy began consolidating several existing small lines in Missouri and Kansas. From 1873 to 1888, the Katy was controlled by railroad magnate Jay Gould, who enabled the line's modest growth through the early years of the twentieth century. Having reached the Texas border by 1872, the line reached Dallas in 1886, Houston in 1893, and San Antonio in 1901. Notably, it was the first railroad in so-called Indian Territory, which became the state of Oklahoma in 1907.

Pushing northward, the Katy reached the crucial St. Louis gateway in the 1880s and Kansas City in 1904. Despite crossing largely flat terrain west of the Mississippi, the railroad suffered from overexpansion and a meandering network. This, combined with

▼ On August 20, 1985, against a stormy sky, Katy freight No. 203 passes a Missouri Pacific freight. Both MP and M-K-T were melded into the Union Pacific system—MP in 1982 and M-K-T in 1988. *John Leopard*

▲ An F3A leading the *Katy Komet* (St. Louis–Ft. Worth fast freight) meets one of the Katy's northward long-distance passenger trains on single-track at Keller, Texas. *Wallace W. Abbey photo, Center for Railroad Photography & Art*

competition from parallel lines, plagued the Katy despite its good freight connections. In 1923, the line was slimmed down and reorganized as the Missouri-Kansas-Texas Railroad. In later years, the M-K-T system consisted of more than a half-dozen railways, with the M-K-T at its core.

The M-K-T acquired its last new steam locomotives in 1925, and after heavy use during World War II, suffered acutely from a tired fleet and well-worn physical plant. Unfortunately, M-K-T took a haphazard approach to dieselization, so by the early 1960s it had to replace or repower much of its fleet. Its hybrid types used Baldwin and Alco bodies and electrical components fitted with Electro-Motive diesel engines. These odd contraptions served the railroad into the early 1980s.

To compete with the trucking industry and parallel lines, the Katy operated named freights *Katy Komet* and *Klipper*. The Katy was never a major passenger carrier, and in 1965 it discontinued its last passenger trains, six years before Amtrak assumed operation of most remaining intercity services, and sold its small fleet of streamlined E-units to Atlantic Coast Line. In 1969, the railroad was put under control of Katy Industries. Despite its difficulties, the railroad survived as an independent line longer than Rock Island, Frisco, and Missouri Pacific, all lines that had served the Katy's region. The Katy was finally swept up by the merger movement. In 1988, it was melded into Union Pacific's Missouri Pacific subsidiary. Since that time, UP has consolidated the Katy into its system.

Headquarters: St. Louis, MO, and Dallas, TX

Years operated: 1870–1988

Disposition: Merged with Union Pacific

Route mileage: 3,293 (c. 1943) and 2,211 (c. 1982)

Locomotives
   Steam: 351 (c. 1943)
   Diesel: 200 (c. 1981)

Reporting mark: MKT

Emblem: Distinctively shaped shield around M-K-T with grain sheaf and diagonal banner reading "Missouri-Kansas-Texas Lines"

Nickname: The Katy

Primary locomotive shop: Parsons, KS

States served: KS, MO, OK, TX

Major cities served: Dallas/Ft. Worth, Galveston, Houston, Kansas City, San Antonio, St. Louis

Flagship passenger train: *Katy Flyer* (St. Louis and Kansas City–Parsons, KS–Dallas/Ft. Worth and Galveston)

Other name passenger trains: *Sooner* (Kansas City–Oklahoma City); *Texas Special* (St. Louis–Ft. Worth with Dallas–San Antonio section operated jointly with Frisco; also carried through sleepers from New York via Pennsylvania Railroad)

Notable freight commodities: Coal, grain, oil, general freight

Principal freight yards: Parsons, KS; Bellmead (Waco) and Denison, TX

191

The Katy's Glen Park Yard office at Kansas City, Kansas. *Scott Muskopf*

The Katy and Frisco jointly operated the *Texas Special*. *Solomon collection*

Timetable, 1937. *Voyageur Press collection*

This rare photograph is believed to depict the M-K-T *Katy Special* at Dennison, Kansas, in 1902. In the lead is 4-4-0 No. 505, a typical passenger locomotive of the late-nineteenth century and adequate power for this three-car passenger train. In the twentieth century, heavier all-steel passenger cars and longer consists would demand much more powerful passenger locomotives. *Author collection*

The M-K-T extended the life of its Baldwin and Alco diesels by rebuilding them with EMD engines. On March 27, 1985, rebuilt Baldwin switchers Nos. 22 and 27 work cab-first at Dallas, Texas. M-K-T Nos. 1000—1010 were originally Baldwin DS-4-4-1000 switchers built in 1946 and 1947. In 1959 and 1960, EMD modified and repowered them with 12-567C engines and they were renumbered 22—32. *John Leopard*

MISSOURI PACIFIC RAILROAD

Missouri Pacific (MP) had its origins in an 1849 Pacific Railroad charter that envisioned a route from St. Louis to Kansas City, then straight west over the Rockies to the West Coast. Although visionary, this scheme was impractical and never reached beyond the Great Plains. Yet, beginning in 1851, the railroad began its ambitious push, using tracks built to the Missouri track standard of 5 feet, 6½ inches.

In 1876, the company reorganized as the Missouri Pacific and came under the wing of railroad mogul Jay Gould, who favored the line and took its traffic and goals to heart. The MP was central to Gould's empire-building strategies, and later those of his son George, who used it as the basis for a planned transcontinental empire. At the time, MP connected St. Louis, Kansas City, and Omaha with a line reaching across Kansas and eastern Colorado to meet the Denver & Rio Grande Western, another Gould property. George's empire crumbled in the years prior to World War I, and MP assembled an empire of its own. In 1917, it merged with its longtime affiliate, St. Louis, Iron Mountain & Southern, with lines extending south from St. Louis into Texas and Louisiana. In the 1920s, MP extended its reach by absorbing the Gulf Coast Lines and International & Great Northern, and taking control of Texas & Pacific, this latter retaining a degree of independence during

▼ *Eagles* were among the most attractive trains of the streamlined era. *Photographer unknown, Robert A. Buck collection*

the middle years of the twentieth century. Although chartered to the West Coast like MP, Texas & Pacific never got within a time zone of its goal and reached only as far west as El Paso, Texas.

After World War II, MP invested in a fleet of classy streamlined passenger trains, most of which operated as its famed *Eagles*. Best known was the *Texas Eagle* domeliner, which connected St. Louis with various cities in the South. In the 1960s, MP made strides toward becoming a modern railroad. It ditched its passenger service, bought modern high-horsepower diesels, and revamped its main lines with continuous welded rail, deep ballast, and Centralized Traffic Control signaling. It furthered its reach by dividing the old Chicago & Eastern Illinois with Louisville & Nashville, with MP taking routes between Chicago and Thebes, Illinois, and St. Louis, Missouri. In 1976, it formally merged with both Chicago & Eastern Illinois and Texas & Pacific. In 1981, the railroad finally realized its Pacific ambitions through a merger with Union Pacific. Despite the fact MP took on Union Pacific's image, it was MP's management style that was the dominant force behind the enlarged UP.

Headquarters: St. Louis, MO

Years operated: 1876–1982

Disposition: Merged with Union Pacific; most surviving routes operated by UP

Route mileage: 10,440 (incl. affiliates)

Locomotives

    Steam: 396 (c. 1952)

    Diesel: 1,488 (c. 1981)

Reporting mark: MP

Emblem: Circular image of sun with MISSOURI PACIFIC LINES or stylized eagle

Nickname: MoPac

Primary locomotive shops: North Little Rock, AR; Ewing Avenue (St. Louis) and Sedalia, MO; Centennial (Ft. Worth), TX

States served: AR, CO, IL, KS, LA, Mo, NE, OK, TX, TN

Major cities served: Dallas/Ft. Worth, Denver, Houston, Little Rock, Memphis, New Orleans, Omaha, St. Louis

◀ In the 1960s and 1970s, MP set the tone for modern railroading. On June 28, 1981, an MP freight is stopped at the Santa Fe Railway station in Sugar Creek, Missouri, on joint MP–Santa Fe track. By the end of 1982, MP would be part of the growing Union Pacific system. *Scott Muskopf*

▲ MP's stylized eagle graces the side of an SD40-2. *John Leopard*

Flagship passenger trains: *Eagles* (see below)

Name passenger trains: *Missouri River Eagle* (St. Louis–Omaha); *The Aztec Eagle* (San Antonio–Mexico City, operated with National Railways of Mexico); *The Colorado Eagle* (St. Louis–Kansas City–Denver); *The Sunshine Special* (St. Louis–Hot Springs, AR, Lake Charles, LA, and San Antonio); *The Sunflower* (Kansas City–St Louis and Omaha); *The Texas Eagle* (St. Louis–Ft. Worth and Houston)

Notable freight commodities: Chemicals, coal, general freight, grain, intermodal, lumber

Principal freight yards: Centennial (Ft. Worth), TX; Dupo (near East St. Louis), IL; Little Rock, AR; Neff (Kansas City), MO

◄ In the 1960s, MP hacked away at its passenger schedules as it focused on long-distance freight. *Solomon collection*

▼ Missouri Pacific ad, November 1946. *Solomon collection*

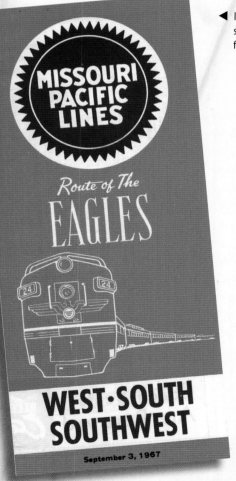

MISSOURI PACIFIC LINES

Route of The EAGLES

WEST·SOUTH SOUTHWEST

September 3, 1967

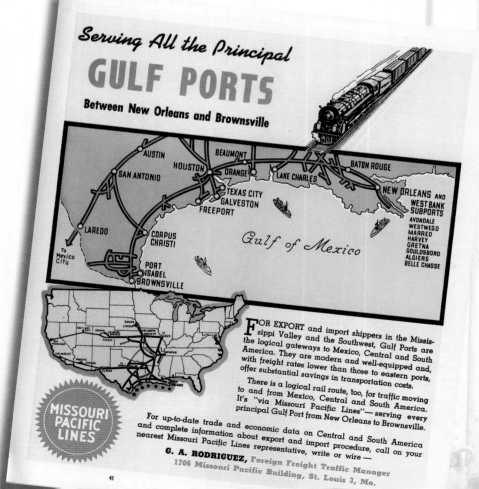

Serving All the Principal GULF PORTS
Between New Orleans and Brownsville

FOR EXPORT and import shippers in the Mississippi Valley and the Southwest, Gulf Ports are the logical gateways to Mexico, Central and South America. They are modern and well-equipped and, with freight rates lower than those to eastern ports, offer substantial savings in transportation costs.

There is a logical rail route, too, for traffic moving to and from Mexico, Central and South America. It's "via Missouri Pacific Lines"—serving every principal Gulf Port from New Orleans to Brownsville.

For up-to-date trade and economic data on Central and South America and complete information about export and import procedure, call on your nearest Missouri Pacific Lines representative, write or wire—

G. A. RODRIGUEZ, Foreign Freight Traffic Manager
1706 Missouri Pacific Building, St. Louis 3, Mo.

MISSOURI PACIFIC LINES

41

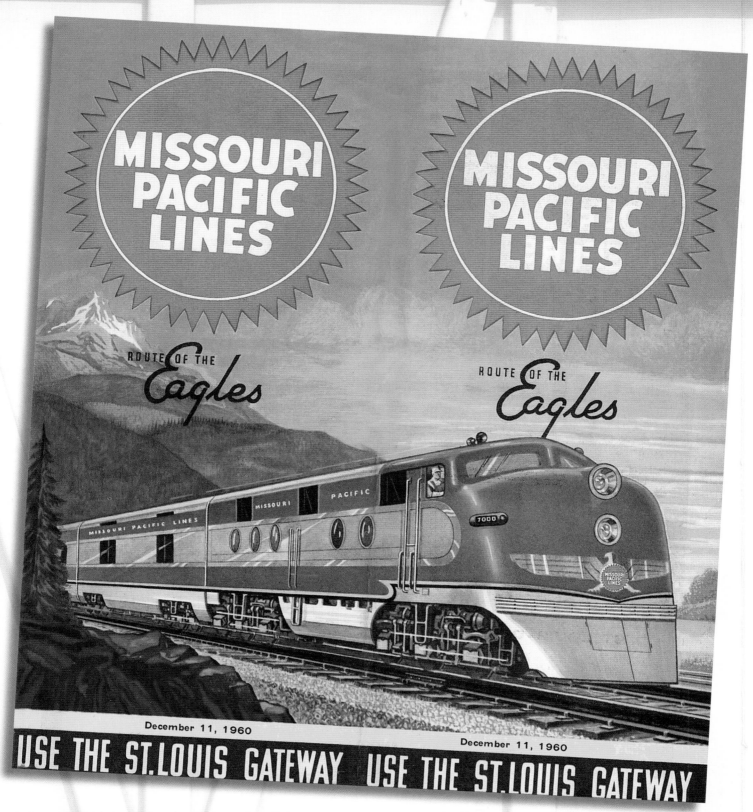

▲ Passenger and freight timetable, December 1960. *Voyageur Press collection*

MONTANA RAIL LINK

Burlington Northern's largest and most significant spin-off resulted in the October 1987 creation of Montana Rail Link, a new regional carved out of some 900 miles of former Northern Pacific lines. This included 588 miles of NP transcontinental line between Jones Junction near Huntley (east of Billings, Montana) and Sandpoint, Idaho, and 66 miles of trackage rights over Burlington Northern across the Idaho panhandle to Yardley Yard in Spokane, Washington. MRL was viewed by some as a labor-busting tactic to avoid traditional crewing arrangements, yet it may well have helped save the core of the old NP route from abandonment. MRL offered more liberal labor arrangements that provided greater flexibility and lower costs than were possible under the existing BN arrangements.

BN and its successor, BNSF Railway, have enjoyed a variety of benefits from the spin-off. As a locally owned and regional railroad, MRL offered superior service to online customers that helped develop local traffic fed to BN and BNSF interchanges. MRL has also kept the NP route open to through BN and BNSF trains moving via the Billings/Laurel gateway while serving as a potential safety valve for traffic via the former Great Northern transcon. Since MRL began operation, the majority of traffic moving over its lines has comprised BN and BNSF through trains. Initially, MRL operated a ragtag fleet of second-hand EMD locomotives, including a significant number of 20-cylinder SD45s, but in 2004, it bought 15 new Electro-Motive SD70ACes for use on mainline trains and as helpers.

▼ A westward MRL freight climbs across the Skyline Trestle on the ascent of Montana's Mullen Pass as an evening thunderstorm brews in the distance over Helena in July 1994. MRL has resulted in a renaissance of the former Northern Pacific route across Montana. *Brian Solomon*

▲ MRL's Livingston-to-Missoula (LM) freight drops downgrade from Mullen Pass at Bradley, Montana, on June 13, 2008. In the lead are two of the railroad's Electro-Motive SD70ACe diesels. MRL is one of a few midsized American railroads to invest in modern diesels in the last few years. *Tom Kline*

Headquarters: Missoula, MT

Years operated: 1987–present

Route mileage: 943 (c. 1996)

Diesel locomotives: 162 (2005)

Reporting mark: MRL

Emblem: Stylized W incorporating lion's head and signifying parent Washington Companies

Primary locomotive shop: Livingston, MT

Notable features: Bozeman Tunnel at Bozeman Pass, 3,015 ft. long; Blossburg Tunnel at Mullen Pass, 3,897 ft. long; Marent Gulch Viaduct (near Missoula), 797 ft. long, 162 ft. tall

States served: MT and ID

64

NEW ENGLAND CENTRAL RAILROAD

New England Central (reporting marks NECR) is a regional startup that assumed operations from Canadian National affiliate Central Vermont Railway (CV) in February 1995. It operates over the former CV main line between East Alburgh, Vermont, and the port of New London, Connecticut. A short branch connects Essex Junction and Burlington, Vermont.

RailTex, NECR's original owner, was acquired by short-line operator RailAmerica in 2000. A north–south railroad in an east–west world, NECR enjoys numerous freight interchanges with regional carriers and robust online business. Interchange partners and points include Canadian National at East Alburgh; Vermont Rail System (VRS) at Bellows Falls, Burlington, Montpelier Junction, and White River Junction, Vermont; Pan Am Southern at Brattleboro, Vermont, and Millers Falls, Massachusetts (the latter connection reactivated in 2010 after decades of disuse); CSX and Mass-Central at Palmer, Massachusetts; and Providence & Worcester (P&W) at Willimantic and New London, Connecticut. Since the 1990s, NECR has served as a link in a chain of carriers, including Canadian Pacific, VRS, and P&W that provide an alternative "Alphabet Route" gateway for freight moving to New England.

▼ A trio of NECR GP38s lead freight No. 610 (Palmer–New London) as it crests Stateline Hill at the Massachusetts–Connecticut state line in October 1999. *Brian Solomon*

Headquarters: St. Albans, VT

Years operated: 1995–present

Route mileage: 394 (2010)

Diesel locomotives: 27 (2010)

Reporting mark: NECR

Emblem: Illustration GP38 locomotive emerging from round shield with NECR banner at top and railroad name beneath

Primary locomotive shop: St. Albans, VT

Notable features: Bridges at Georgia, VT; Claremont, NH; and East Northfield and Millers Falls, MA; short tunnels at Bellows Falls, VT, and Yantic, CT

States served: CT, MA, NH, VT

▲ A set of NECR GP38s work in "run 8" (maximum throttle) on the ascent of State Line Hill at Stafford Hollow Road in Monson, Massachusetts, in October 1999. Compare this photo with that on page 74 of a CV freight in the same spot. *Brian Solomon*

In addition to local and through freight services, NECR hosts Amtrak's Washington, D.C.–St. Albans *Vermonter* between Palmer and the train's terminus. At the time of its startup, NECR briefly hosted Amtrak's *Montrealer* overnight service between Washington, D.C., and Montreal before that train was canceled due to a budgetary shortfall. In 2010, NECR received federal stimulus money to begin upgrading Vermont portions of its main line to allow for faster speeds, greater axle-loading, and increased passenger business.

► On the morning of August 7, 2010, a pair of NECR GP38s leads a southward freight working from Brattleboro, Vermont, to Palmer across the 1906 deck truss over the Millers River at Millers Falls, Massachusetts. A second freight followed with a mix of leased locomotives and those borrowed from sister RailAmerica short line Connecticut Southern. *Brian Solomon*

65

NEW YORK CENTRAL SYSTEM

New York Central was created in 1853 by grouping the series of relatively short railroads operating between Albany and the Niagara frontier. In the 1860s, steamboat magnate Cornelius Vanderbilt—popularly known as "the Commodore"—took control of NYC and combined it with New York & Hudson River Railroad and New York & Harlem, both of which he already controlled. Vanderbilt extended NYC through acquisition, lease, and new construction, establishing it as one of America's foremost railroads and dynastic enterprises.

In the first half of the twentieth century, New York Central was America's second-largest railroad after its chief competitor, Pennsylvania Railroad. The two companies vied for traffic throughout the Northeast. The New York Central System controlled the Boston & Albany; Cleveland, Cincinnati, Chicago & St. Louis (a.k.a., the Big Four); Michigan Central; Toledo & Ohio Central; and West Shore Railroads, and maintained close affiliations with Pittsburgh & Lake Erie, Indiana Harbor Belt, and Chicago River & Indiana, lines that retained a greater degree of independence.

▼ One of NYC's iconic T-motors glides by Yankee Stadium in the Bronx in October 1964. Following a wreck on approach to Grand Central in 1902, Central electrified its lines serving New York City. Today these are operated by Metro-North.
Richard Jay Solomon

On October 15, 1947, NYC Class L3a 4-8-2 Mohawk No. 3002 leads train 49, *The Knickerbocker*, upgrade on the Boston & Albany at Twin Ledges west of Middlefield, Massachusetts. *Robert A. Buck*

Who's who on the *Century*. In the glory days, the *20th Century Limited* was the finest means of travel between New York and Chicago. This ad depicts the train in 1945. *Solomon collection*

As a major freight and passenger carrier, NYC was a transportation powerhouse that developed some of the most intensive heavy-rail infrastructure in North America. New York Central's largely four-track New York City–Chicago main line connected cities across the heavily industrialized central and western New York and Great Lakes regions. Lines around New York City were electrified using under-running third rail, as were Michigan Central's Detroit River tunnel operations, while Cleveland Union Terminal was wired with overhead catenary.

Central's late-era steam locomotives were considered among the finest ever built and noteworthy for their efficient design and high availability for service. The railroad had the largest fleet of 4-8-2s—known as Mohawks—and pioneered the 2-8-4 Berkshire type (named for the Boston & Albany grade) and the 4-6-4 Hudson type. After World War II, it developed and embraced an exceptional 4-8-4 design called the Niagara that exceeded the capabilities of diesels (but couldn't match diesel operational costs). Despite these magnificent machines, New York Central was fully dieselized by 1957.

Headquarters: New York, NY

Years operated: 1853–1968

Disposition: Merged with Pennsylvania Railroad to form Penn Central in 1968; PC operations conveyed to Conrail in 1976; Conrail bought and divided between CSX and Norfolk Southern, with independent operations ending in 1999; most surviving NYC routes east of Cleveland and route to St. Louis went to CSX; main line west of Cleveland went to NS; New York suburban operations part of Metro North; secondary lines and branches operated by various short lines

Route mileage: 10,740 (c. 1950)

Locomotives (1950)

Steam: 3,500

Diesel: 850

Electric: 160

Reporting mark: NYC

Emblem: Oval encircling NEW YORK CENTRAL SYSTEM

Nickname: The Water Level Route and the Central

Primary locomotive shops: Harmon, West Albany, and DeWitt, NY; West Springfield, MA (Boston & Albany); Collinwood (Cleveland), OH; McKees Rocks, PA (P&LE); Beech Grove, IN (car shops)

Notable features: Grand Central Terminal (New York City); Ohio River bridges at Louisville, KY, and Beaver, PA (P&LE); Hudson River bridges at Castleton and Albany, NY; Niagara Gorge Bridge (Niagara Falls, NY); Park Avenue viaduct and tunnel (New York City); tunnels under Detroit River and on West Short Railroad at Weehawken, NJ, and West Point, NY

States and provinces served: IL, IN, KY (Big Four), MA (B&A), MI, MO (Big Four), NY, OH, PA, WV, plus ON and QC

Major cities served: Albany, Boston, Buffalo, Charleston, Chicago, Cincinnati, Cleveland, Columbus, Detroit, Erie, Indianapolis, Montreal, New York, Peoria, Pittsburgh, Springfield, Syracuse, Toledo, Worcester, Youngstown

As America's second-largest passenger carrier (behind Pennsylvania Railroad), New York Central fielded an array of famous named trains collectively known as its Great Steel Fleet. Most exclusive was its all-Pullman, extra-fare New York–Chicago express train, *20th Century Limited*, remembered as the setting for Alfred Hitchcock's 1959 thriller *North by Northwest*. The railroad's Grand Central Terminal in New York City, which it shared with the New Haven Railroad, survives today and is arguably the world's most famous passenger station and a testimony to the industrial might of the railroad in its heyday.

► Cover of New York Central children's menu, 1940s. *Voyageur Press collection*

▲ Most famous of the Central's Great Steel Fleet was its exclusive extra-fare *20th Century Limited*, seen here in September 1962 on the first leg of its journey to Chicago, passing at Mott Haven Yards in the Bronx. *Richard Jay Solomon*

▲ EMD E-units in the classic "lightning stripe" lead one of NYC's long-distance passenger trains as it exits the tunnels at Breakneck Ridge along the east shore of the Hudson on the sprint from Grand Central to Albany. *Richard Jay Solomon*

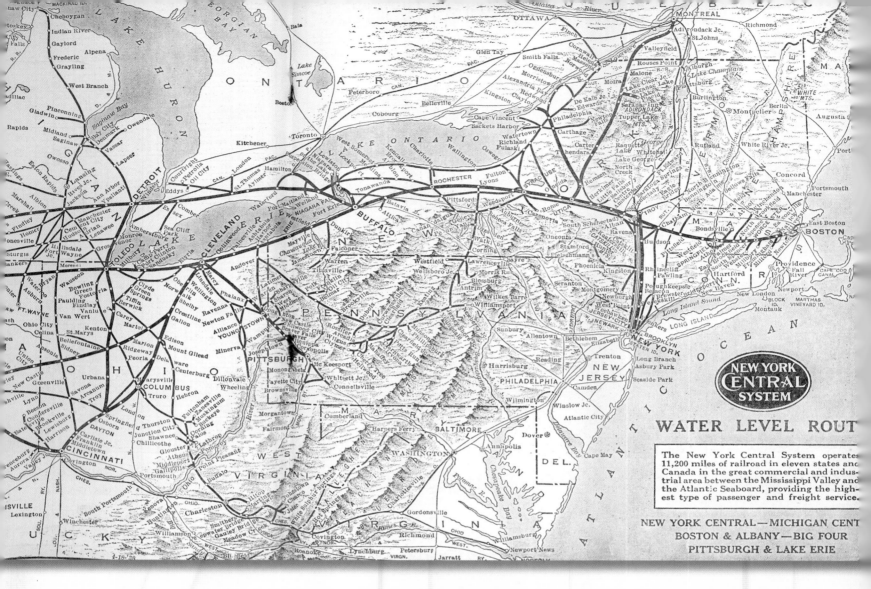

▲ This New York Central System map distinguishes main passenger routes from secondary routes by line thickness. Also shown are its affiliate routes, including the Pittsburgh & Lake Erie. *Solomon collection*

Flagship passenger trains: *20th Century Limited* (New York–Chicago) and *Empire State Express* (New York–Buffalo and Detroit)

Other name passenger trains: *Commodore Vanderbilt*, *The DeWitt Clinton* (New York–Syracuse); *The James Whitcomb Riley* (Cincinnati–Chicago); *Lake Shore Limited* and *The Pacemaker* (New York–Chicago); *The Laurentian* (New York–Montreal, operated with Delaware & Hudson); *The Niagara* (New York–Niagara Falls); *New England States Limited* (Boston–Chicago); *Southwestern Limited* and *The Knickerbocker* (New York and Boston–St. Louis); *The Paul Revere* (Boston–Chicago, Detroit and St Louis)

Named freight train: *The Pacemaker* (New York–Buffalo)

Notable freight commodities: Merchandise and manufactured goods, steel and metals (P&LE), coal and mineral ores, dairy products, perishables (fruit and vegetables), livestock, timber, paper products

Principal freight yards: Avon (Indianapolis) and Elkhart, IN; Beacon Park (Boston), MA; DeWitt (Syracuse), Frontier (Buffalo), Selkirk (Albany), and West Albany, NY; Collinwood (Cleveland), OH

◀ Mixed in with NYC's vast fleet of Alco and Electro-Motive cab units were a handful of Baldwin "sharks," which tended to work Big Four routes in Ohio and Indiana. Here, an A-B set of RF16 sharks in Central's lightning stripe paint rolls through Sandusky, Ohio, in June 1954. *J. R. Quinn collection*

◀ NYC's last gasp of steam was its 4-8-4 Niagara, which pushed the limits of conventional steam power. In August 1948, a powerful Niagara leads the eastbound *Lake Shore Limited* at Stuyvesant, New York. *Frank Quinn photo, Jay Williams collection*

66

NEW YORK, CHICAGO & ST. LOUIS RAILROAD

▼ NKP No. 750 works its way through Continental, Ohio. Built by Lima in 1944, this S-2 class 2-8-4 was sold for scrap in 1964. *Don Krofta photo, Voyageur Press collection*

In 1870, New York Central's domination in northern Ohio and Indiana spawned the consolidation of several midwestern lines into the Lake Erie & Western . In February 1881, LE&W's promoters chartered the New York, Chicago & St. Louis Railroad (NYC&StL),

▲ NKP's late-era passenger timetables featured its Alco PA streamlined locomotives.
Solomon collection

Headquarters: Cleveland, OH

Years operated: 1881–1964

Disposition: Merged into
Norfolk & Western; surviving
routes now operated by
Norfolk Southern

Route mileage c. 1952:
2,192 (c. 1952, incl. Wheeling
& Lake Erie)

Locomotives
Steam: 465 (c. 1929)
Diesel: 408 (c. 1962)

Reporting mark: NKP

Emblem: NICKEL PLATE ROAD
in dark square bordered by
three white rules

Trade name: Nickel Plate Road

Primary locomotive shops:
Bellevue and Connaught, OH

Notable features:
Cuyahoga River Viaduct
(Cleveland), 2,991 ft. long,
157 ft. high; 33-span Elk
Creek Trestle (near Girard,
PA) and numerous other
tower-supported
plate-girder trestles

States served: IN, IL, MO, NY,
OH, PA

Major cities served:
Buffalo, Chicago,
Cleveland, Erie, Indianapolis,
St. Louis, Toledo

which rapidly built a 524-mile route between Buffalo and Chicago running large parallel with NYC's lines. NYC&StL's unusually high construction standard (some might say it was overbuilt) seems to have been the inspiration for its trade name, the Nickel Plate Road (NKP). While finely engineered, with tall tower-support, plate-girder bridges crossing river valleys, and long stretches of tangent rights-of-way, NKP was constructed as largely a single-track line and remained so.

Despite its intent to compete with NYC, in the mid-1880s both NKP and LE&W came under Vanderbilt control; however, federal monopoly concerns during World War I encouraged NYC to sell LE&W and NKP to Cleveland developers Oris P. and Mantis J. Van Swearingen. The "Vans," as the two brothers became known, used the Nickel Plate Road as the basis for an extensive and well-planned railroad empire. In the 1920s, the Van Swearingens greatly expanded NKP by consolidating it with LE&W and the "Clover Leaf Route," the trade name for the Toledo, St. Louis & Southwestern. They also leveraged control of the Chesapeake & Ohio, Pere Marquette, and the Erie Railroad, all of which they planned to combine into a first-class trunk line. The Interstate Commerce Commission squashed this plan, but the lines continued to benefit from a family relationship. This

Flagship passenger train:

Nickel Plate Limited
(Chicago–Buffalo–
Jersey City via DL&W)

Other name passenger train:

The Westerner
(Chicago–Buffalo–
Jersey City via DL&W)

Notable freight commodity:

General freight

Principal freight yard:

Bellevue, OH

included a well-thought-out motive power plan that resulted in some of the finest engine designs operated in the eastern United States.

In the 1930s, the Vans' empire unraveled, orphaning NKP. In 1949, NKP acquired control of the Wheeling & Lake Erie, and during the 1950s it famously clung to steam longer than many roads, operating its late-era Lima-built Berkshires on fast freight through 1958; NKP was among just a few railroads noted for running piggyback trailers behind steam.

NKP's strategic route structure made it ripe for a merger. While it discussed options with a variety of roads, the end came in 1964, when Norfolk & Western acquired the line, along with Wabash, as part of a planned grouping designed to counter the anticipated Penn Central consolidation. NKP's core Buffalo–Chicago route remained an important line, first for N&W, and then for Norfolk Southern.

▶ NKP held onto mainline steam longer than many roads. While it was famous for its excellent Lima 2-8-4 Berkshires, it also had eight 4-6-4 Hudsons. Leading a Cleveland–Bellevue, Ohio, local in the 1950s is No. 174, one of four Hudsons built by Lima in 1929 for passenger service but used as "universal" locomotives in later years. *J. William Vigrass*

◀ NKP operated steam very late, completing dieselization by mid-1958, much to the sadness of some operating officials and many railroad enthusiasts. *Solomon collection*

THE NEW YORK, CHICAGO AND ST. LOUIS RAILROAD COMPANY

TERMINAL TOWER · CLEVELAND 1, OHIO

C. B. BENNETT
ASSISTANT TO PRESIDENT - PUBLIC RELATIONS

July 1, 1958

File 115

Mr. Richard J. Solomon
85 McClellan Street
New York 52, New York

Dear Mr. Solomon:

Thank you for your recent letter and we are pleased to know of your interest in the Nickel Plate.

We are not operating any steam power as the conversion to diesel power has recently been completed.

Sincerely,

C. B. Bennett

BUF
222

▲ In the mid-1950s, NKP No. 802, a 2-8-4 Berkshire acquired through the lease of Wheeling & Lake Erie, leads a coal train 222 miles west of
Buffalo, New York. *J. William Vigrass*

67

NEW YORK, NEW HAVEN & HARTFORD RAILROAD

▼ In July 1962, New Haven FL9 No. 2019 rolls east under wire at South Norwalk, Connecticut, with a train bound for Pittsfield, Massachusetts. New Haven's overhead catenary was energized at 11,000 volts alternating current and represented the first large-scale high-voltage AC mainline electrification in the United States. *Richard Jay Solomon*

The New York, New Haven & Hartford has its origins in the New York & New Haven, a line chartered in 1844 to connect its namesakes. Gradually, the railroad merged with, leased, or otherwise absorbed dozens of affiliated and competing properties. In 1872, the NY&NH merged with the Hartford & New Haven, resulting in the New York, New Haven & Hartford. By the early twentieth century, the New Haven, as it was more commonly known, had a virtual transportation monopoly in southern New England. Not only did the New Haven control all the steam railroads in Connecticut and Rhode Island (except for Central Vermont Railway in Connecticut and a few Rhode Island short lines), but it controlled the street railways and some steamship companies as well. This near domination of transport was unusual in the eastern United States, where railroad operations tended to feature rival companies vying for traffic.

Because New Haven's territory was among the most densely populated in the United States, the railroad had an abnormally high percentage of passenger revenue compared to freight. New Haven's "Shore Line" main line developed as a principal intercity passenger route between Boston and New York City, and, along with other lines, as an intensive suburban line as well. Yet, in its heyday, New Haven was a major freight carrier, too, serving as a gateway and terminal line for traffic to southern New England—a major manufacturing center through the World War II period, after which it declined.

New Haven invested heavily in its infrastructure during the late nineteenth and early twentieth centuries, making its main line one of the best-built lines of the era. In the 1890s, it expanded its New Haven–New York line to four main tracks and grade-separated most of the route. In the early twentieth century it embarked on an ambitious electrification scheme, making it one of the first lines to pioneer the application of high-voltage alternating current (now a common power-transmission system for railways in continental Europe, Asia, and elsewhere). While, New Haven envisioned electrifying its New York–Boston trunk and its New Haven–Springfield line, in the end its electrification only covered New York to New Haven, and its Danbury and New Canaan branches.

▲ NH's last new passenger locomotives were 10 GE-built EP-5 electrics and 60 dual-mode (diesel-electric/electric) FL9s. On July 25, 1964, an EP-5 is ready to depart New Haven westbound for New York, while a pair of FL9s that brought the train down from Boston reverses into the engine-servicing tracks.
Jim Shaughnessy

Headquarters: New Haven, CT
Years operated: 1872–1969
Disposition: Absorbed by Penn Central in 1969; remaining lines divided by Conrail and Amtrak in 1976; Providence & Worcester component reclaimed independence in 1973 and gradually pieced together a portion of former NH freight network; surviving lines operated by more than a dozen railroads
Route mileage: 1,790 miles (c. 1950)
Locomotives (1950)
  Steam: 179
  Diesel: 300
  Electric: 110
  Electric multiple-units: 200
Reporting mark: NH
Emblems: "New York, New Haven and Hartford" in embellished type; stacked N and H in wide serif font
Nickname:
  The Shore Line Route
Primary locomotive shops:
  New Haven, CT;
  Van Nest (the Bronx), NY
Notable features:
  Poughkeepsie (NY) Bridge over Hudson River; Hell Gate Bridge (New York City), 19,233 ft. long, 135 ft. high; 22-span Canton (MA) Viaduct; four-track New Haven, CT–Woodlawn, NY, electrified mainline
States served: CT, MA, RI, NY
Major cities served: Boston, Hartford, Providence, Springfield, Worcester

Flagship passenger train: *Merchants Limited* (Boston–New York)

Other name passenger trains: *The Comet* (Boston–Providence); *The Senator* and *The Federal* (Boston–Washington, D.C., operated with Pennsylvania Railroad); *State of Maine Express* (Portland–Washington, D.C., operated with Boston & Maine and Pennsylvania Railroad); *Yankee Clipper* (Boston–New York)

Notable freight commodities: Merchandise and manufactured products

Principal freight yards: Cedar Hill (New Haven), CT

Antitrust legislation, combined with fundamental economic changes and the rise of the highway economy, doomed New Haven's prosperity. Despite heavy traffic, the line was in chronic financial trouble from World War I onward. In later years, the line was characterized by fading early twentieth-century heavy infrastructure and quirky experiments intended to lower costs and attract new traffic. It was a pioneer of intermodal freight railroading, for example, and was among the first to adopt lightweight high-speed passenger trains. Its efforts failed, and the bankrupt line was forced into Penn Central in 1969. Today its Shore Line route is part of Amtrak's Northeast Corridor, while other routes serve myriad freight railroads and commuter agencies.

▲ On August 9, 1958, a New Haven EP4 leads a westward passenger train at Stamford, Connecticut. The powerful GE double-ended streamlined electric was then 20 years old. Six were built in 1938, based on NH's EP-3 boxcab design and intended for a top speed of 93 miles per hour. *Richard Jay Solomon*

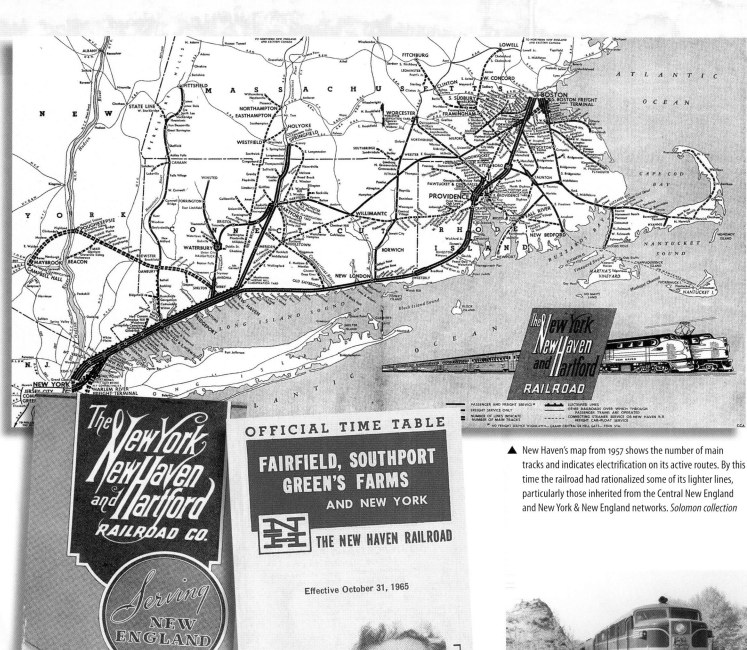

▲ New Haven's map from 1957 shows the number of main tracks and indicates electrification on its active routes. By this time the railroad had rationalized some of its lighter lines, particularly those inherited from the Central New England and New York & New England networks. *Solomon collection*

▲ The cover of New Haven's July 21, 1935, public timetable features an artist's view of a modern heavy Pacific-type steam locomotive leading a passenger train along the Shore Line route. *Solomon collection*

▲ A 1965 passenger timetable featured several ads for the theater crowd. *Voyageur Press collection*

▲ A pair of New Haven's attractively painted Alco PAs leads a Railroad Enthusiasts excursion returning from Maybrook, New York, in July 1956. New Haven's Maybrook Line was an important freight line until the mid-1960s. *Jim Shaughnessy*

68

NEW YORK, ONTARIO & WESTERN RAILWAY

The New York, Ontario & Western's mystique reflects its troubled history, unusual and eclectic locomotives, challenging route structure that traversed some the finest scenery in the East, and financial collapse in 1957 that resulted in near total abandonment. The O&W (or "Owen W"), as it was more commonly known, was born from difficulty. In 1880, it was formed from the financial wreckage of Dewitt C. Littlejohn's New York & Oswego Midland, a railway conceived at the end of the Civil War as an "air line route" (i.e., "straight" route) between New York City and the Lake Ontario port at Oswego. This route proved anything but straight, and the O&W was plagued by one of the most difficult profiles of any mainline railroad in the East.

O&W negotiated trackage rights over the West Shore from Cornwall, New York, to Weehawken, New Jersey, gaining more efficient access to New York City, and it built a 54-mile branch between its main line at Cadosia, New York, and Scranton, Pennsylvania. For the next half-century, coal traffic from Scranton, milk traffic from central New York State, and seasonal holiday traffic to the Catskills were O&W's lifeblood. Passenger trains operated from New York Central's West Shore Station in Weehawken, using ferry connections to serve New York City. At one time the O&W served as part of a through route to Chicago, with sleepers running west of Oswego on the Rome, Watertown & Ogdensburg, with connections west via Niagara Falls, but this business dried up by the 1920s.

▼ O&W dieselized right after in World War II in a desperate attempt to cut costs. Yet, diesels only put off liquidation by a dozen years, and most of its diesels outlasted the railroad. On September 1, 1947, O&W FTs lead freight over the long trestle at Carbondale, Pennsylvania. *John E. Pickett*

Headquarters: New York, NY

Years operated: 1880–1957

Disposition: Abandoned

Route mileage: 541 (c. 1952)

Locomotives

    Steam: 177 (c. 1929)

    Diesel: 35 (c. 1952)

Reporting mark: OW

Emblem: Letter O encircling
bowed W

Trade name:

    Ontario & Western

Primary locomotive shop:

    Middletown, NY

Notable features:

    Carbondale (PA) Viaduct;

    Lyon Brook (NY) Trestle

States served: NJ, NY, PA

Major cities served:

    New York and Scranton

▲ O&W's quaint pastoral settings and subsequent total abandonment have lent to its mystique. On August 7, 1948, Electro-Motive NW2 No. 48 leads the southward O&W Delhi Branch train near Colchester, New York. Within a decade scenes like this had become just a memory. *John E. Pickett*

Like other anthracite railroads, O&W also used this commodity as locomotive fuel. To make good use of anthracite, locomotives required an exceptionally broad firebox, which typically necessitated a twin-cab arrangement commonly known as a "camelback." O&W operated a large fleet of these in addition to other types. In the late 1930s, O&W's anthracite business collapsed, and the line was reorganized, which led to cost-savings through early dieselization and installation of Centralized Traffic Control signaling, and attempts to promote the route as a bridge line for through freight traffic. These measures did little more than prolong O&W's misery, however. In its final years, O&W's colorful fleet of Electro-Motive FT and F3 road diesels contrasted with its decaying track structure and light traffic. Virtually every place O&W served had better rail connections via other railroads. The end came in March 1957, and all tracks, save a few short segments, were torn up. Only vestiges remain today.

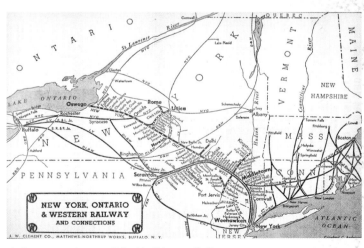

▲ System map, circa 1949. *Richard Jay Solomon collection*

69

NEW YORK, SUSQUEHANNA & WESTERN RAILWAY

New York Susquehanna & Western's antecedents originally served as eastern connections to New York, Ontario & Western precursor New York & Oswego Midland. Later, NYS&W was affiliated with the Wilkes Barre & Eastern, with which it served as a conduit for anthracite coal moving east to the New York City market. This arrangement ended in the late 1930s when declines in the anthracite market resulted in the abandonment of the WB&E. Between 1898 and the 1940s, NYS&W was controlled by the Erie Railroad. In the early 1940s, it dieselized rapidly, becoming one of the first American lines to achieve complete diesel operation, thanks to a small fleet of Alco switchers, RS-1 road switchers, and American Car & Foundry diesel railcars. Despite this progress, the loss of coal traffic, declining passenger business, and a general decline in the region caused NYS&W hardship. The line withered in the 1960s and was forced to trim back operations and end New York–area suburban services.

Although bankrupt by 1976, NYS&W stayed out of Conrail. Its salvation as an independent line came in the early 1980s when control passed to short-line operator Delaware Otsego. DO reversed NYS&W's decline and expanded operations by acquiring from Conrail former Delaware, Lackawanna & Western lines running from Binghamton to Syracuse and Utica, New York, along with trackage rights on the former Erie east of Binghamton

▼ In the 1980s, NYS&W fulfilled the "& Western" part of its moniker by expanding operations well beyond its historic limits into New York State. In 1988, the railroad was appointed the designated operator of the Delaware & Hudson. On April 30, 1989, brand-new GE-built B40-8s lead a D&H Sea-Land double-stack train eastward on Conrail's former Erie route near Swain, New York. *Brian Solomon*

to link with its existing New Jersey lines. In the mid-1980s, under the management of Walter Rich, NYS&W was developed as a transcontinental link in an intermodal corridor that offered an alternative route to Conrail's stranglehold on the New York City market. In this arrangement, NYS&W served as the easternmost part of a bridge route for double-stacks, working with Delaware & Hudson to move trains between Buffalo, Binghamton (and in the 1990s via Syracuse), and its Little Ferry, New Jersey, intermodal yard. In 1986, to avoid congestion on the commuter-intensive Erie line east of Campbell Hall, it rebuilt the moribund line over Sparta Mountain and reactivated a portion of the former Lehigh & Hudson River.

NYS&W was the designated operator of Delaware & Hudson from 1988 until 1990 when Canadian Pacific took control of Delaware & Hudson. In 1997, CSX and Norfolk Southern agreed to divide Conrail, and NYS&W arranged for the two giants to buy it as well, in an arrangement that allowed NYS&W to retain its independent management and image. Although it lost the intermodal business, NYS&W has continued other operations and expanded control of the Erie route with the 2005 acquisition from NS of the line east of Binghamton.

▲ A pair of NYS&W suburban trains is tied up at Butler, New Jersey, the western terminus for the railroad's commuter service, 38 miles from New York City. In 1949, the railroad provided 10 roundtrips daily between Erie's Jersey City terminal and Butler, with a more frequent service as far as Hawthorne. Passengers to Manhattan could also make a bus connection from Susquehanna Transfer. *Richard Jay Solomon*

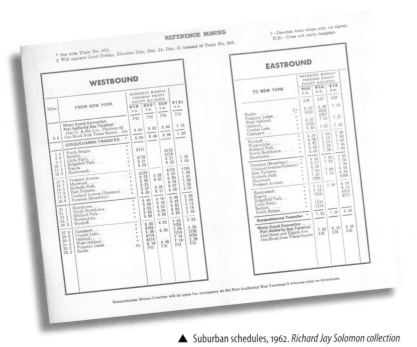

▲ Suburban schedules, 1962. *Richard Jay Solomon collection*

Headquarters: Cooperstown, NY

Years operated: 1881–2011

Disposition: Controlled by Erie Railroad until 1940; acquired by Delaware Otsego in 1980; jointly owned by CSX and NS since 1997

Route mileage: 120 (1952) and 400+ (2011)

Diesel locomotives: 20 (c. 1950) and 19 (2005)

Reporting mark: NYSW

Emblem: Letter *S* in circle

Nickname: Susie-Q

Trade name: Susquehanna

Primary locomotive shop: Little Ferry, NJ

Notable feature: Starrucca Viaduct (Lanesboro, PA), 1,040 ft. long, 100 ft. high (since 2005)

States served: NJ, NY, PA

70

NORFOLK SOUTHERN RAILWAY

Norfolk Southern Railway is a subsidiary of Norfolk Southern Corporation, which came about through the 1982 merger of Norfolk & Western and Southern Railway. In the 1960s and 1970s, when most other railway systems in the eastern United States were suffering from declining traffic and deferred maintenance and were threatened with insolvency, Norfolk & Western and Southern were among the industry's shining stars. N&W in particular thrived on the movement of Pocahontas coal, while the Southern was famous for its innovative management, well-groomed track, and excellent service.

▶ A trio of NS General Electric-built Evolution-series diesels (model ES40DC) leads a loaded coal train at Stewartsville, Virginia, on December 11, 2009. NS is a healthy modern railroad operating heavy trains with modern locomotives over most of its eastern network.
T. S. Hoover

▲ The west slope of the former Pennsylvania Railroad "Main Line" over the Allegheny Divide at Gallitzin sees a continual parade of freight most days. In July 2010, eastward NS freight symbol 18N passes a westward double-stack train at Lilly, Pennsylvania. Conrail raised clearances on the Pennsy route in the mid-1990s, and today it is major double-stack corridor. *Brian Solomon*

In the 1960s, Southern had pioneered the unit-train concept and introduced high-volume coal hoppers, so it was little surprise that these industry leaders faired well in the post-Staggers environment. Their networks complemented each other well with relatively little duplication and interchanged at several developing gateways.

Unlike other large eastern carriers, Norfolk Southern resisted many of the industry trends of the 1980s and 1990s; when other big railroads were spinning off branch lines, consolidating dispatching offices, and embracing new technologies such as three-phase alternating current traction locomotives and distributed power, NS retained a more traditional philosophy. From the mid-1990s to the mid-2000s, it built a standard motive power fleet based on General Electric's Dash 9 model and was the last of the large carriers to embrace the now standard North American Safety Cab. NS finally began purchasing AC traction diesels in 2008.

Headquarters: Norfolk, VA

Years operated: 1982–present

Route mileage:
approx. 21,500 (2010)

Diesel locomotives:
3,976 (2009)

Reporting mark: NS

Emblem: Italic *NS* and
five horizontal lines
superimposed with
silhouette of
thoroughbred horse

Nickname: The Thoroughbred
of Transportation

Primary locomotive shops:
Altoona, PA, Chattanooga and
Knoxville, TN; Roanoke, VA

Notable features: Horseshoe
Curve (near Altoona,
PA); Natural Tunnel (near
Duffield, VA); Portage Bridge
over Letchworth Gorge (near
Castile, NY); Rockville Bridge
over Susquehanna River
(Rockville–Marysville, PA),
3,820 ft.

States and province served:
AL, DE, FL, GA, IL, IN, IA, KS,
KY, LA, MD, MI, MO, NJ, NY,
NC, OH, PA, SC, TN, VA, WV,
plus ON

Major cities served: Atlanta,
Baltimore, Birmingham,
Buffalo, Chattanooga,
Charleston, Chicago,
Cincinnati, Cleveland,
Columbus, Des Moines,
Detroit, Erie, Harrisburg,
Indianapolis, Jacksonville,
Kansas City, Memphis,
Mobile, Newark, New
Orleans, Philadelphia,
Peoria, Pittsburgh, Raleigh,
Richmond, St. Louis,
Washington, D.C.

Notable freight commodities:

Coal, automobiles, intermodal

Principal freight yards:

Bellevue, OH; Bison (Buffalo), NY; Brosnan (Macon) and Inman (Atlanta), GA; Conway and Enola, PA; DeButts (Decatur), IL; Elkhart and Fort Wayne, IN; Norris (Birmingham) and Sheffield (Muscle Shoals), AL; Roanoke, VA; Sevier (Knoxville), TN; Spencer (Linwood), NC

In 1997, NS and CSX opted to purchase and divide the gigantic Conrail system. NS largely acquired former Pennsylvania Railroad lines, along with surviving portions of the old Erie Railroad east of Buffalo and bits of Reading, Lehigh Valley, and Central Railroad of New Jersey, along with the New York Central Water Level Route between Berea, Ohio (west of Cleveland), and Chicago. The purchase was approved in 1998, and NS operations of Conrail lines commenced in spring 1999. Since then, NS has advanced its influence on eastern railroading through partnerships with other railroads in the region, including joint operating arrangements on Canadian Pacific's Delaware & Hudson and a partnership called Pan Am Southern with Pan American Railways on the Boston & Maine route. Although, NS built its reputation largely as a coal hauler, since the 1980s, it has diversified its traffic base and has been carrying a growing volume of intermodal traffic, a move aided by its Conrail acquisition and development of new corridors.

▼ Eastward unit coal train 862, led by an Evolution-series GE diesel, meets a westward intermodal near Cresson, Pennsylvania, on the former Pennsylvania Railroad Main Line in June 2010. Among the lines inherited from Conrail, this is the busiest route on Norfolk Southern. *Brian Solomon*

▲ On June 23, 2004, lone Dash 9-40CW No. 9468 hauls a long westward RoadRailer on the former Wabash at Philo, Illinois. Four thousand horsepower is just enough to keep this comparatively lightweight train moving across the rolling cornfields of Indiana and Illinois. *Brian Solomon*

NORFOLK SOUTHERN

NS

Safety is our Keystone

Pittsburgh Division

▶ For 19 years running, NS has won the highly acclaimed Edward H. Harriman Memorial Gold Medal railroad safety award. *Brian Solomon*

71

NORFOLK & WESTERN RAILWAY

Although its earliest predecessor dated to 1838, the Norfolk & Western was created in 1881 when Frederick J. Kimball embarked on the development of bituminous coal fields in southwestern Virginia, West Virginia, and eastern Kentucky. The railroad expanded rapidly over the next two decades while providing key connections to move coal to principal gateways. It reached northeast to Hagerstown, Maryland; east to deepwater ports at Hampton Roads, Virginia; west to Columbus, Ohio; and south from Roanoke to North Carolina. By 1901 it reached Cincinnati, its western terminus at the time. Operations were focused at Bluefield, West Virginia, and at Roanoke and Lambert Point, Virginia. At the latter point the railroad operated intensive deepwater coal docks. Heavy traffic on its Elkhorn grade led the railroad to electrify this portion of its main line in 1912; however, with massive rebuilding, electric operations were discontinued in favor of steam in 1950.

▼ On July 31, 1958, one of N&W's A-class simple-articulated locomotives leads a manifest freight eastward over Blue Ridge Summit, east of Roanoke, Virginia, while another locomotive works at the back as a pusher. Although N&W was best known as a coal hauler, it also carried general freight. *Richard Jay Solomon*

The classic N&W was devoted to steam a decade longer than most American railroads and only in 1954 did N&W make the decision to begin its conversion to diesel operations; its final steam runs were 1960. Notably, N&W built many of its own steam locomotives, including streamlined J-class 4-8-4s, massive late-era Y-class 2-8-8-2 Mallet types, and fast "high-stepping" A-class simple articulateds. N&W dieselized with large purchases of Alco and Electro-Motive Division road switchers. For many years, N&W was affiliated with the Pennsylvania Railroad, leading to its decision to adopt a variation of Pennsy's distinctive position-light signaling.

In 1959, N&W bought the Virginian Railway to make use of its superior and largely parallel eastward grade. By integrating parallel main lines, N&W made the best advantage of ascending and descending grades to more efficiently move coal. In a prelude to the Penn Central merger, Pennsy broke its affiliation with N&W. Then, in 1964, N&W merged with Nickel Plate Road and Wabash while acquiring a key north–south route to Sandusky, Ohio, from the Pennsy, thus allowing it to link with its new acquisitions and move coal directly to the Great Lakes. Also related to the Penn Central deal, the U.S. Supreme Court encouraged N&W to support the Erie-Lackawanna and Delaware & Hudson during the mid-1960s. As a result, N&W created the Dereco holding company to shield N&W from these weak lines' financial liabilities, while also giving it control of them. N&W assumed control of EL in April 1968 but allowed EL to retain its identity. This arrangement was short-lived, and EL joined Conrail in 1976.

In 1982, N&W and Southern Railway merged to form Norfolk Southern, which emerged as the strongest line in the eastern United States.

Headquarters: Roanoke, VA

Years operated: 1896–1982

Disposition: Merged with Southern Railway; currently principal component network of Norfolk Southern; most routes remain active

Route mileage: 2,129 (c. 1949) and 7,659 (c. 1977)

Locomotives

    Steam: 462 (c. 1952)

    Diesel: 1,377 (c. 1981)

Reporting mark: N&W

Emblems: Letters N and W separated by vertical "& Ry" and conformed inside circle; NW in large block letters

Primary locomotive shop: Roanoke, VA

Notable feature: Elkhorn tunnel, 7,052 feet long.

States and province served: KY, MD, NC, OH, VA, WV (1949); IN, IL, IA, MI, MO, NE, NY, PA, plus ON (after 1964)

Major cities served: Cincinnati, Columbus, Norfolk, Roanoke (1949); Buffalo, Chicago, Cleveland, Des Moines, Detroit, Erie, Kansas City, Omaha, Peoria, Pittsburgh, St. Louis, Toledo (after 1964)

▶ Passenger timetable, 1951. *Voyageur Press collection*

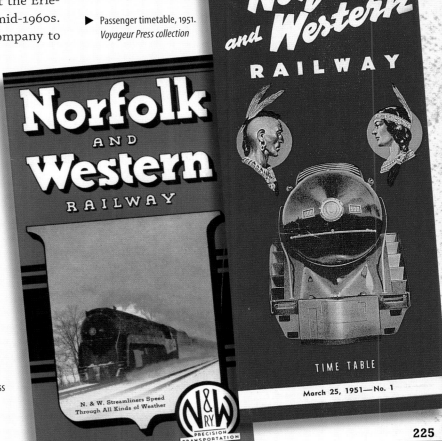

▶ This N&W 1946 passenger timetable features one of the railroad's famous J-class streamlined 4-8-4s. *Solomon collection*

▶ On July 30, 1958, an N&W K2-class 4-8-2 Mountain type rests at the locomotive-servicing facility at Bluefield, West Virginia. Though similar in appearance, N&W's streamlined K-class Mountains were less well-known than the railroad's famous J-class 4-8-4s. *Richard Jay Solomon*

▼ In 1960, the same year N&W conducted its final steam runs, it ran this ad depicting an engineer at the controls of a thoroughly modern diesel-electric locomotive. *Voyageur Press collection*

Looking just one way...

forward!

Take a forward look with the new N&W! Here is a railroad that's going all-out to improve efficiency and serv- ice—to create new savings in time and money for shippers. Nation's newest fleet of diesels. Plenty of freight cars in tiptop condition. Fast, dependable freight schedules. A railroad con- stantly looking forward to find new ways to give better service to its cus- tomers. Come aboard the new N&W— the nation's going-est railroad.

N&W

NORFOLK & WESTERN RAILWAY

GENERAL OFFICES • ROANOKE, VIRGINIA

Flagship passenger train: *The Powhatan Arrow* (Norfolk—Cincinnati)

Other name passenger trains: *The Pocahontas* (Norfolk— Cincinnati, with through cars to Chicago via Pennsylvania Railroad); *Cavalier* (Norfolk—Cincinnati, carried through cars from New York and Richmond via Pennsylvania Railroad, Richmond, Fredericksburg & Potomac, and Southern Railway)

Notable freight commodities: Automobiles and coal

Principal freight yards: Bluefield, WV; Lambert Point and Roanoke, VA; Portsmouth, OH; Williamson, KY; also Bellevue, OH; Bison (Buffalo), NY; Decatur, IL; Ft. Wayne, IN (after 1964)

◀ Working as intended—long hood first—an N&W SD40-2 leads a loaded coal train eastbound at Roderfield, West Virginia, sometime in the early 1980s. N&W moved coal like a conveyor belt from Appalachian mines east to the Hampton Roads port at Lambert Point, Virginia. *George S. Pitarys*

NORTHERN PACIFIC RAILWAY

The early days of Northern Pacific were marked by precarious finances precipitated by the worldwide panic of 1873. Once completed, its lines spanned the wide expanses of North Dakota and Montana and crested numerous mountain passes. In addition, NP operated some of the world's largest steam locomotives and the famed *North Coast Limited*—one of the finest trains ever to roll on American rails.

NP was chartered in 1864 to link the Pacific Northwest to the Great Lakes at Duluth, Minnesota, yet took several years to get moving. Financier Jay Cooke propelled NP forward, beginning construction in northern Minnesota at Thompsons Junction, near the present-day town of Carlton, in 1870. To encourage investment, he offered imaginative descriptions of the Pacific Northwest that earned the region the facetious moniker "Jay

▼ Just a few months after the Burlington Northern merger of 1970, a trio of NP U25Cs leads a BN unit coal train. *Wallace W. Abbey, Center for Railroad Photography & Art*

Cooke's Banana Belt." When Cooke's finances collapsed, it sparked a chain reaction of failures that led to the Panic of 1873, an event that redrew the map of American finance and temporarily halted North American railroad construction. Visionary financier Henry Villard took the reins of NP in the early 1880s, putting it under common management with Oregon Railway & Navigation Company (OR&N), which later became part of Union Pacific. On August 22, 1883, a golden spike ceremony at Independence Gulch, Montana, marked completion of NP's transcontinental route, which relied on a link with OR&N at Wallulla, Washington.

But Villard lost control of NP in 1884 and the NP network was further challenged by the completion of James J. Hill's Great Northern in the 1890s. By 1901, Hill controlled both NP and Great Northern, and together these lines bought control of their chief eastward connection, Chicago, Burlington & Quincy, giving Hill dominance in Chicago–Pacific Northwest trade. This consolidation pitted him against the similar designs of Edward H. Harriman, and to keep his rival in check, Hill created a holding company called Northern Securities to unify management of his railroad empire. This raised the ire of "trust-buster" President Theodore Roosevelt, and in 1904, the U.S. Supreme Court found Hill's empire in violation of the Sherman Antitrust Act. Despite this, Hill's lines retained

▼ Alco built this prototype 2-8-8-4 for NP in 1928, and Baldwin built 11 more of the locomotives for NP in 1930. Designed to work NP's difficult Yellowstone District between Glendive, Montana, and Mandan, North Dakota, the Z-5-class locomotives became known as "Yellowstones" and were the world's largest locomotives until Union Pacific's Big Boy was introduced 1941. *Robert A. Buck collection*

Headquarters: St. Paul, MN

Years operated: 1870–1970

Disposition: Merged with Chicago, Burlington & Quincy, Great Northern, and Spokane, Portland & Seattle to form Burlington Northern; surviving routes now operated by BNSF, Montana Rail Link, and various short lines

Route mileage: 6,883 (c. 1952)

Locomotives (1952)

    Steam: 622

    Diesel: 134

    Self-propelled railcars: 16

Reporting mark: NP

Emblem: Yin and yang surrounded by NORTHERN PACIFIC

Nickname: Main Street of the Northwest

Primary locomotive shops: Brainerd, MN; Glendive and Livingston, MT

Notable features: Bozeman Tunnel at Bozeman Pass, 3,015 ft. long; Blossburg Tunnel at Mullen Pass, 3,897 ft. long; Marent Gulch Viaduct (near Missoula), 797 ft. long, 162 feet tall; Sheyenne River Viaduct (Valley City, ND), 3,863 ft. long, 162 ft. tall; Stampede Tunnel in Washington Cascades, 9,834 ft. long; St. Louis Bay Bridge (Duluth, MN–Superior, WI), 2,650 ft. long

States and provinces served: ID, MN, MT, ND, OR, WA, WI, plus MB and BC

Major cities served: Duluth, Fargo, Minneapolis/St. Paul, Portland, Seattle, Spokane

Flagship passenger train: *North Coast Limited* (Chicago–Seattle and Portland via SP&S, operated with CB&Q)

Other name passenger trains: *Mainstreeter* (Chicago–Seattle and Portland via SP&S, operated with CB&Q)

Notable freight commodities: Perishables and general freight

Principal freight yards: Billings, MT, and Pasco, WA

a family relationship and were ultimately rejoined by the Burlington Northern merger of 1970.

NP played a second fiddle to Great Northern, yet maintained robust freight traffic and carried its share of transcontinental passengers to the Pacific Northwest. Introduced in 1928, NP's famed 2-8-8-4 Yellowstones were the largest locomotives in the world until superseded by Union Pacific's Big Boy in 1941. In 1926, NP was first to adopt the 4-8-4 wheel arrangement, and the type was commonly known as the Northern in the railroad's honor.

Period advertisements tout NP's Vista-Dome service. *Voyageur Press collection*

SCENERY UNLIMITED The Northern Pacific Railway traverses some of the finest scenery in America. And passengers on its North Coast Limited, famous streamliner which operates between Chicago and the North Pacific Coast, are being given an extraordinary opportunity to see and enjoy it.

Now, the North Coast Limited features Budd stainless steel Vista-Dome cars. They let you see ahead, both sides, behind and above you, as you seem to glide past towering mountains, through evergreen forests, along rushing rivers.

Nearly a hundred of these Budd-built dome cars are now in service on United States railroads.

They are symbolic of the imagination and investment railroads are devoting to make your journey by rail safe, convenient and enjoyable. And they are also symbolic of the contributions Budd brings to the field of transportation. The Budd Company, Philadelphia, Detroit, Gary.

Automobile and Truck Bodies and Wheels, Railway Passenger Cars **Budd**

PIONEERS IN BETTER TRANSPORTATION

Now...a friendly stewardess welcomes you aboard the *VISTA-DOME* North Coast Limited

Another thoughtful *Extra* on one of the world's *Extra Fine* trains

NEW EXTRA SERVICE! A charming stewardess makes you feel at home on the Vista-Dome North Coast Limited. What's more, she's also a registered nurse!

4 VISTA-DOMES! You get a thrilling, all-around view. See the rugged Rockies, the Cascades, great rivers, forests and rolling plains as you never could see them before.

LOW FAMILY PLAN FARES save you money. Bring the children—enjoy an extra fast, extra comfort trip in reclining coach seats or private Pullman rooms.

Extra comfort...no extra fare

 *VISTA-DOME* **North Coast Limited**

SEND for free booklet "Northwest Adventure". Includes Alaska, California trips. Please write G. W. Rodine, 844 Northern Pacific Railway, St. Paul 1, Minnesota.

 NORTHERN PACIFIC RAILWAY

CHICAGO • TWIN CITIES • SPOKANE • PORTLAND • TACOMA • SEATTLE

MAIN STREET

Transcontinental Conveyor Belt

Every few hours, day and night, another section of No. 603 pulls westward out of the Twin Cities along the Main Street of the Northwest. Somewhere, at any given moment, some section of this famous Northern Pacific hot-shot is on the move.

This "chain-train" and her eastbound twin No. 602 are now on schedules 24 hours faster than during wartime . . . they are, in effect, constantly moving conveyor belts, 1900 miles long, carrying whopping big loads of food, timber, fuel, minerals, machinery, and merchandise on Main Street.

By efficient, dependable operation of these and other fast freight trains, by constant improvement of our rail-road and by active assist... ... agriculture and indus-try, Northern Pacific doe... ... bright along Main Stree...

NORTH...

F5111 MADE IN U. S. A.

◀ A 1946 artist's portrayal of NP's "Main Street of the North West" depicts a brand-new set of Electro-Motive FTs meeting one of NP's late-era 4-8-4 Northerns. *Solomon collection*

▼ NP's 1961 public timetable provides an advertisement for its flagship *North Coast Limited*. In 1946, NP ordered new lightweight streamlined equipment for this train and the new trainsets entered service a year later. NP subsequently equipped the service with luxurious Vista-Domes. It was considered among the finest trains to grace American rails and remained a classy operation until Amtrak assumed operation of most American long-distance services in May 1971. Today, most of the route once served by the *North Coast Limited* is used strictly for freight. *Richard Jay Solomon collection*

On the *Vista-Dome*
NORTH COAST LIMITED . . .

Stewardess-Nurse Service
All-Room Slumbercoaches
Vista-Dome Sleepers
Vista-Dome Coaches
Exciting Traveller's Rest
Buffet-Lounge

PASSENGER TRAIN SCHEDULES

Route of the Vista-Dome
NORTH COAST LIMITED

Time Folder issued May 28, 1961

Time Folder issued May 28, 1961

▲ NP's famed herald incorporated the Asian yin-yang symbol to evoke the railroad's role in trade with Asia. *Brian Solomon*

73

PAN AM RAILWAYS

Without context, the sudden emergence of Pan Am Railways (PAR) may seem like an incongruous development, but today's PAR was the result of the renaming of the Guilford Rail System (GRS) in 2006. GRS had principally operated surviving freight services on the old Boston & Maine and Maine Central networks. In 1998, GRS's corporate parent, Guilford Transportation Industries, had bought the Pan American World Airways name and trademarks and for a few years even operated a limited commercial airline service. GRS railway cars began appearing in Pan Am paint prior to 2006, and that year a few locomotives were painted in a Pan Am livery remarkably similar to that used on historic Pan Am jet aircraft. (Interestingly, for a few years beginning in the late 1920s, B&M and Pan Am Airways had offered joint services; however, this curious connection is mere coincidence between the two companies.)

In 2008, PAR and Norfolk Southern entered a joint venture called Pan Am Southern (PAS), known by the marketing name Patriot Corridor. This covers 281 route miles, largely of former Boston & Maine lines, with a focus on B&M's 155-mile Fitchburg Division main line between terminal facilities at Ayer, Massachusetts, and a connection with Canadian Pacific's Delaware & Hudson route near Mechanicville, New York. This has allowed Norfolk Southern to offer better services in the New England region and facilitated infrastructure investment on the old B&M route. Track work and signaling improvements have speeded transit times over the B&M route, and traffic levels have improved. NS through trains on this route tend to operate with NS road locomotives.

▼ On a clear and very cold January 2011 morning, Pan Am Railway's weekly eastward clay slurry train NBWA (North Bennington, Vermont, to Waterville, Maine) crosses the Connecticut River on the former Boston & Maine Fitchburg Division main line at East Deerfield, Massachusetts. *Brian Solomon*

Headquarters: North Billerica, MA

Years operated: 2006–present

Route mileage: approx. 500 (PAR) and 281 (PAS)

Diesel locomotives: 115

Reporting marks: BM, MEC, PTM, ST

Emblem: Adaptation of Pan Am Airways globe logo

Primary locomotive shop: Waterville, ME

Notable features: Connecticut River Bridge (East Deerfield, MA); Hoosac Tunnel (near North Adams, MA); Hudson River Bridge (Mechanicville, NY)

States served: CT, ME, MA, NH, NY, VT

Major cities served: Boston, Portland, Springfield

Principal freight yards: East Deerfield, MA; Rigby (Portland) and Waterville, ME

◀ Pan Am operates a moderate-sized fleet of secondhand Electro-Motive diesels. Brian Solomon

◀ Pan Am symbol freight EDMO (East Deerfield, Massachusetts, to Mohawk Yard, Schenectady, New York) works west through a snow squall near Charlemont, Massachusetts. *Brian Solomon*

74

PENN CENTRAL RAILROAD

Pennsylvania Railroad and New York Central, the Northeast's two largest railroads, and historically the two most influential carriers in the United States, suffered financial distress after World War II. By the mid-1950s they began discussing merger as a panacea to their mounting woes. After a decade of discussions, the railroads sealed their union in 1968 and in 1969 accepted bankrupt New Haven Railroad into their struggling network.

In short, Penn Central was a total catastrophe, and its black paint scheme had appropriately funereal connotations. Today Penn Central is remembered as the low point in American railroading. Its problems ran deep—managers had failed to fully consider details of integrating differing operating practices, and disparate operating cultures led to numerous

▼ Despite its bankruptcy, Penn Central moved an astonishing volume of freight. PC No. 6529, a former Pennsylvania Railroad U28C, leads freight OPV-1 (Oak Point to Selkirk, New York) on the former New Haven Railroad electrified main line at Bridgeport, Connecticut, on April 14, 1971. *George W. Kowanski*

incompatibles. Worse, savings proved illusory while the merger induced inefficiencies that resulted in widespread service failures. But Penn Central's problems went deeper. It suffered from the combination of years of stifling and inequitable rate regulation, obsolete and overly restrictive labor arrangements that forced the cost of labor to untenable levels, growing passenger deficits, inappropriate infrastructure-based taxation, poorly maintained lines, and routes parallel with new federally sponsored interstate highways.

Lost traffic combined with the increased expenses accelerated Penn Central's cash shortage, and by 1970, the carrier declared bankruptcy—the largest ever at that time. To sort out Penn Central's mess, and that of other bankrupt northeastern lines, Congress created Conrail in 1976, which assumed operation of many Penn Central routes on April 1 of that year.

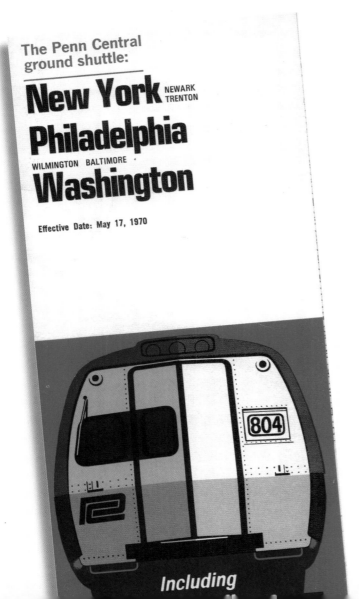

Headquarters: Philadelphia, PA

Years operated: 1968–1976

Disposition: Operations conveyed to Conrail; surviving routes operated by Amtrak, CSX, Norfolk Southern, and various suburban agencies and short lines

Route mileage: 22,000 (c. 1970)

Locomotives (c. 1970)

   Diesel: 3,982

   Electric: 225

   Electric railcars: 853

Reporting mark: PC

Emblem: Intertwined letters PC colloquially known as the "mating worms"

Primary locomotive shops: Altoona, PA; Collinwood (Cleveland), OH; DeWitt (Syracuse) and Harmon, NY; Wilmington, DE

Notable features: Horseshoe Curve (near Altoona, PA); Rockville Bridge over Susquehanna River (Rockville–Marysville, PA), 3,820 ft.; Smith Memorial Bridge over Hudson River (Castleton-on-Hudson–Selkirk, NY)

States and provinces served: CT, DE, IL, IN, KY, MD, MA, MI, MO, NJ, NY, OH, PA, RI, VA, WV, plus ON and QC

Major cities served: Baltimore, Boston, Buffalo, Cincinnati, Cleveland, Columbus, Detroit, Indianapolis, Montreal, New York, Philadelphia, Pittsburgh, Rochester, St. Louis, Syracuse, Toledo, Washington, D.C.

Principal freight yards: Altoona, Conway, Enola (near Harrisburg), Northumberland, and West Philadelphia PA; Avon (Indianapolis), Elkhart, and Piqua (Ft. Wayne), IN; Bay View (Baltimore), MD; Beacon Park (Boston), MA; Cedar Hill (near New Haven), CT; Chicago (various facilities) and Rose Lake (Washington Park), IL; Collinwood (Cleveland) and Undercliff (Cincinnati), OH; DeWitt (Syracuse), Frontier (Buffalo), and Selkirk (Albany), NY; Greenville (near Jersey City), Meadows (near Newark), and Morrisville, NJ

◄ With a top line-speed of 120 miles per hour, Penn Central's Budd-built Metroliner was America's fastest train in 1970. *Solomon collection*

75

PENNSYLVANIA RAILROAD

The Pennsylvania Railroad had its origins in April 1846, when the commonwealth's governor signed legislation that authorized its construction across the state to Pittsburgh. PRR was by no means the state's first railroad. By 1846, railways in various forms had been operating in the state for the better part of 20 years, but PRR intended to improve east–west commerce in recognition of the inadequacies of the state-sponsored Main Line of Public Works, an awkward system of canals, railways, and inclined planes (steeply grade cabled-hauled lines) built in the 1830s to connect Philadelphia with the Ohio River at Pittsburgh.

PRR hired J. Edgar Thomson to survey its line in 1847. Thomson had learned his trade on the ground, having spent 15 years building and operating railways, most significantly having worked on both the Camden & Amboy and the Philadelphia & Columbia—lines later integrated into the PRR system under his leadership. Thomson rose to become PRR's third president and set standards for knowledgeable leadership that remained with the company for generations. In 1855, PRR opened its mountain line via the Horseshoe Curve to Pittsburgh that reduced transit time from Philadelphia from four to five days (via the old Main Line of Public Works) to as little as 13 hours by express train.

▼ PRR's flagship was its exclusive extra-fare *Broadway Limited* (New York–Philadelphia–Chicago). In May 1928, the westward train pauses at the suburban Chicago station at Englewood, Illinois. *Solomon collection*

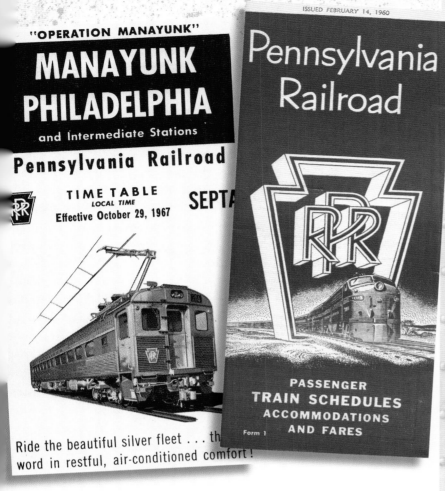

"OPERATION MANAYUNK"

MANAYUNK PHILADELPHIA

and Intermediate Stations

Pennsylvania Railroad

TIME TABLE
LOCAL TIME
Effective October 29, 1967

SEPTA

Ride the beautiful silver fleet . . . th[e] word in restful, air-conditioned comfort!

Pennsylvania Railroad

PRR

PASSENGER TRAIN SCHEDULES ACCOMMODATIONS AND FARES

Form 1

▲ A Budd Silverliner graces the cover of this 1967 Philadelphia-area suburban schedule. *Solomon collection*

▲ PRR E8A diesels feature on the cover of the railroad's February 14, 1960, public timetable. *Solomon collection*

PRR expanded rapidly by building, leasing, and acquiring lines across Pennsylvania and the region, including the Northern Central (connecting Baltimore and Harrisburg), the Philadelphia & Erie (built west from Sunbury via Renovo and Emporium to Erie, Pennsylvania), and the Cumberland Valley Railroad (working west from Harrisburg toward Hagerstown, Maryland). PRR also bought the old Main Line of Public Works from the commonwealth in 1857. This included the Philadelphia & Columbia line, which effectively served as PRR's eastward connection.

PRR secured western connections to reach the Midwest and rapidly developed as one of the four major east–west trunk lines. It bridged the Allegheny River in 1858 and reached Chicago through its Pittsburgh, Ft. Wayne & Chicago Railway affiliate in 1859. PRR ultimately leased two parallel Pittsburgh–Chicago routes: the famed Panhandle Line serving as a southern route, and the aforementioned Ft. Wayne serving as the northern route. Philadelphia was the focus of PRR's early charter, but during the second half

Headquarters: Philadelphia, PA

Years operated: 1846–1968

Disposition: Merged with New York Central to form Penn Central; Penn Central melded into Conrail in 1976 with former PRR electrified New York–Washington, D.C., and Philadelphia–Harrisburg lines going to Amtrak; Conrail divided between CSX and NS in 1999, key portions of former PRR routes to NS; other portions operated by short lines and regional railways

Route mileage: 10,113 (c. 1950)

Locomotives (1950)

  Steam: 4,460

  Diesel: 545

  Electric: 321

Reporting mark: PRR

Emblem: Keystone with intertwined "PRR"

Slogan: The Standard Railroad of the World

Nicknames: The Pennsy and P-Company

Primary locomotive shop: Altoona, PA

Notable features: Allegheny and Gallitzin tunnels (Gallitzin, PA), 3,604 ft.; New Portage Tunnel (Gallitzin, PA), 1,629 ft; B&P tunnels (Baltimore), 4,962 and 2,190 ft.; Union tunnels (Baltimore), 3,405 and 3,394 ft.; Pennsylvania Station (New York City) and approach infrastructure, including the East River tunnels, four 13,446-ft. parallel bores and North River tunnels, two 13,380-ft. parallel bores; Hell Gate Bridge (New York City), 19,233 ft. long, 135 ft. high; Ohio River Bridge (Louisville), 5,263 ft. long, 101 ft. high; Ohio River Bridge (Pittsburgh), 4,555 ft. long, 95 ft. high; Rockville Bridge over Susquehanna River (Rockville–Marysville, PA), 3,820 ft.; Safe Harbor (PA) Viaduct, 1,560 ft. long, 148 ft. tall; Horseshoe Curve (near Altoona, PA); Sunnyside Yard (Queens, NY), largest passenger coach yard of its era

States served: DE, IL, IN, KY, MD, MI, MO, NJ, NY, OH, PA, VA, WV, WI (via car ferries)

Major cities served: Baltimore, Buffalo, Chicago, Cincinnati, Cleveland, Columbus, Detroit, Erie, Harrisburg, Indianapolis, Milwaukee (via car ferries), Newark, New York, Peoria, Philadelphia, Pittsburgh, Rochester, Scranton, St. Louis, Toledo, Washington, D.C.

Flagship passenger train: *Broadway Limited* (New York–Philadelphia–Chicago)

Some named passenger trains: *The Admiral, Gotham Limited, Manhattan Limited, Pennsylvania Limited, The Trail Blazer* (New York–Chicago); *The American, The Jeffersonian, The Penn-Texas* (with through cars via Missouri Pacific to Dallas/Ft. Worth, El Paso, and San Antonio), *Spirit of St. Louis, The St. Louisan* (New York–Washington, D.C., and St. Louis); *The Colonial* (with through cars to Springfield), *The Federal, The Patriot* (Boston–New York–Washington, D.C., operated with New Haven Railroad); *The Red Arrow* (Detroit–New York); *The Golden Triangle* (Chicago–Pittsburgh); *The Clevelander* (Cleveland–Philadelphia)

Notable freight commodities: Chemicals, coal, general freight, intermodal, mineral ore, perishables

Principal freight yards: Altoona, Conway, Enola (Harrisburg), Northumberland, Pitcairn (near Pittsburgh), and West Philadelphia, PA; Bay View (Baltimore); Chicago (various facilities) and Rose Lake (near St. Louis), Washington Park, IL; Greenville (near Jersey City), Meadows (near Newark), and Morrisville, NJ; Hawthorn (Indianapolis), Jeffersonville (near Louisville, KY), and Piqua (Ft. Wayne), IN; Kinsman (Cleveland) and Undercliff (Cincinnati)

of the nineteenth century, it moved to control lines from New York to Washington, D.C, as well as across its expanding territory, so by the end of the century it was America's largest and busiest railroad. Its lines linked New York, Philadelphia, Baltimore, and Washington to Chicago and St. Louis; reached north to Buffalo; and radiated throughout Pennsylvania and the Midwest.

In the twentieth century, PRR focused on improving its infrastructure. It grade-separated junctions to ease traffic flow, expanded key main lines to four-track operation, and constructed major new terminals in New York City, Philadelphia, Pittsburgh, Baltimore, and Washington. It also improved connections with affiliated lines. PRR was the foremost proponent of electrification, wiring hundreds of miles of multiple-track main line; its electric operations ultimately extended from New York City to Alexandria, Virginia; between Philadelphia and Harrisburg; and from Harrisburg to Baltimore. Electrification also included low-grade cutoffs and yard trackage, as well as key Philadelphia- and New York–area suburban routes.

PRR's practice of establishing a standardized parts supply and using standardized locomotive, passenger car, and freight car designs, led it to proclaim that it was the "Standard Railroad of the World," an oft misunderstood slogan. Its locomotives were especially noteworthy for their design excellence. Among PRR's best-known steam locomotives were its K4s Pacifics, L1s Mikados, M1 Mountains, and I1s Decapods, all among the finest of their respective types. (The "s" in the model names indicated the engines were superheated.) Additionally, PRR's famed GG1 was one of the finest electrics to work American rails. PRR dieselized in the late 1940s and 1950s, dumping the fires on its last steam power in 1957. By this time the company was straining from a difficult financial position and considering merger with New York Central, its longtime chief competitor. Following a decade of negotiations that realigned the northeastern railroad network, PRR and NYC finally merged in 1968 to form the ill-fated Penn Central.

◀ A wartime advertisement features an artist's stylized rendering of a T1 streamlined locomotive while alluding to PRR's role in the war effort. *Voyageur Press collection*

PRR's double-end streamlined GG1 electrics were the mainstay of its electrified main line. In the early 1960s, GG1 No. 4924 leads a Washington, D.C.–bound long-distance train near Secaucus, New Jersey.
Richard Jay Solomon

▶ A PRR stock certificate portrays the railroad's famous four-track Horseshoe Curve west of Altoona, Pennsylvania. *Solomon collection*

▼ PRR played a crucial role during World War II, a fact that was heralded in this March 1943 timetable. *Solomon collection*

Groundwork

Millions will be needed for "Deferred Maintenance"

TODAY's mighty war loads are riding on foundations like that pictured . . . "highways" into which the railroads have put more than 4 billion dollars for improvements since the last war.

But wear and tear on roadway, bridges, locomotives, cars and equipment have been terrific. And material and labor for needed mainte-

nance are not obtainable now beyond the minimum necessary for safe, continued operation. As a result, much work that should be done has had to be deferred.

Money from current revenue should be saved to pay for the needed repairs and replacements when material and labor are available. But the tax law forbids. If money for needed repairs cannot be spent as it is earned it is considered "profit" and practically taxed

away. But it isn't profit. It is the life-blood of the railroads.

To tax this money away, simply because it cannot be spent now due to war conditions, threatens the backbone of American transportation.

Congressional amendment of the tax law to permit this money to be put aside for replacements would mean strong postwar railroads and thousands of jobs for returning fighting men.

▶ PRR was famous for its heavily built infrastructure. After World War II this advertisement advised the public on the investment required of the railroad to bring its tracks back up to standard. *Solomon collection*

▲ In July 1963, a PRR N-8 cabin (as cabooses were known on the Pennsy) marks the back of a westward freight entering the tunnels at Gallitzin, Pennsylvania. This is the summit of the railroad, having ascended the famous Horseshoe Curve. Gallitzin also sits atop the Allegheny Divide: From here, water flows east to the North Atlantic and west to the Gulf of Mexico. *Richard Jay Solomon*

PITTSBURGH & LAKE ERIE RAILROAD

Pittsburgh & Lake Erie got its start in 1875, and by 1879 connected steel centers at Pittsburgh, Pennsylvania, and Youngtown, Ohio. Its strategic route pierced the heart of the Pennsylvania Railroad's empire, naturally attracting Pennsy rival New York Central, which bought control of the line in 1889. P&LE retained a higher degree of independence than the big railroad's other affiliates: It had its own management and maintained its own car and locomotives shops, and locomotives and equipment were lettered to identify both the P&LE and New York Central System. Significantly, P&LE had one of the most intensely developed main lines that served the thriving coal and steel industries in the Mahoning, Monongahela, and Ohio River valleys.

In 1934, Baltimore & Ohio arranged for trackage rights on a 61-mile-long section of P&LE between McKeesport and New Castle Junction that allowed B&O passenger trains better access Pittsburgh while providing a shorter and low-grade route for its freight.

▼ On July 9, 1958, a freshly painted P&LE GP7 rests at McKees Rocks, Pennsylvania. This scheme was unusual. During the New York Central era, most P&LE diesels wore NYC colors with P&LE sub-lettering. *Richard Jay Solomon*

◀ Pittsburgh & Lake Erie GP7 No. 1501 leads the railroad's afternoon westward commuter train on July 30, 1981. Pittsburgh's West End Bridge is seen against the city skyline in the background. P&LE operated a single roundtrip commuter train between State College (Beaver Falls) and Pittsburgh, Pennsylvania, until July 1985. Also in the background is the confluence of the Ohio River with the Allegheny and Monongahela rivers.
Gordon Lloyd Jr., Lloyd Transportation Library

Headquarters: Pittsburgh, PA

Years operated: 1875–1992

Disposition: Assets transferred to Three Rivers Railway, then absorbed by CSX

Route mileage: 404 (c. 1987)

Locomotives

   Steam: 326 (1923)

   Diesel: 100 (1981)

Reporting mark: PLE

Emblem: "P&LE RR" intertwined script within a circle featuring full railroad name and nickname

Nickname: The Little Giant

Primary locomotive shop: McKees Rocks, PA

States served: PA and OH

Major cities served: Pittsburgh and Youngstown

P&LE was not part of the Conrail reorganization 1976, but instead remained a private line that remained profitable through the 1970s. P&LE's profits evaporated with the collapse of Pittsburgh's steel industry in the early 1980s. By the mid-1980s, P&LE was essentially only operating a single through freight daily; the majority of traffic on its lines belonged to B&O. In 1991, CSX purchased the crucial 61-mile section on which B&O operated, and in 1992 purchased significant additional P&LE assets via its new Three Rivers Railway subsidiary, including P&LE's main line from Brownsville to McKeesport, Pennsylvania, and from New Castle Junction, Pennsylvania, to Youngstown, Ohio, plus Conrail trackage rights to Ashtabula, Ohio. CSX was not interested in the remaining P&LE lines, subsidiaries, and assets, which P&LE sold separately.

77

PITTSBURGH & WEST VIRGINIA RAILWAY

G eorge Gould's transcontinental ambitions resulted in the stringing together of a network of railroads, the core of which featured the Missouri Pacific and Wabash systems inherited from his father, Jay Gould, in the late nineteenth century. To penetrate the Pittsburgh steel-producing territory and forge a link between his Wheeling & Lake Erie and Western Maryland lines, Gould financed an expensive and highly engineered line called the Wabash Pittsburgh Terminal Railway (WPTRy). This venture extended his empire into Pittsburgh by 1904, but fell short of reaching the Western Maryland. Over the next decade Gould's financial empire unraveled, and in 1916, the Pittsburgh & West Virginia was formed to succeed the WPTRy and related properties. In 1931, P&WV finally reached a connection with the Western Maryland at Connellsville, Pennsylvania, essentially fulfilling Gould's plan.

▼ P&WV was one of only a few railroads to buy 2-6-6-4 simple articulated locomotives. On July 25, 1950, P&WV No. 1100 works with a freight alongside Monessen & Southwestern No. 11 at Monessen, Pennsylvania. In the early 1950s, P&WV replaced its steam with new Fairbanks-Morse diesels. *George C. Corey*

While P&WV discontinued all passenger services on November 1, 1931, during the 1930s, it became part of the "Alphabet Route" freight bridge route—consisting of the P&WV, Nickel Plate Road, Wheeling & Lake Erie, WM, and Reading Company—that offered an alternative trunk route to shippers. Coal was a key commodity on this line.

The railroad was famous for its Baldwin 2-6-6-4 locomotives introduced in 1934, and in the 1950s it made the unusual choice to dieselize with Fairbanks-Morse road switchers. In 1964, when Norfolk & Western merged with the Wabash and Nickel Plate Road (including the Wheeling & Lake Erie), it leased the P&WV. In 1990, Norfolk Southern sold off lines to an 840-mile regional spin-off that adopted the name Wheeling & Lake Erie, which included historic P&WV and W&LE trackage.

Headquarters: Pittsburgh, PA

Years operated: 1916–1964

Disposition: Leased by Norfolk & Western; PV&W lines spun off by Norfolk Southern in 1990, creating 575-mile regional railroad named for the historic Wheeling & Lake Erie

Route mileage: 204 (c. 1952)

Locomotives

    Steam: 30 (c. 1929)

    Diesel: 24 (c. 1952)

Reporting mark: P&WV

Emblem: Railroad initials enclosed by a circle

Primary locomotive shop: Rook, PA

Notable features: Speers Bridge over Monongahela River (Belle Vernon, PA), Monongahela River Bridge (Pittsburgh), and several other massive steel trestles; Mt. Washington Tunnel (Pittsburgh)

States served: PA, OH, WV

Major city served: Pittsburgh

▲ In 1959 P&WV entered into an agreement with Greenville Steel Car to sell the Pennsylvania company 100 hoppers for rebuilding. The railroad used the funds from the sale to lease back the rebuilt and renumbered (700–799) cars. *Voyageur Press collection*

◄ P&WV matchbook. *Voyageur Press Collection*

78

PROVIDENCE & WORCESTER RAILROAD

The Providence & Worcester's roots lie in the nineteenth-century New England railroad that connected its namesakes and was absorbed into the comprehensive New Haven Railroad system. Its modern independence began in 1973, when it withdrew from the faltering Penn Central and reassumed operation of its historic lines in Massachusetts and Rhode Island. As Conrail experienced the 1976 bailout of northeastern bankrupt lines and the Boston & Maine scaled back its New England operations, P&W expanded its territory. By the late 1980s, it was operating a significant network of former New Haven Railroad lines, including routes between Worcester and Providence, Worcester to Groton, Connecticut (with rights on Amtrak's former New Haven Shore Line route between Old Saybrook, Connecticut, and Attleboro, Massachusetts), and the former B&M route between Worcester and Gardner, Massachusetts, the latter point serving as its primary Guilford connection.

▼ Rolling southward along the Thames River in December 1992, Providence & Worcester freight NR-2 passes the preserved USS *Nautilus* at the Submarine Force Library and Museum in Groton, Connecticut. In its modern form, P&W began operations in 1973 and is a rare example of a short line that bought new locomotives from three builders: Electro-Motive, GE, and Montreal Locomotive Works. *Brian Solomon*

Much of P&W's freight traffic was interchanged at Worcester with Conrail (CSX after 1999). P&W based local freights at its Worcester yard, with additional trains working out of yards at Valley Falls, Rhode Island, and Plainfield, Connecticut. During the 1990s, P&W expanded further. It picked up more lines discarded by Conrail, while assuming Conrail trackage rights on Amtrak and Metro-North to New York City. In 1997, it merged with Middletown, Connecticut–based Connecticut Central. Today P&W provides freight service and operates occasional excursions with its company passenger train.

Headquarters: Worcester, MA
Years operated: 1973–present
Route mileage: 470 (c. 1996)
Diesel locomotives: 20 (1996)
Reporting mark: PW
Primary locomotive shop:
    Worcester, MA
Notable feature: Trackage
    rights on Amtrak's Thames
    River Bridge (New London–
    Groton, CT)
States served: CT, MA, NY, RI
Major cities served:
    Providence, New Haven,
    New York, Worcester

▲ Providence & Worcester bought this B23-7 new from General Electric. *Brian Solomon*

READING COMPANY

One of America's earliest railroads, Philadelphia & Reading was incorporated on April 4, 1833, to connect its namesake cities. Engineered by Moncure Robinson, the railroad initially emphasized passenger traffic (which began between Reading and Pottstown in May 1838), but soon became synonymous with anthracite coal. It reached Philadelphia in December 1839, and although it continued to expand, it remained intensely focused on Philadelphia and the anthracite region of eastern Pennsylvania. As its routes radiated from hubs at Philadelphia and Reading, its territory stretched from the lower Delaware River to the Susquehanna, extending north from Philadelphia to Allentown and Bethlehem, and northwest from Reading to dozens of coal-producing towns. A few routes extended beyond the anthracite fields to reach nearby interchange gateways; one ran from Harrisburg to Shippensburg and Gettysburg, reaching the Western Maryland; another ran northwest to Newberry Junction near Williamsport, connecting with New York Central's Fallbrook Route. A northeasterly route crossed New Jersey to the Atlantic Coast port at Port Reading.

At various times the P&R controlled the Central Railroad of New Jersey and Lehigh Valley, both large anthracite roads. After the panic of 1893, however, the P&R lost its

▼ In the 1960s, Reading Rambles proved popular with railway enthusiasts and the public. In June 1964, one of several surviving T-1 4-8-4s leads an excursion in eastern Pennsylvania. Steam locomotives had been out of revenue service just long enough for the novelty to attract lots of attention. *Richard Jay Solomon*

▲ In the 1880s, Reading master mechanic John E. Wootten developed a broad, shallow firebox ideal for burning anthracite coal as a locomotive fuel. Many Reading locomotives used this type of firebox, first with divided-cab "camelbacks," such as 2-8-0 No. 1575 pictured here, and later with a more conventional end-cab arrangement. *Photographer unknown, Solomon collection*

independence, and financier J. P. Morgan took control. In 1896, Reading Company was formed to control the assets of the P&R. Over time the railroad came to be known as the Reading Company rather than P&R. Further consolidation occurred in 1923, when Reading Company sold the Reading Coal & Iron Company. In the twentieth century it remained the foremost anthracite line, yet its operation and finances were closely tied to the Baltimore & Ohio (which by now controlled it), and the Central Railroad of New Jersey, using these lines to reach the New York metro area. In addition to coal traffic, Reading was part of the "Alphabet Route," which served as an alternative to trunk lines in the East. It also operated an intensive Philadelphia suburban service based out of Reading Terminal, with its massive balloon shed on Philadelphia's Market Street. From the early 1930s, Reading Company and Pennsylvania Railroad jointly owned the Pennsylvania-Reading Seashore Lines, a group of lines radiating south and east from Philadelphia and serving southern New Jersey. In the late 1950s and early 1960s, Reading Rambles excursions were popular with regional railway enthusiasts and saw a revival of Reading steam power using several of the company's home-built Class T-1 4-8-4s.

As with the other anthracite carriers, Reading's fortunes waned with the decline of hard coal, and it was one of six major carriers folded into Conrail in April 1976.

▶ Reading's September 1946 timetable advertises its Budd-streamlined *Crusader*, powered by a Class G-1 4-6-2 adorned with stainless-steel shrouds. *Solomon collection*

Headquarters: Philadelphia, PA

Years operated: 1833–1976

Disposition: Merged into Conrail

Route mileage: 1,185 (c. 1970)

Locomotives

    Steam: 917 (1928)

    Diesel: 254 (c. 1970)

    Electric railcars: 125 motorcars and 28 trailers (1970)

    Self-propelled diesel cars: 16 (1970)

Reporting mark: RDG

Emblem: Diamond with "Reading Lines" inside

Trade names: Reading Lines and Reading Railway

Primary locomotive shop: Reading, PA

Notable features: Harrisburg (PA) Viaduct over Susquehanna River, 3,507 ft. long, 74 ft. tall; Mahanoy Tunnel (Tamaqua, PA), 3,409 ft.; Muncy Bridge over West Branch of Susquehanna River (Muncy, PA), 1,300 ft. long, 91 ft. tall; Reading Terminal (Philadelphia)

States served: DE, NJ, PA

Major cities served: Harrisburg, Philadelphia, Reading

Flagship passenger train: *Reading Crusader* (Philadelphia–Jersey City, operated on Central Railroad of New Jersey to Jersey City)

Other name passenger trains: *Queen of the Valley* (Jersey City–Harrisburg, operated with CNJ) and *Scranton Flyer* (Philadelphia–Scranton, operated with CNJ)

Notable freight commodity: Anthracite coal

Principal freight yards: Philadelphia, Port Reading (coal pier), Reading, and Rutherford (Harrisburg), PA

THROUGH SERVICE

Reading
Railway System

Crusader
CLAD IN SHINING ARMOR

LUXURIOUS COMFORT WITH ECONOMY

STAINLESS STEEL

Streamlined Train
between
PHILADELPHIA
and **NEW YORK**

RICHMOND, FREDERICKSBURG & POTOMAC RAILROAD

Richmond, Fredericksburg & Potomac was chartered in 1834 and developed to connect its namesakes while retaining a virtual monopoly in this territory. For most of its twentieth-century existence, RF&P served as a 113-mile double-track link connecting Virginia gateways at Alexandria and Richmond.

RF&P traditionally had six-principal connections: Baltimore & Ohio and Pennsylvania Railroad on the north, and the Atlantic Coast Line, Chesapeake & Ohio, Seaboard Air Line, and Southern Railway on the south. These lines jointly controlled RF&P through the Richmond-Washington Corporation, which held three-fourths voting stock. The collapse of Penn Central ended Pennsylvania Railroad's influence, and by 1990, other mergers and changes found CSX owning roughly 80 percent of Richmond-Washington Corporation. By then, more than 80 percent of RF&P's traffic was overhead business, and the line strategically connected CSX's former B&O routes with those of the former

▼ RF&P's relatively level profile allowed it to assign Pacific-type locomotives to freight service. While other railroads occasionally used 4-6-2 for freight, the type was generally a passenger locomotive. The sign below the smoke box indicates the locomotive is equipped with automatic train stop. *John E. Pickett collection*

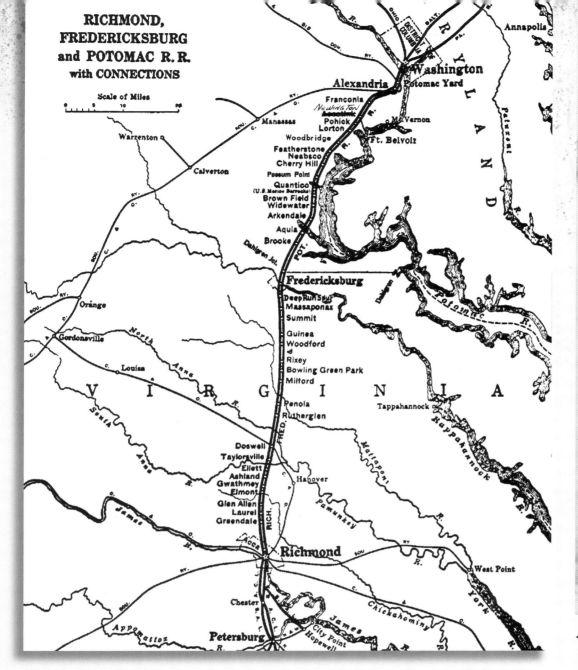

RICHMOND, FREDERICKSBURG and POTOMAC R.R. with CONNECTIONS

Scale of Miles

Headquarters: Richmond, VA

Years operated: 1834–1991

Disposition: Merged with CSX; remains integral component of the CSX network

Route mileage: 116

Locomotives

    Steam: 105 (1932)

    Diesel: 34 (1981)

Reporting mark: RFP

Primary locomotive shop:

    Bryan Park (Richmond), VA.

Notable feature: Concrete open-spandrel arch bridge over Rappahannock River (Fredericksburg, VA)

Major cities served:

    Richmond and Washington, D.C.

Principal freight yards:

    Acca (Richmond) and Potomac (Alexandria), VA

◀ RF&P's double-track line formed a strategic link between Washington, D.C. and Richmond, Virginia. *Solomon collection*

▼ Freight schedules, April 1957. *Richard Jay Solomon collection*

Seaboard Coast Line and C&O. In February 1990, CSX set the wheels in motion to merge the RF&P into its vast network. RF&P's sprawling Potomac yards across the river from Washington, D.C., had been its greatest single asset but were deemed worth more as commercial property than as a classification yard, so following RF&P's absorption into CSX in 1991, the yards were gradually phased out. The once vast and bustling sea of freight cars is now completely gone.

Initially under CSX, RF&P trains didn't look much different than they had under independent operation. This was a function of the railroad's restrictive cab-signal system that required specialized equipment on lead locomotives. The former RF&P route remains a vital artery for CSX, as well as Amtrak and Virginia Rail Express, and by 2011, it was nearing the limits of capacity.

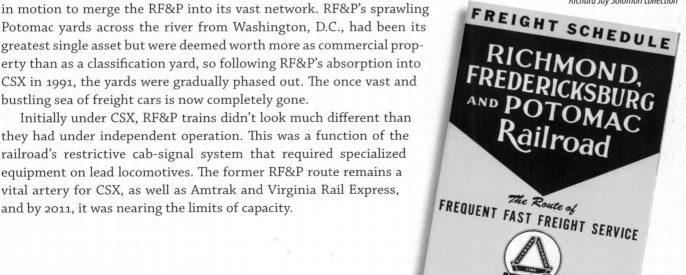

FREIGHT SCHEDULE

RICHMOND, FREDERICKSBURG AND POTOMAC Railroad

The Route of FREQUENT FAST FREIGHT SERVICE

RUTLAND RAILROAD

Vermont-based Rutland Railroad traced its origins to the 1840s with construction of the Rutland & Burlington (R&B). For most of its existence, Rutland and its predecessors were linked with other railroads in the region. R&B was partially financed by the Fitchburg Railroad, and in 1867 was reorganized by Vermont interests as the Rutland Railroad while acquiring the route between the towns Rutland and Bellows Falls, Vermont. Between 1871 and 1896, Rutland Railroad was leased by Central Vermont interests, at which time it was also affiliated with Delaware & Hudson.

In 1896, regional railroad visionary Percival W. Clement took control, and over the next five years expanded the line into its twentieth-century form. He built across the Grand Isles of northern Lake Champlain to connect Burlington and Rouse Point while acquiring the Ogdensburg & Lake Champlain to form a through route from Bellows Falls and Ogdensburg, New York. Meanwhile, the Rutland also acquired the Bennington & Rutland and Chatham & Lebanon Valley lines, giving it a through connection to Chatham, New York, where it connected with the New York Central System and its Boston & Albany

▼ This classic night shot of a Chatham, New York–bound freight crossing the Walloomsac River near the Vermont–New York state line typifies the Rutland's short-lived diesel era. *Jim Shaughnessy*

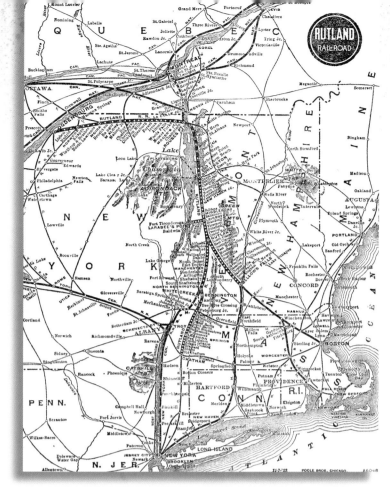

▲ A Rutland system map, 1923. *Richard Solomon collection*

Headquarters: Rutland, VT

Years operated: 1867–1961

Disposition: Ended operations following steep decline in traffic and crippling strikes; surviving routes in Vermont acquired by the state; significant portions between Burlington, Rutland, Bellow Falls, and North Bennington operated by Vermont Rail System; 25-mile fragment of Ogdensburg route has been run by various short lines

Route mileage: 415 (c. 1949)

Locomotives

    Steam: 85 (c. 1929)

    Diesel: 15 (c. 1960)

Reporting marks: R and RUT

Emblems: A circle around RUTLAND RAILROAD; colonial-shaped shield bearing legend GREEN MT GATEWAY with RUTLAND in broad band across center

Nickname: The Green Mountain-Lake Champlain Route

Primary locomotive shop: Rutland, VT

States served: VT and NY

Flagship passenger train: *Green Mountain Flyer* (New York and Boston–Montreal, operated with New York Central to New York City, Boston & Maine to Boston, and Canadian National between Rouse Point, VT, and Montreal)

Other name passenger trains: *Arlburgh Express* (New York–Burlington–Ogdensburg, operated with NYC); *The Cheshire* (Boston–Bellows Falls–Rutland, operated with B&M); *The Mount Royal* (Boston–Rutland–Montreal, operated with B&M and CNR)

Notable freight commodities: Marble, milk, general freight

Principal freight yards: Bellows Falls and Rutland, VT

subsidiary. In 1902, Rutland came under Vanderbilt control, and for a dozen years enjoyed prosperity as an affiliate of the New York Central System. The New Haven Railroad and Interstate Commerce Commission objected to New York Central domination, so the Central conveyed half interest in Rutland to New Haven in exchange for a similar arrangement with New York, Ontario & Western.

Rutland thrived as the link in through New York–Montreal and Boston–Montreal services, while handling a significant volume of dairy traffic to both Boston and New York. But improved highways hit Rutland hard, and by the end of World War II its prospects seemed dim. Reorganization as Rutland Railway in 1950 and subsequent dieselization with a fleet of Alco road-switchers offered a glimmer of hope. The railroad retrenched, abandoning its "Corkscrew Line" between Bennington and Chatham in favor of trackage rights on Boston & Maine and ending passenger services on June 26, 1953. Strikes in 1960 and 1961 doomed the line. Although Rutland faded from the scene, the state of Vermont acquired key portions, allowing Vermont Railway to begin operation in 1964 on the Burlington–Rutland–Bennington route, and Green Mountain Railroad to assume operation of the Rutland–Bellows Falls leg a year later. In New York State, the Norwood–Ogdensburg segment was revived by the Ogdensburg Bridge Authority in 1967. Today it is a VRS-operated short line.

ST. LOUIS–SAN FRANCISCO RAILWAY

The St. Louis–San Francisco Railway, more commonly known by its equally misleading trade name, the Frisco, never reached farther west than the Texas panhandle. In 1866, the Atlantic & Pacific was chartered to connect Springfield, Missouri, with the California coast along a route following the 35th parallel. A&P spawned the St. Louis & San Francisco Railway to construct the eastern portion, while the Santa Fe Railway planned to construct the western portion. While the Santa Fe moved aggressively on the western part of the A&P, the Frisco stalled and the route was neither completed nor unified.

▼ On the eve of merger with Burlington Northern, Frisco train 33 passes Pacific, Missouri. *Mike Abalos, courtesy Friends of Mike Abalos*

Headquarters: St. Louis, MO

Years operated: 1875–1980

Disposition: Merged with Burlington Northern; most surviving routes operated by BNSF

Route mileage: 4,645 (c. 1979)

Locomotives

    Steam: 880 (c. 1929)

    Diesel: 441 (c. 1980)

Reporting mark: SLSF

Emblem: Distinctive shield with FRISCO

Nicknames: The Frisco and F-F-F (for Frisco Faster Freight)

Trade Name: Frisco Lines

Primary locomotive shops: North Side Shops (Springfield), MO

States served: AL, AR, FL, KS, MS, MO, OK, TN, TX

Major cities served: Birmingham, Dallas/Ft. Worth, Kansas City, Memphis, Mobile, Oklahoma City, St. Louis, Tulsa

Flagship passenger trains: *Texas Special* (St. Louis–Ft. Worth with Dallas–San Antonio section operated jointly with M-K-T; also carried through sleepers from New York City via Pennsylvania Railroad)

Other name passenger trains: *The Black Gold* (Tulsa–Dallas); *Firefly* (Kansas City–Oklahoma City); *Streamlined Meteor* (St. Louis–Oklahoma City, through cars via New York Central to New York City, and via Baltimore & Ohio to Washington, D.C., and Jersey City); *The Sunnyland* (St. Louis–Memphis); *The Will Rogers* (Chicago–St. Louis–Oklahoma City operated with GM&O)

Notable freight commodities: General freight and oil

Principal freight yards: Birmingham; Memphis; Rosedale (Kansas City), Springfield, and Lindenwood (St. Louis), MO; Tulsa, OK

In the 1880s, the Frisco was jointly controlled by Southern Pacific's C. P. Huntington and Jay Gould. Santa Fe bought control of the line in 1890, but lost it as a result of the Panic of 1893. It was reorganized as St. Louis & San Francisco Railroad in 1896, and again after 1913 as the St. Louis–San Francisco Railway.

In the twentieth century, its network resembled a flattened butterfly, with principal routes emanating from its Springfield, Missouri, hub. These routes ran northwest to Kansas City; northeast to St. Louis; southeast to Memphis, and beyond to Birmingham and Mobile, Alabama, and Pensacola, Florida; and southwest to various gateways in Oklahoma and Texas. This route structure allowed it to participate in the movement of both east–west transcontinental traffic and north–south traffic.

As with other lines operating in the middle of the nation, Frisco vied fiercely with other lines and suffered from growing highway competition. The Great Depression hit it hard, and it operated under bankruptcy protection from 1932 until 1947. In the 1950s, it tried to expand by acquiring the Central of Georgia, but the Interstate Commerce Commission didn't approve the proposal and the Frisco sold out to Southern Railway.

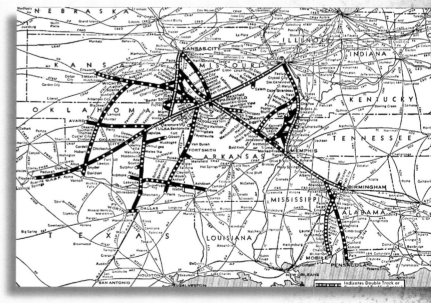

▲ Route map, circa 1959. *Richard Jay Solomon collection*

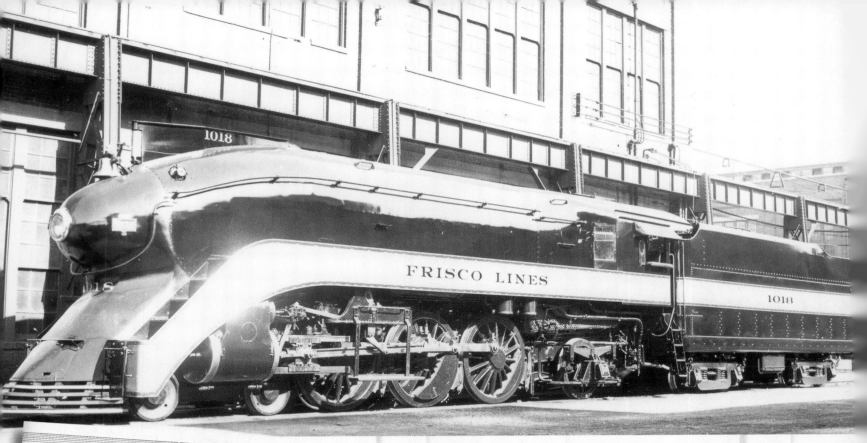

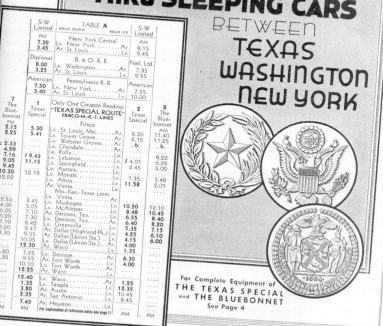

▲ In 1939, the Frisco applied distinctive streamlined shrouds to three pre–World War I Pacific types for service on the Kansas City–Tulsa–Oklahoma City *Firefly*. *Robert A. Buck collection*

◄ A 1947 advertisement for the *Texas Special*. *Richard Jay Solomon collection*

In the 1930s, the Frisco embraced streamlining in a low-cost fashion by equipping some older Pacific-type locomotives with stream-styled shrouds. More conventional streamlining came after the war when it bought Electro-Motive E- and F-units, along with commercially produced lightweight passenger cars. Although never a major passenger route, it operated several noteworthy trains, including the *Texas Special* and *The Bluebonnet* in conjunction with Missouri-Kansas-Texas, and its famous *Meteor*. The line began phasing out long-distance passenger trains in the late 1950s and ended passenger services altogether before the creation of Amtrak in 1971. Frisco merged with Burlington Northern in 1980.

February, 1959

FRISCO

Condensed Schedules

February, 1959

FRISCO

Condensed Schedules

▲ Frisco's February 1959 public timetable featured an elegant streamlined train.
Richard Jay Solomon collection

ST. LOUIS SOUTHWESTERN RAILWAY

▼ On June 2, 1991, General Electric Dash 8-40B No. 8046 leads intermodal freight CHEGA (Chicago to Eagle Pass, Texas) at East St. Louis, Illinois. The Cotton Belt finally reached Chicago in 1989 when SP purchased the former Alton Route between St. Louis and Chicago from bankrupt Illinois Central spin-off Chicago Missouri & Western Railway. *Scott Muskopf*

St. Louis Southwestern (SSW), best known by its trade name, the Cotton Belt, was largely the creation of rail baron Jay Gould, who in 1891 reorganized a network of lines that began in 1871 as a Texas narrow gauge scheme. It was a few more years before Cotton Belt actually reached the important St. Louis gateway, but by the 1920s, the railroad connected St. Louis and Memphis with Arkansas cities; Shreveport, Louisiana; Dallas, Ft. Worth, and Waco, Texas; and other Southwest destinations.

The SSW was a weak railroad, but its network was a promising combination for other lines. Rock Island took control in 1925, but soon sold it to Kansas City Southern. In 1932, Southern Pacific assumed control and operated the line as a subsidiary for the next 60 years. Unlike many of SP's properties, the SSW retained considerable independence. It maintained a distinct locomotive policy in the steam era, and the SP continued to letter locomotives for SSW into the 1990s (largely for tax reasons). Yet, SSW's six-motor EMDs were as likely to be found working on Donner Pass as on SSW's own lines.

Where many railroads were famous for named passenger trains, the SSW is best known for its hot less-than-carload fast freight of the 1930s called the *Blue Streak*. SP continued this tradition, extending it to Los Angeles and Memphis. On several occasions, SP's *Blue Streak* was deemed the fastest freight train in the world. SP melded the SSW into its corporate structure before merging with Union Pacific in 1996.

▶ In 1952, the Cotton Belt issued this pocket-sized history to mark the railroad's 75th anniversary. *Voyageur Press collection*

▶ Cotton Belt logo. *Richard Jay Solomon collection*

Headquarters: St. Louis, MO

Years operated: 1891–1992

Disposition: Operated as a Southern Pacific subsidiary until melded with SP in 1992; SP merged with Union Pacific in 1996; surviving routes largely operated by UP

Route mileage: 1,569 (c. 1949)

Locomotives
    Steam: 212 (c. 1945)
    Diesel: 407 (c. 1952)

Reporting mark: SSW

Emblem: "Cotton Belt Route" in oddly shaped shield

Trade name: The Cotton Belt

Primary locomotive shop: Pine Bluff, AR

Notable feature: Former Rock Island Lines Cimarron River Bridge (near Liberal KS), 1,269 ft. long

States served: AR, IL, LA, MO, TN, TX; KS, NM, OK (after 1980)

Major cities served: Dallas/Ft. Worth, Little Rock, Kansas City (after 1980), Memphis, St. Louis

▲ Route map, mid-1950s. *Richard Jay Solomon collection*

SEABOARD AIR LINE

The Seaboard Air Line was pieced together by northern business interests following the Civil War; however, it didn't assume its classic form until the early twentieth century. In the age of commercial air travel, the railroad's name may seem strange, but the term "air line" predates the invention of the airplane and once referred to a tangent alignment (i.e., one without curves).

SAL's earliest component was the Portsmouth & Roanoke, which dated to 1834 and connected the Roanoke River at Weldon, North Carolina, with Portsmouth, Virginia. During the 1870s and 1880s, Baltimore business mogul John M. Robinson assembled a railroad network that included the Seaboard & Roanoke (which had absorbed the assets of the Portsmouth & Roanoke), Raleigh & Augusta Air Line, Raleigh & Gaston, Carolina Central, and Georgia, Carolina & Northern. By 1892, this network was collectively known as the

▼ SAL was among the first railroads to use Electro-Motive E-units in intensive long-distance passenger service. Its fleet of E4s worked from Washington, D.C., to Florida hauling the *Sunshine Special, Orange Blossom Special*, and other name trains. Here, an A-B-A set of Es roll by a Pennsylvania Railroad GG1 near Ivy City in Washington, D.C. *S. P. Davidson photograph, Jay Williams collection*

▲ SAL 4-6-0 No. 284 goes for a spin on a turntable. *Solomon collection*

Seaboard Air Line System. It formed a northeast-southwest route connecting Portsmouth with Atlanta, and during the 1890s expanded rapidly by absorbing Georgia & Alabama, Florida Central & Peninsular, and the newly built Richmond, Petersburg & Carolina. During this time it arranged to forward its traffic over Richmond, Fredericksburg & Potomac between Richmond and Washington, D.C.

Consolidation in 1900 simplified the network's corporate structure and resulted in the Seaboard Air Line Railway, while construction of a 90-mile link from Cheraw and Columbia, South Carolina, allowed SAL to connect Richmond, Virginia, and Jacksonville, Florida, on a tangential north–south axis.

Headquarters: Norfolk, VA

Years operated: 1881–1967

Disposition: Merged with Atlantic Coast Line; old SAL route structure gradually gave way to ACL's, while some former SAL routes are still operated by CSX; many lines have been downgraded, truncated, abandoned, or sold to short lines

Route mileage: 4,150 (c. 1949)

Locomotives

  Steam: 726 (c. 1929)

  Diesel: 470 (c. 1952)

Reporting mark: SAL

Emblem: Circle with railroad name and heart at the center with railroad slogan (see below)

Slogan: Through the Heart of the South

Primary locomotive shop: Hamlet, NC

Notable feature: Hardwick (AL) Tunnel, 1,326 ft. long

States served: AL, FL, GA, NC, SC, VA

Major cities served: Atlanta, Birmingham, Charleston, Charlotte, Jacksonville, Miami, Orlando, Richmond, Savannah, Tampa/St. Petersburg

Name passenger trains: *Orange Blossom Special* (New York–Washington, D.C.–Miami, operated seasonally with Pennsylvania Railroad and Richmond, Fredericksburg & Potomac); *The Silver Comet* (New York–Washington–Birmingham, operated with PRR and RF&P); *The Silver Meteor* (New York–Washington–Miami/St. Petersburg, operated with PRR and RF&P); *The Silver Star* (New York–Washington, D.C.–Miami, operated with PRR and RF&P)

Notable freight commodities: Perishables and general freight

Principal freight yard: Hamlet, NC

SAL's east–west and north–south axes crossed at Hamlet, North Carolina, and this key junction was developed as the base of freight operations. SAL's inland routes suffered from a hill-and-dale profile that was more costly to operate than those of its chief competition, Atlantic Coast Line.

In 1908, SAL was reorganized as the Seaboard Air Line Railroad, and it continued expansion into the 1920s by linking cities across Florida, ultimately reaching from Tallahassee and Jacksonville to Tampa, St. Petersburg, West Palm Beach, and Miami. SAL thrived on perishable traffic to northern cities, and as southern industry flourished after World War II, it carried an increasing amount of manufactured products, as well as Florida phosphates

▲ SAL's Class Q3 2-8-2 Mikados were based on a World War I–era U.S. Railroad Administration light Mikado design and were constructed by various builders in 1923 for freight services. *Robert A. Buck collection*

Among SAL's most distinctive steam locomotives were fast 2-6-6-4 simple articulateds. The railroad was among lines to avail of Electro-Motive's pioneering FT road diesel, and after World War II it dieselized rapidly, with steam largely finished by 1953. In the diesel era, it also operated 10 Baldwin Centipedes, a type it had urged Baldwin to develop.

In 1967, SAL merged with its long-time competitor, ACL, to form Seaboard Coast Line.

▲ Passenger traffic remained robust on SAL through its merger with ACL in 1967. This well-maintained streamlined SAL coach was photographed in July 1965. *Richard Jay Solomon*

▲ SAL's April 1958 timetable featured its classy streamlined trains. *Solomon collection*

85

SEABOARD COAST LINE

In the late 1950s, W. Thomas Rice of Atlantic Coast Line and John Smith of Seaboard Air Line proposed the merger of their largely parallel and historically competitive railroads. These well-run lines had been enjoying general prosperity since the end of World War II but faced the ominous threat of increased highway and airline competition. They had thrived on perishable freight, especially Florida citrus, and seasonal passenger traffic between the Northeast and Florida. They agreed to merge in 1960, but two factors, healthy parallel routes and Atlantic Coast Line's interest in Louisville & Nashville, delayed the Interstate Commerce Commission's approval until December 1963, and the merger was not consummated until July 1, 1967.

▼ SCL Alco C-420 No. 1218 works a westward local freight at Plymouth, Florida, in April 1974. By blending two formerly competitive systems into a single strong network, it was hoped that SCL would be in better position to tackle growing highway and airline competition. *Terry Norton*

SCL, which blended the names of its predecessors, began with 9,624 route miles, but planned to achieve savings by rationalizing redundant routes. ACL's double-track main line was preferred over SAL's hill-and-dale single-track main, and over the next two decades, SAL's once formidable route structure was pruned back.

Less than two years after the SCL merger, SCL absorbed the North and South Carolina–based Piedmont Northern. Then, in 1972, SCL, L&N, the Clinchfield, and the Georgia Railroad were jointly marketed as the Family Lines. As the name suggested, these independently managed railroads enjoyed a close relationship with each other. In 1980, SCL's parent company, SCL Industries, merged with Chessie System to form an umbrella company called CSX Corporation. Before the numerous railroads were all merged, SCL took the interim step in 1983 of consolidating the Family Lines through the merger of L&N and SCL into the Seaboard System.

▲ SCL drink coaster. *Voyageur Press collection*

▼ An SCL advertisement that appeared on the eve of Amtrak. *Richard Jay Solomon collection*

Headquarters: Richmond, VA, and Jacksonville, FL

Years operated: 1967–1982

Disposition: Melded with Louisville & Nashville, Clinchfield, and related properties to form Seaboard System, one of CSX's constituent railroads; surviving portions now key parts of the CSX network

Route mileage: 9,260 (c. 1970)

Diesel locomotives: 2,675 (c. 1972)

Reporting mark: SCL

Emblem: Stylized SCL

Primary locomotive shop: Jacksonville, FL

Notable feature: James River Bridge (Richmond, VA), multi-span open-spandrel arch, 2,278 ft. long

States served: AL, FL, GA, NC, SC, VA

Major cities served: Atlanta, Birmingham, Charleston, Jacksonville, Montgomery, Raleigh, Savannah, St. Petersburg

◀ One of SCL's last public timetables. *Richard Jay Solomon collection*

86

SOUTHERN PACIFIC RAILROAD

▼ Unique to the Southern Pacific were its oil-fired, cab-forward articulated steam locomotives that were introduced in 1911 to overcome smoke problems in the tunnels and snow sheds on Donner Pass in the California Sierra Nevada range. Here, SP cab-forward Class AC-4 No. 4100 poses with its crew. *C. Edward Hedstrom photo, Solomon collection*

The complex story of Southern Pacific has not one beginning but many, and it involves the numerous companies that ultimately came under SP's corporate influence.

In 1861, railroad visionary Theodore D. Judah convinced four successful Sacramento, California, business owners—Collis P. Huntington, Leland Stanford, Charles Crocker, and Mark Hopkins (popularly known as the "Big Four")—to support his concept for a transcontinental railroad link over the Sierra. Together, they created the Central Pacific Railroad (CP). Later that year, Stanford was elected governor of California. Key to the railroad's construction was passage of the Pacific Railroad Act of July 1862 that provided federal land grants and cash incentives to CP and its eastern counterpart, Union Pacific. Construction began at Sacramento and concluded on May 10, 1869, with the famed Golden Spike ceremony at Promontory, Utah. Once the transcontinental was complete, the Big Four set out to connect numerous points in California, Oregon, and the Southwest with railroads and rapidly dominated transportation in these areas.

In June 1864, a railroad called the San Francisco & San Jose opened on the San Francisco Peninsula; in 1866, the principals behind this railroad incorporated the Southern Pacific, which they envisioned as a connection between San Francisco and San Diego and later as part of a southern transcontinental scheme. Like most potential Big Four competitors in the nineteenth century, this line was soon swallowed up by the Big Four. Ultimately, the Southern Pacific name, rather than Central Pacific, predominated over the Big Four's collective enterprise.

After the 1900 death of Huntington, the last of the Big Four, Edward H. Harriman assumed control of SP, adding it to his already powerful Union Pacific system. Harriman's farsighted plans greatly improved SP and its affiliates through investment in low-grade lines, new cutoffs, automatic signaling, and other modern infrastructure, as well as the establishment of standards for locomotives, cars, stations, and small bridges. His plans to unify UP and SP were foiled, however, by the Interstate Commerce Commission, which viewed the combination as anti-competitive.

SP flourished in the mid–twentieth century, dieselizing in the 1940s and 1950s, and transforming its network into that of a modern freight carrier in the 1960s and 1970s. Santa Fe Railway attempted to merge with SP in the 1980s, but this enterprise was also denied by the ICC, after which SP entered a period of decline, despite common management with the Denver & Rio Grande Western beginning in 1988. SP spun off a variety of secondary lines in the 1980s and 1990s, then finally merged with UP in 1996.

Headquarters: San Francisco, CA

Years operated: 1866–1996

Disposition: Merged with Union Pacific in 1996; most routes today operated by UP

Route mileage: 12, 399 (c. 1952) and 11,143 (c. 1995)

Locomotives (1950)
    Steam: 1338
    Diesel: 1,153

Reporting mark: SP

Emblem: Tracks heading into a setting sun in a circle with words "SOUTHERN PACIFIC LINES"

Nicknames: Espee and The Friendly

Primary locomotive shops: Bay Shore (San Francisco), Los Angeles, and Sacramento, CA; Lafayette, LA; Sparks, NV; El Paso and Houston, TX; Ogden, UT

Notable features: Benicia Bridge (Martinez, CA), 5,603 ft. long; Huey P. Long Bridge (New Orleans), 22,997 ft. long; Lucin Cutoff across Great Salt Lake, originally a wooden pile trestle and earthen-fill estimated at 28 mi. long; Pecos River (TX) Bridge, 1,390 ft. long, 374 ft. tall; Pit River (CA) Bridge, 2,754 ft. long; Tunnel 41 on Donner Pass, 10,326 ft. long

States served: AZ, AR, CA, LA, MO, NV, NM, OR, TX, UT; also OK and KS (after 1980); CO and IL (after 1988)

Major cities served: San Francisco, Los Angeles, Salt Lake City, Portland, New Orleans, Houston, Dallas/Ft. Worth, San Diego, St Louis; also Kansas City and Chicago (from 1980)

◄ One of Southern Pacific's most famous features is the Tehachapi Loop at Waylong, California. The loop was chief engineer William Hood's clever means of gaining elevation while maintaining a steady gradient. In 1991, a 12,000-ton SP coal train works upgrade around the loop with locomotives at the front (top), middle (not pictured), and back (bottom) of the train. *Brian Solomon*

Flagship passenger trains:

Daylight (San Francisco–
Los Angeles); Sunset Limited
(San Francisco–New
Orleans; Los Angeles–
New Orleans in later years);
Overland Limited (Chicago–
Omaha–Oakland, with ferry
connection to San Francisco,
operated jointly with
Chicago & North Western
and Union Pacific)

Other name passenger trains:

Lark (San Francisco–
Los Angeles); City of San
Francisco and Pacific Limited
(Chicago–Omaha–Oakland,
operated jointly with C&NW
and UP); Golden State
Limited (Chicago–Tucumcari,
NM–Los Angeles, jointly
operated with Rock Island);
Cascade and Shasta Daylight
(Portland––Oakland);
Fast Mail (Sparks, NV–
Oakland) (Note: Oakland
trains had ferry connections
San Francisco at the
Oakland Mole)

Notable freight commodities:

Chemicals, forest products,
general freight, intermodal,
perishables

Principal freight yards:

Colton, Roseville, and Taylor
(Los Angeles), CA; El Paso,
TX; Eugene, OR; Houston, TX;
Ogden, UT

▲ California's Donner Pass can receive
up to 800 inches of snow annually. To
keep the pass clear, SP used a variety
of special plows. The largest and
most powerful were steam-era Leslie
rotary plows that were converted
to diesel-electric operation in the
1950s. In February 1993, rotaries plow
upgrade near Soda Springs in northern
California. *Brian Solomon*

◀ Southern Pacific diesels featured a
distinctive headlight arrangement
that included a pair of twin-sealed
beams, dual oscillating headlights,
and a red oscillating warning light.
Brian Solomon

▲ In 1953, Southern Pacific's Lima-built Class Gs4 4-8-4 No. 4431 rests under the shed at the Oakland Mole with the *San Joaquin Daylight* passenger train. This cavernous shed was a transfer point for passengers continuing by ferry to San Francisco. *Robert O. Hale photo, Jay Williams collection*

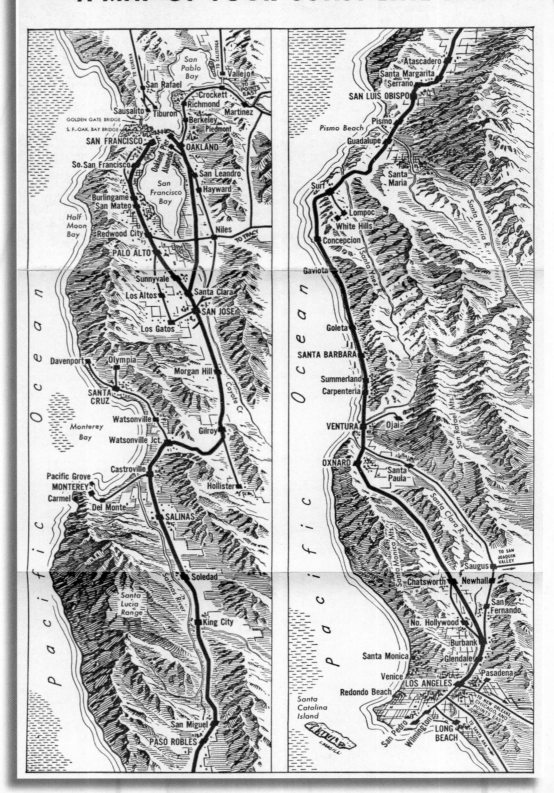

▶ An SP brochure from the 1950s shows the route of the *Daylight* passenger service between San Francisco and Los Angeles. *Solomon collection*

A MAP OF YOUR COAST LINE TRIP

SUNSET LIMITED

ACROSS THE CONTINENT
TO
CALIFORNIA
The Land of Sunshine, Fruit and Flowers
where there are *no sudden changes* in the temperature, but a cool, bracing, balsamic air, the year round, where you can indulge in Boating, Bathing, Driving, Riding, Golfing, Tennis, and all outdoor sports, *every day in the year.*

REACHED VIA

SOUTHERN PACIFIC
ALL THE WAY THROUGH

Louisiana, Texas, New Mexico, Arizona
DELIGHTFUL OCEAN TRIP FROM
NEW YORK to NEW ORLEANS
Elegant New Passenger Steamers Sailing Every Wednesday at Noon

NEW YORK, 349 Broadway   INQUIRE   PHILADELPHIA, 632 Chestnut Street
" " 1 Broadway   BALTIMORE, 210 No. Charles Street
BOSTON, 170 Washington Street   SYRACUSE, 129 So. Franklin Street

▲ *Sunset Limited* service was inaugurated in 1893. This stunning ad appeared in 1904, and the railroad touted their rails as the preferable southern routing for New York travelers headed for "The Land of Sunshine." *Voyageur Press collection*

▲ On June 10, 1994, SP's brand-new General Electric Dash 9s descend California's Donner Pass at Yuba Pass using track 1, the original 1860s Central Pacific alignment. Within a few days of this photograph, SP discontinued operation on the old alignment in favor of the newer 1920s alignment of track 2, seen to the right of the trains. This was a result of single-tracking of portions of the Overland Route. Since that time traffic has blossomed on Donner, and Union Pacific has restored some track capacity. *Brian Solomon*

Children's Menu

S.P.

Now just before you eat, please look
At all the pictures in this book.
It only takes one little minute
To introduce the people in it.

◄ Children's menu cover, 1938.
Voyageur Press collection

87

SOUTHERN RAILWAY

Southern Railway was created in 1894 by J. P. Morgan, a titan of American finance and the visionary banker behind many North American railway systems. At that time, the Southern assumed control of the financially destitute Richmond & West Point Terminal Railway and its numerous affiliates. Morgan appointed the highly skilled Samuel Spencer to manage the new network, and over the next dozen years, Spencer expanded the Southern's route structure, rehabilitated its physical plant, and built new yards, thus transforming the railroad into a first-class property.

Southern's earliest component was South Carolina Canal & Rail Road (SCC&RR), one of America's earliest commercial railways that dated from the 1820s. On January 15, 1831, SCC&RR became the first U.S. railroad to run a scheduled steam-hauled passenger service, using its American-built locomotive, *Best Friend of Charleston*. Another early Southern component, the Richmond & Danville, was an antebellum giant dating to 1856, which by the 1890s had expanded into the core of the Richmond & West Point Terminal network, subsequently the Southern Railway under Morgan's influence.

▼ Southern Railway's *Crescent Limited*, led by 4-6-2 No. 6561, specially lettered for the service, poses at Lexington, North Carolina, for what may have been a special occasion or an inaugural run in the 1920s. *Photographer unknown, Solomon collection*

Headquarters: Richmond, VA

Years operated: 1894–1982

Disposition: Merged with Norfolk & Western in 1982 to form Norfolk Southern

Route mileage: 7,570 (c. 1953, incl. affiliates) and 10,494 (c. 1977)

Locomotives

    Steam: 1,743 (1929)

    Diesel: 1,419 (1980)

Reporting mark: SOU

Emblem: Stylized SR ringed by a double circle

Slogan: Southern Serves the South

Primary locomotive shops: Spencer (Salisbury), NC, and Birmingham, AL

Notable feature: Natural Tunnel (near Duffield, VA)

States served: AL, FL, GA, IL, IN, KY, LA, MS, MO, NC, OH, SC, TN, VA

Major cities served: Atlanta, Birmingham, Charlotte, Chattanooga, Cincinnati, Memphis, New Orleans, Richmond, St. Louis, Washington, D.C.

▼ Timetable, May 1958. *Solomon collection*

▲ This 1967 advertisement took a novel approach to convincing the public to ride the Southern. *Solomon collection*

Serving as an umbrella organization to a host of smaller Class 1 lines, including its namesake Southern Railway, was the Southern Railway System. Other family roads included the Georgia & Florida Railway, New Orleans & Northeastern Railroad, Alabama Great Southern Railroad, and the Cincinnati, New Orleans & Texas Pacific Railway. In 1963, the Southern system added Central of Georgia to its family and in 1974 added the Virginia- and North Carolina–based Norfolk Southern Railway.

The Southern Railway was a classy operation, remembered for its innovative and efficient operations. After World War II it embraced Centralized Traffic Control and dieselized rapidly, with the last of its steam retired in the early 1950s. Yet, the company was sympathetic with its past and in the 1960s revived steam operations with a popular program that operated excursions across its system. In the 1960s, Southern's dynamic leader, D. William Brosnan, transformed the railroad into one of America's finest transportation networks through such trendsetting innovations

Flagship passenger train: *Crescent Limited* (New York–Washington, D.C.–Atlanta–New Orleans)

Other name passenger trains: *Birmingham Special* (New York–Birmingham, operated with Pennsylvania Railroad and Norfolk & Western; also incl. a Chattanooga–Memphis segment); *Peach Queen* (New York–Atlanta, operated with PRR); *Pelican* (Washington, D.C.–New Orleans, operated with N&W); *Tennessean* (Washington, D.C.–Memphis, operated with N&W)

Notable freight commodities: Coal, general freight, perishables

Principal freight yards: Brosnan (Macon) and Inman (Atlanta), GA; Citco (Chattanooga) and Sevier (Knoxville), TN; Norris (Birmingham) and Sheffield, AL; Potomac (Alexandria), VA; Spencer (Linwood), NC

as high-capacity "Big John" coal hoppers and mine-to-plant unit coal trains. Yet, in the 1970s, when many railroads conveyed money-losing long-distance passenger services to Amtrak, the Southern continued to run its own handsome trains, among them its streamlined *Crescent*, with origins in the old *Crescent Limited* that debuted in 1925. The Southern final capitulated to Amtrak in 1979, and then in 1982 it merged freight operations with Norfolk & Western to become Norfolk Southern (a new corporation unrelated to the line the Southern absorbed in 1974).

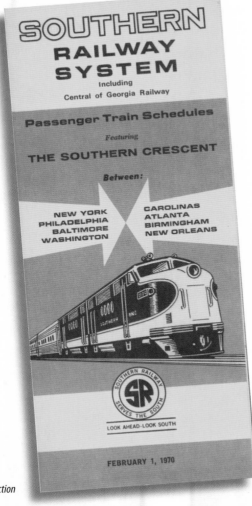

▶ Passenger timetable, 1970. *Solomon collection*

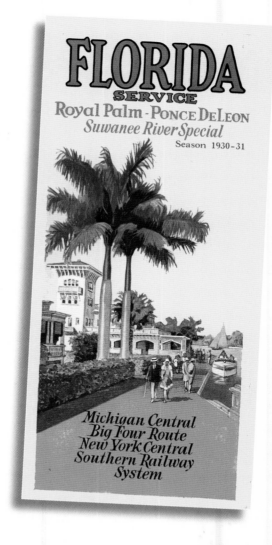

▲ A 1930–1931 winter timetable offered information on services the Southern provided in cooperation with other railroads. *Voyageur Press collection*

◀ The Southern was one of only a few railroads that preferred a long-hood-first diesel orientation with a high short hood. The railway continued to order locomotives like this through its merger with Norfolk & Western. Here, Southern Railway EMDs lead the St. Charles job at Keokee, Virginia, in the early 1980s. *George W. Kowanski*

◀ Passenger timetables, 1914. *Voyageur Press collection*

88

SPOKANE, PORTLAND & SEATTLE RAILWAY

The Spokane, Portland & Seattle Railway was created to fill gaps in James J. Hill's northern transcontinental network formed by his Great Northern and Northern Pacific lines. It began as the Portland & Seattle in 1905 but was amended to the Spokane, Portland & Seattle in February 1908. Interestingly, although its parent railroads served the Puget Sound port in its name, SP&S never reached Seattle on its own rails.

The railway's Columbia River route connecting Portland, Oregon, and Pasco, Washington, opened to traffic in March 1908, and the highly engineered Spokane leg opened in May 1909. The 379-mile main line followed a largely water-level route and had a maximum gradient of just 0.2 percent (2 feet gained for every 1,000 traveled) and gentle curves with a maximum of 3 degrees. North of Pasco, SP&S used five huge tower-supported steel trestles to span deep gulches, and six tunnels to maintain an even gradient. Significantly, SP&S provided James J. Hill with a jumping-off point to reach deep into central Oregon. In fact, Hill's Oregon Trunk and later extensions were the final chapters in a struggle between his system and Harriman's Union Pacific–Southern Pacific empire.

▼ SP&S's Z-6 Challengers were built by Alco to the same specifications as Northern Pacific's 4-6-6-4s of the same class. The primary difference was that NP's Z-6's were coal burners, while SP&S's were oil-fired.
Robert A. Buck collection

Operationally, the SP&S low-grade route was ideal for moving heavy freight, while it also offered a shortcut for passenger trains to Portland and so forwarded passenger trains to that city for both Great Northern and Northern Pacific. It used Northern Pacific's terminal facilities at Pasco and Great Northern's Hillyard terminal at Spokane rather than maintaining its own terminals. The SP&S primary yards were at Wishram and Vancouver, Washington, and it dieselized primarily with Alco, whose diesels it continued to purchase until the locomotive builder concluded domestic production in 1969.

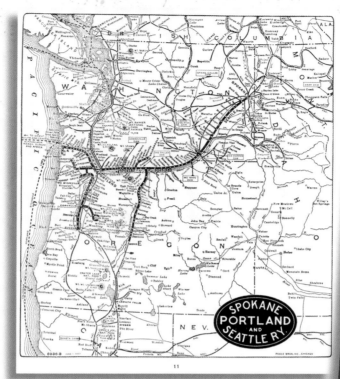

◀ System map, 1957. *Richard Jay Solomon*

▼ Timetables, 1961.
Richard Jay Solomon collection

Headquarters: Portland, OR

Years operated: 1905–1970

Disposition: Merged with Chicago, Burlington & Quincy, Great Northern, and Northern Pacific to form Burlington Northern; highly engineered Spokane–Pasco line abandoned in 1987; Pasco–Portland route along the Columbia River remains part of BNSF

Route mileage: 963 (1950)

Locomotives

    Steam: 112 (c. 1930)

    Diesel: 99 (c. 1970)

Reporting mark: SPS

Emblem: Oval encircling SPOKANE, PORTLAND AND SEATTLE RY

Slogan: The Northwest's Own Railway

Notable features: Crooked River (OR) High Bridge, 464 ft. long, 295 ft. high; numerous tall steel-plate-girder viaducts

States served: OR and WA

Major cities served: Eugene (via Oregon Electric Subsidiary), Portland, Spokane

▲ SP&S used several tall-tower–supported plate-girder viaducts. This ad depicts SP&S FA diesels on a viaduct along Snake River. *Richard Jay Solomon collection*

STRASBURG RAILROAD

Pennsylvania's pastoral 3 1/2-mile Strasburg Railroad holds the title of America's oldest railway line operating under its original charter. This unusual line dates to 1832, when it was chartered as the Strasburg Rail Road, yet it was another two decades before grading was completed, tracks were laid, and operations commenced.

For its first century, the line served as a Pennsylvania Railroad feeder, connecting the village of Strasburg with the Pennsy's "Main Line" at Leaman Place. In addition to passenger trains, it hauled freight for local businesses, including coal, grain, and timber products. The motor age took its toll on the line, as it did on so many others, and by the 1950s it was nearly finished. The Strasburg may have been relegated to scrap had it not been for a group of forward-thinking railway enthusiasts who acquired the property and

▼ Since 1960, the Strasburg Railroad has offered steam excursions on a short but pastoral route between its namesake and its junction with the former Pennsylvania Railroad Main Line at Lehman Place. Here, Strasburg No. 475, a former Norfolk & Western 4-8-0, leads a late-November excursion on its return trip in late November 2008. *Brian Solomon*

Headquarters: Strasburg, PA

Years operated: 1851–present

Disposition: Operates as tourist railway and common-carrier freight line

Route mileage: 3.5

Locomotives

    Steam: 9

    Diesel: 2

    Light gasoline locomotives: 3

    Railcars: 2

Reporting mark: SRC

Emblems: Historically STRASBURG RAILROAD inside oval with profile of a rail; currently STRASBURG RAIL • ROAD inside rectangle with the legend SINCE 1832

Primary locomotive shop: Strasburg, PA

▲ Strasburg Railroad's operations are based at facilities in East Strasburg, Pennsylvania, located across the road from the Railroad Museum of Pennsylvania, making this one of the best places in the eastern United States to study steam locomotives. *Brian Solomon*

developed it as one of America's earliest tourist lines. Excursions began in early 1959, and steam service began a year later.

During the next half-century the Strasburg Railroad emerged as one of the world's foremost preserved railways. It operates steam excursions during most of the year and benefits from its location amid the popular Pennsylvania Dutch Country, as well as from other nearby railroad attractions, such as the Railroad Museum of Pennsylvania, located across the street from the railroad's East Strasburg Station. In addition to excursion trains, Strasburg still functions as a common carrier, and moves carload freight as needed.

UNION PACIFIC RAILROAD

▼ UP still moves large volumes of long-distance freight across the American West. On July 28, 1991, a new General Electric Dash 8-40CW leads a westward freight through Utah's Echo Canyon. *Brian Solomon*

Three years after it was authorized by the Pacific Railroad Act of 1862, the Union Pacific was building westward from its eastern anchor at Omaha/Council Bluffs to meet the Central Pacific, which was building east from Sacramento, and help form America's first transcontinental rail line. The two railroads were famously joined at Promontory, Utah, on May 10, 1869. (Because this location was an unsuitable interchange point, the junction between the two lines was relocated east of Ogden, Utah, near Salt Lake City.)

▲ Among the railroad's finest steam locomotives were Union Pacific's Alco-built 800-class 4-8-4s. One these magnificent engines leads a set of Electro-Motive diesels in about 1956. *Robert O. Hale photo, Jay Williams collection*

Headquarters: Omaha, NE

Years operated: 1862–present

Route mileage: Approx. 9,700 (c. 1977) and 32,094 (2009)

Locomotives

    Steam: 2 (2010)

    Diesel: 7,700 (2005)

Reporting mark: UP

Emblem: Badge-shaped shield with red and white vertical stripes at bottom half and blue field at top with railroad name

Primary locomotive shops: North Little Rock, AR, Omaha, NE; Pocatello, ID

Notable features: Concrete viaduct over Santa Ana River (near Riverside, CA); numerous bridges and tunnels previously part Chicago & North Western, Missouri Pacific, Southern Pacific, and Western Pacific systems

States served: CA, CO, ID, IA, KS, MO, NE, NV, OR, WA, WY; also, AR, AZ, IL, LA, MN, MT, NM, OK, TN, TX, UT, WI (2011)

Major cities served: Dallas/Ft. Worth, Denver, Des Moines, Houston, Kansas, Los Angeles, Las Vegas, Memphis, Milwaukee, Minneapolis/St. Paul, New Orleans, Oklahoma City, Omaha, Phoenix, Portland, Salt Lake City, San Antonio, San Francisco, Seattle, Spokane, Tucson

Despite serving as a crucial link to the West Coast, Union Pacific suffered in its early years, plagued by scandals and suffering from shoddy construction. In 1897, UP's fortunes changed when the railroad came under the control of Edward H. Harriman, who invested heavily in improvements and aggressively expanded the line. He also acquired Southern Pacific, but Harriman's dream of a unified UP and SP unraveled in the face of early–twentieth-century trust-busting actions.

The classic Union Pacific encompassed several key affiliated lines, including the Oregon Railway & Navigation Company and the Oregon Short Line (forming a through route via Granger, Wyoming, on the UP main line to the Pacific Northwest), the Los Angeles & Salt Lake (providing a transcontinental link via its namesakes), and the Kansas Pacific, connecting Kansas City and Denver via Salina, Kansas.

Union Pacific expanded in 1958 by assuming control of the Spokane International, which connected to Canadian

Flagship passenger trains: *Overland Limited* and *San Francisco Overland* (Chicago–Oakland, operated with Chicago & North Western and Southern Pacific, with ferry connections to San Francisco)

Other name passenger trains: *City of San Francisco, Gold Coast, Pacific Limited,* and *Treasure Island* (Chicago–Oakland, operated with Chicago & North Western and Southern Pacific, with ferry connections to San Francisco); *City of Denver* (Chicago–Denver), *City of Los Angeles* (Chicago–Los Angeles), *City of Portland* (Chicago–Portland), and *Utahn* (Chicago–Salt Lake City) (all operated with C&NW); *City of St. Louis* (St. Louis–Kansas City–Denver, operated with Wabash)

Notable freight commodities: Automotive, chemicals, coal, general freight, grain, intermodal, perishables

Principal freight yards: North Little Rock, AR; Colton (ex-SP), Roseville (ex-SP), Yermo, CA; Hinkle and Pocatello, ID; Dupo (ex-Missouri Pacific) and Proviso (ex-C&NW at Chicago); North Platte and Omaha, NE; Eugene (ex-SP), OR; Ft. Worth and Houston, TX (ex-MP)

Pacific Railway in British Columbia. The Union Pacific system expanded even more significantly as result of mergers in 1981 with Western Pacific, in 1982 with Missouri Pacific, and in 1988 with Missouri-Kansas-Texas. In 1995, UP absorbed Chicago & North Western, its longtime eastern connection to Chicago, and then finally fulfilled Harriman's vision by merging with Southern Pacific in 1996 (which by that time also included UP's one-time nemesis, Denver & Rio Grande Western).

UP's desire to move long freights over great distances led it to push locomotive designs to extremes. In the 1920s, it bought three-cylinder 4-12-2s steam designs; in the 1930s, it was first to adopt the 4-6-6-4 Challenger, a type it expanded in 1941 into the famous 4-8-8-4 Big Boy. UP experimented with a General Electric coal-fired steam turbine in the late 1930s, and in the 1950s, it acquired a large fleet of enormously powerful GE gas turbines. In the 1960s, the railroad bought powerful double diesels culminating with the DDA40X Centennials. Then, in the 1990s, it bought two fleets of 6,000-horsepower AC-traction diesels.

▶ In the mid-1980s, UP began moving unit double-stack container trains between Pacific Coast ports and Chicago. A westward American Presidents Line stack crosses Altamont Pass in northern California on the former Western Pacific route. In 2009, UP improved clearances on the former Southern Pacific Donner Pass, crossing to facilitate double-stack trains on that portion of the Overland Route. *Brian Solomon*

▲ In 1996, UP merged with SP, resulting in two parallel routes between Salt Lake City/Ogden, Utah, and California's Bay Area. In 2009–2010, improvements to the old SP route resulted in a de-emphasis of the former WP route. On July 26, 1993, however, the old WP was alive with trains. This westward UP freight was one of four crawling west across the Nevada desert. It is seen navigating the Arnold Loop at Silver Zone Pass Nevada. WP's main line was engineered to keep the maximum gradient to just 1 percent. *Brian Solomon*

▲ The view of UP's Bailey Yard in North Platte, Nebraska, as seen from the eight-story-tall Golden Spike visitor's tower. Bailey Yard is considered the world's largest freight classification yard and covers 2,850 acres. UP claims that 10,000 to 15,000 cars pass through the yard each day, that the yard's double hump sorts 3,000 cars daily, and that the yard services up to 8,500 locomotives monthly. *Michael L. Gardner*

Streamliner
"CITY OF SAN FRANCISCO"

▶ *City of San Francisco* brochure, late 1950s. *Solomon collection*

▼ In the early 1960s, the construction of the Oroville Dam on the Middle Fork of California's Feather River forced the relocation of Western Pacific's main line in the lower portion of the Feather River Canyon. UP acquired the route in 1981. On May 18, 1990, an eastward UP freight crosses the North Fork Bridge near where the new alignment rejoins the historic routing. The train is exiting one of two tunnels—among the longest on the UP system—built as part of the line relocation. *Brian Solomon*

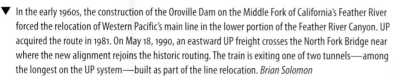

▲ The cover of UP's brochure for the 1934 Chicago World's Fair played off the fair's theme—A Century of Progress—by featuring the railroad's brand-new M-10000, "America's first fully streamlined lightweight high speed passenger train." The M-10000 boasted obvious automotive-inspired styling and all-aluminum construction. *Voyageur Press collection*

UTAH RAILWAY

Utah Railway was organized in 1912 to tap coal fields in Utah's Carbon and Emery counties and built to connect with Union Pacific's San Pedro, Los Angeles & Salt Lake, effectively giving Union Pacific access to rich coal mines otherwise solely in Denver & Rio Grande Western territory. Rather than construct its own expensive mountain crossing, Utah Railway negotiated a mutually beneficial arrangement with the Rio Grande involving the Soldier Summit crossing in Utah's Wasatch Mountains. This arrangement expanded the capacity of this key mountain pass and provided Utah Railway with joint access and trackage rights between Utah Railway Junction (near Helper) and Provo.

▶ In the 1990s, Utah Railway assembled a fleet of secondhand Electro-Motive six-motor diesels to work its unit coal trains. A westward loaded train climbs through Kyune on its way over Soldier Summit in July 1995. Four units on the head-end are assisted by four more located midtrain. *Brian Solomon*

▲ Six-motor diesels lead the way in this photo taken on July 1995. Nos. 9003 and 9006 were former CSX SD40s that Utah Railway leased from Morrison Knudsen. No. 9013 was an F45, also on lease from MK. In 2001, 11 SD40s were returned to M-K and were replaced by MK5000Cs purchased from Motive Power Industries, and SD50Ss purchased from National Railway Equipment. *Brian Solomon*

Headquarters: Provo, UT

Years operated: 1912–present

Disposition: Acquired by Genesee & Wyoming in 2002

Route mileage: 112 (c. 1950, incl. 70.5 mi. jointly operated with Denver & Rio Grande Western); 47 (2011, plus 378 mi. of trackage rights)

Locomotives

   Steam: 6 (c. 1950)

   Diesel: 22 (2005)

Reporting mark: UTAH

Nickname: Utah Coal Route

Emblem: Adaptation of Genesee & Wyoming logo incorporates two outward facing arrows with the letters U and R atop a circle with a beehive in the middle

Primary locomotive shop: Martin, UT

Notable features: Soldier Summit crossing of Wasatch Mountains, incl. Kyune tunnels and Gilluly loops

States served: UT and CO

Major city served: Salt Lake City

Utah Railway steam locomotives tended to embrace Union Pacific designs. In the early 1950s, it dieselized with six-motor Alco road-switchers and continued to employ unusual Alco six-motors (both its original fleet, and later former Santa Fe units) into the late 1980s.

As a result of the Union Pacific and Southern Pacific merger, Utah Railway gained extensive trackage rights in 1996, allowing it to operate to Grand Junction, Colorado, and serve more mines. Utah Railway acquired the 25-mile Salt Lake City Southern Railway in 1999, and in 2002, Genesee & Wyoming added Utah Railway to its list of short-line and regional railroads. Today, the Utah interchanges trains at both Provo and Grand Junction and connects with both UP and BNSF. Coal remains its lifeblood, and 105-car unit trains are common. Its westward trains over Soldier Summit typically run with a four-unit midtrain helper.

VERMONT RAIL SYSTEM

▼ Vermont Rail System represents a re-unification of surviving portions of the old Rutland Railroad network. Here, VRS freight 263 (Rutland to Bellows Falls, Vermont), running with a mix of Green Mountain and Vermont Railway Electro-Motive diesels, crosses the Cuttingsville Trestle on its ascent of Mt. Holly in October 2005. *Brian Solomon*

When the Rutland Railroad ended operations in 1961, it left a gaping hole in the Vermont rail map. The state stepped in and acquired key portions of Rutland infrastructure in an effort to preserve rail service. Vermont Railway (VTR) was incorporated on October 25, 1963, to operate the section from Burlington to Rutland and south to North Bennington. Later, it acquired additional trackage, including the former Boston & Maine branch from North Bennington to Hoosick Junction, New York.

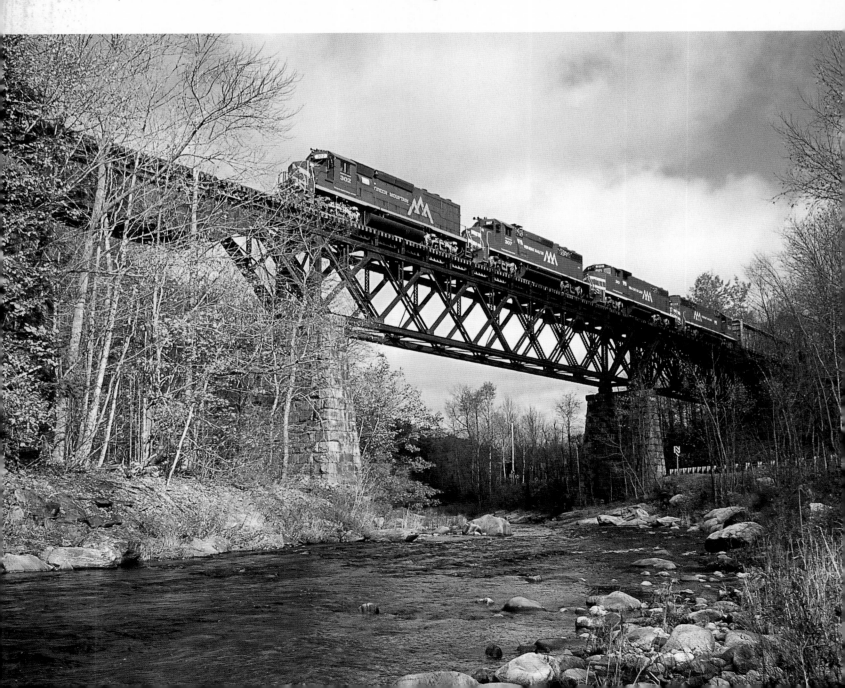

Green Mountain Railroad (GMRC) was formed in 1964 and began operations over 52 miles of line between Rutland and Bellows Falls, Vermont, over the old Rutland Railroad's Mount Holly grade. In addition, it operated some short segments of the old Boston & Maine, including the connection from its North Walpole roundhouse, across the Connecticut River from Bellows Falls. Between the 1960s and 1983, GMRC hosted Steamtown, USA, which was based at Riverside near Bellows Falls. Subsequently, GMRC began its own tourist-train operation using historic cars and vintage diesels.

In 1997, the umbrella company Vermont Rail System (VRS) was formed to group several affiliated lines, including VTR and GMRC, which the former had recently purchased. The Washington County Railroad was added in 1999, and today VRS also operates the New York & Ogdensburg, another former Rutland line. A joint marketing arrangement with Canadian Pacific and New England Central has allowed the VRS to serve as a bridge line for heavy freight coming in and out of the New England region, while also serving online customers. Clay slurry traffic and unit ethanol trains are among the freight carried by the network. VRS continues to operate seasonal excursions on various parts of the system.

▲ While Vermont Railway and Green Mountain operations were characterized by small fleets of secondhand Alco diesels, today's Vermont Rail System is dominated by classic second-generation EMD products. Red and white is the predominant paint scheme, but VRS System GP40 No. 302 is dressed for Green Mountain Railroad. *Brian Solomon*

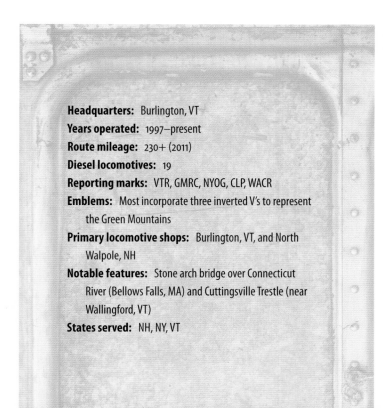

Headquarters: Burlington, VT

Years operated: 1997–present

Route mileage: 230+ (2011)

Diesel locomotives: 19

Reporting marks: VTR, GMRC, NYOG, CLP, WACR

Emblems: Most incorporate three inverted V's to represent the Green Mountains

Primary locomotive shops: Burlington, VT, and North Walpole, NH

Notable features: Stone arch bridge over Connecticut River (Bellows Falls, MA) and Cuttingsville Trestle (near Wallingford, VT)

States served: NH, NY, VT

VIRGINIA & TRUCKEE RAILROAD

By John Gruber

The Virginia & Truckee Railroad—the classic Nevada short line made famous by the writings and photographs of Lucius Beebe and Charles Clegg—opened from Virginia City to Carson City in 1870 to serve the Comstock silver and gold mines. It was extended north to Reno in 1872 to connect with the transcontinental railroad and south to Minden in 1906 to reach an agricultural and grazing area.

With the decline in mining and auto and truck competition, the V&T lost traffic. A McKeen motor car, an economical alternative to a steam passenger train, operated from 1910 to 1945 and has been restored by the Nevada State Railroad Museum. The tracks between Carson City and Virginia City were removed in 1941.

▼ A Virginia & Truckee train is high above Mound House, Nevada, headed for Virginia City in 2010 on the portion of the V&T rebuilt by the Nevada Commission for the Reconstruction of the V&T Railway.
John Gruber

The V&T embodied all the classic Beebe and Clegg elements, especially their mutual love of the Old West and traditional steam railroading. But Beebe could not change the owner's decision to scrap the line, and on May 31, 1950, the V&T made its last scheduled run from Minden to Reno. Later, in *Steamcars to the Comstock* (1957), Beebe concluded his V&T tribute with an uncharacteristic, simple statement: "For railroads such as the V&T do not die but live on in the hearts of men forever."

But the V&T did return. The Gray family reopened 2 miles between Virginia City and Gold Hill in 1976. In 2009, a Nevada commission extended tracks 12.8 miles to the Carson River Canyon near Mound House (East Gate station). Nine V&T locomotives plus equipment are displayed in museums.

▲ V&T No. 27 is a 4-6-0 Ten-Wheeler type built for the railroad by Baldwin in 1913. It pulled its last revenue train in 1950 and is currently on display at the Nevada State Railroad Museum in Carson City. *Voyageur Press collection*

▲ V&T's short entry in The Official Guide of the Railways lists key traffic officials and the railroad's nominal passenger service. *Solomon collection*

Headquarters: Carson City, NV

Years operated: 1870–1950

Disposition: Parts still operate as tourist line

Route mileage: 46

Steam locomotives: 3

Reporting mark: V&T

Primary locomotive shop: Carson City, NV

Notable feature: Crown Point Trestle (near Virginia City, NV)

94

VIRGINIAN RAILWAY

▼ A General Electric–built EL-C electric locomotive leads a coal train across the high bridge at Glen Lyn, Virginia, on July 11, 1959, in the Virginian Railway's final year. Norfolk & Western discontinued the Virginian's high-voltage AC electrification in 1962.
Richard Jay Solomon

The Virginian Railway began in 1896 as a short line called the Deepwater Railway. Visionary Henry Huttleson Rogers expanded the line as Tidewater Railway, and in 1907 changed its name to the Virginian Railway. When completed in 1909, it ran 443 miles from the Appalachian mountain town of Deepwater, West Virginia, via Roanoke to its purpose-built coal port at Sewell's Point, Virginia, on Hampton Roads.

Although completed relatively quickly, the railroad was largely content to remain this size for the next 50 years. It primary purpose remained, as designed, the transport of bituminous coal. Its main line was highly engineered to very heavy standards, as was typical of late-era American railroad construction, and featured gentle curves, numerous tall plate-girder trestles supported by steel towers, and 34 tunnels.

Operations required some of the heaviest trains in the United States, and the Virginian owned the largest and most powerful locomotives of the era. Among its steam locomotives were record-breaking 2-10-10-2s and a Baldwin triplex. Having pushed the limits of steam, beginning in 1922 it electrified 134 miles of mountain main line between Mullens, West Virginia, and Roanoke, Virginia. Late in the steam era it ordered near copies of Chesapeake & Ohio's massive 2-6-6-6 Allegheny types, which were some of the heaviest steam locomotives ever built. To carry maximum volumes of coal, the Virginian had massive six-axle hoppers.

The parallel Norfolk & Western acquired the Virginian in 1959 for its superior grades and lucrative coal traffic.

▼ System map, 1924. *Voyageur Press collection*

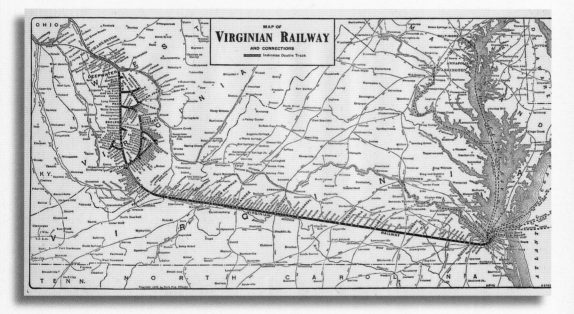

▼ The Virginian operated some of the largest steam locomotives ever built, including massive 2-10-10-2 Mallets featuring low-pressure cylinders measuring 4 feet in diameter. These provided tremendous pulling power, delivering up to 176,600 pounds of starting tractive effort (when worked as simple engines)—the greatest tractive effort of any reciprocating steam locomotive ever built. *Robert A. Buck collection*

Headquarters: Norfolk, VA
Years operated: 1907–1959
Disposition: Acquired by Norfolk & Western; integrated the two parallel routes into uni-directional lines to maximize use of grades; discontinued electrification in 1962
Route mileage: 661 (c. 1949)
Locomotives (c. 1952)
  Steam: 101
  Electric: 16
Reporting mark: VGN
Emblem: Circle with letters VGN in turn encircled by VIRGINIAN RAILWAY
Primary locomotive shop: Princeton, WV
Notable features: Kanawa River Bridge (near Deepwater, WV), 1,820 ft. long; Black Lick Viaduct (Princeton, WV), 910 ft. long, 192 ft. high; 48 tunnels (34 on the main line), incl. Alleghany Tunnel (Merrimac, VA), 5,175 ft.
States served: VA and WV

95

WABASH RAILROAD

The Wabash Railroad was unusual among major carriers because its main lines operated both east and west of Chicago and St. Louis, cities that functioned as major terminal gateways for freight and passenger traffic. The railroad had it origins in a variety of smaller lines that were joined between the 1850s and 1880s. Among these were the Lake Erie, Wabash & St. Louis, the first railroad to incorporate "Wabash" in its name. Over the years, the Wabash was reorganized several times and variously known as the Wabash Railroad and Wabash Railway. Unlike the Nickel Plate Road and Monon, whose colorful trade names took the place of complicated official names, "Wabash" was the railroad's official name.

▼ Wabash reached Buffalo, New York, via southern Ontario from Detroit. It had a small fleet of F7s built by General Motors Diesel in London, Ontario, to serve its Canadian trackage. On August 1, 1957, one of its Canadian F7As worked at Welland Junction. *Jim Shaughnessy*

In 1879, financier Jay Gould added the Wabash to his empire. When he died in 1892, control passed to his son, George, who in the early twentieth century used the Wabash in his ambitious transcontinental scheme. This extended Wabash's reach eastward and included Gould's highly engineered Wabash Pittsburgh Terminal. But the young Gould's costly expansion, ineffective traffic management, and fights with other systems caused his network to unravel before World War I.

After the Gould era, Wabash continued as a major midwestern bridge line well-connected with principal traffic gateways. In 1925, it took control of the Michigan-based Ann Arbor Railroad and was later controlled by the Pennsylvania Railroad, although it maintained its independence. Pennsy control was relinquished in the early 1960s as part of a power play to make way for a merger with New York Central that would go unrealized until the end of the decade. In 1964, Wabash and Nickel Plate Road merged with Norfolk & Western.

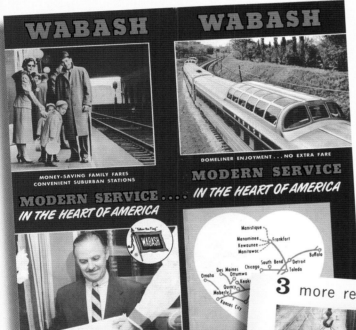

▲ Passenger timetable, April 26, 1959.
Solomon collection

▶ Wabash was synonymous with fast freight, a service it trumpeted in this late 1950s ad.
Solomon collection

3 more reasons shippers like **WABASH**

Under-cover move for industry on the Wabash!

New covered gondola cars on the Wabash protect aluminum extrusions, flat steel and anything else that might suffer from exposure in open-car shipment. Special equipment like this for each shipping job helps Wabash serve better. Shippers save time and money.

It's a truck . . .
It's a train . . .
It's "Piggy-Back"!

A leader in Piggy-Back, Wabash serves the industrial heart of America . . . meets shippers' needs with specialized equipment for fast, all-weather, door-to-door delivery almost anywhere in the U.S.A. Modern Wabash equipment helps shippers save time and money.

Look . . . no hands! New Wabash cars unload by suction

As easy as sipping soda through a straw —and just as sanitary. That's the way these jumbo-sized (3500 cubic ft.) cars can be drained of plastics, peanuts, malt and other dry products. These new cars keep Wabash modern. Shippers save time and money.

WABASH . . . the

Headquarters: St. Louis, MO
Years operated: 1853–1964
Disposition: Merged with Norfolk & Western; some lines abandoned; surviving routes operated by Norfolk Southern and various short lines
Route mileage: 2,393 (c. 1949)
Locomotives
  Steam: 660 (c. 1929)
  Diesel: 337 (c. 1963)
Reporting mark: WAB
Emblem: Flying flag with the name WABASH
Nickname: The Banner Route
Slogan: Follow the Flag
Trade Name: Wabash
Primary locomotive shop: Decatur, IL
States and province served: IL, IN, IA, MI, MO, NE, NY, OH, plus ON
Major cities served: Buffalo, Chicago, Des Moines, Detroit, Kansas City, Omaha, St. Louis, Toledo

06

WESTERN MARYLAND RAILWAY

By Patrick Yough

Western Maryland Railway began as the Baltimore, Carroll & Frederick Railroad in 1852, intending to reach from Baltimore to western Maryland. The following year its name was changed to Western Maryland, and by 1862, WM reached Union Bridge, Maryland, before the Civil War stopped westward progress.

In 1902, George Gould acquired control of the WM as part of his grand scheme to span the continent. Grain and coal piers built at Port Covington along the middle branch of the Patapsco River were to serve as the primary East Coast port for the transcontinental line. Gould melded the West Virginia, Cumberland & Pittsburg into WM in 1905. This line tapped timber- and coal-rich areas between Cumberland and Elkins, West Virginia, and featured a 3.05 percent ruling grade—one of the steepest in the East. Unfortunately, WM's Cumberland Extension was completed with the Gould empire on the brink of collapse due in part to overambitious expansion, and in 1907, some of the Gould roads went into receivership.

Begun in 1906, WM's Connellsville Extension was completed in 1912, giving the railroad connections with the Pittsburgh & Lake Erie and Pittsburgh & West Virginia. This involved crossing the Alleghenies west of Cumberland with 1.75 percent ruling grade westbound, and crossing the Eastern Continental Divide at Deal, Pennsylvania, 300 feet lower than the rival Baltimore & Ohio's crossing at Sand Patch farther north.

▼ Western Maryland completed dieselization in 1955 with Electro-Motive F-units, GP7s, and GP9s, and Alco RS-3s handling most road trains. Four of the RS-3s were equipped with steam generators for passenger service. This pair of unusual EMD BL2s worked the hump yard in Hagerstown. In later years, they were paired with homebuilt slug units, as seen in this 1982 view. *Doug Eisele*

WESTERN MARYLAND RAILWAY
in Miniature

Here in miniature are some of the excellent facilities responsible for Western Maryland's highly efficient freight service.

◄ This pocket-size brochure from the 1950s highlighted WM facilities on one side and rolling stock and motive power on the other. *Voyageur Press collection*

▼ The Western Maryland logo played up its freight services, which represented the vast bulk of its business. *Solomon collection*

Headquarters: Baltimore, MD

Years operated: 1852–1983

Disposition: Merged into Baltimore & Ohio in 1983; eastern portions operated by CSX and Maryland Midland; much of right-of-way west of Hagerstown, MD, given over to Rails-to-Trails conservancy

Route mileage: 717 (c. 1950)

Locomotives (c. 1950)

   Steam: 132

   Diesel: 83

Reporting mark: WM

Nicknames: Fast Freight Line and Wild Mary

Primary locomotive shop: Hagerstown, MD

Notable features: Horseshoe curves at Cash Valley and Lap (Helmstetters), MD; Salisbury (PA) Viaduct over Cassleman River Valley, 1,903 ft. long, and adjacent Keystone Viaduct, 910 ft. long; Blackwater River Canyon (near Douglas, WV)

States served: MD, PA, WV

Cities served: Baltimore, Cumberland, and Hagerstown, MD; York, PA; Elkins, WV

Notable freight commodities: Cement, coal, iron ore, limestone, manufactured products, timber

Principal freight yards: Port Covington (Baltimore) and Jamison (Hagerstown), MD; Connellsville, PA; Elkins and Knobmount (near Ridgeley), WV

In 1927, B&O purchased 44 percent of WM's common stock, but in 1930 the Interstate Commerce Commission directed B&O to place the stock into a trust. In the early 1960s, as Chesapeake & Ohio was taking control of B&O, it also acquired 21 percent of WM stock and in 1964 filed with the ICC to exercise direct control. This motion was approved on March 6, 1967, and WM was included in the C&O/B&O Chessie System of 1972 and fully merged into B&O in 1983.

WM played a central role in the "Alphabet Route," a joint route involving several smaller railroads that competed against major trunks for through traffic (see Chapter 77). Premier freights were known as "Alpha-Jets."

Passenger service on the Western Maryland was minimal, and by February 1959, the last remaining passenger operation was a pair of three-days-a-week mixed trains running the 47 miles between Elkins and Durbin, West Virginia.

07

WESTERN NEW YORK & PENNSYLVANIA RAILROAD

In 1851, when Erie Railroad connected its Piermont, New York, terminus on the Hudson River with Dunkirk, New York, on Lake Erie, it was the longest railroad in the world. Erie expanded to reach Buffalo, Rochester, Cleveland, and ultimately Chicago. In the early years of the twentieth century, Erie Railroad constructed low-grade cutoffs and grade-separated main lines in western New York and Pennsylvania to improve upon its original line. Yet, Erie remained the weakest of the four main east–west trunks. In 1960, it merged with Delaware, Lackawanna & Western, and in 1976 the resulting Erie Lackawanna was melded into Conrail. Conrail had little use for the Erie route and abandoned much of the infrastructure. But New York State insisted that Conrail retain the New York portions of the Erie route, so in the 1990s, Conrail invested in Erie's Binghamton–Hornell–Buffalo segment. However, the old main line west from Hornell to Olean, New York, and Meadville, Pennsylvania, was downgraded and portions were closed to traffic.

▼ WNY&P Alco No. C-430 wears parent company Livonia, Avon & Lakeville's corporate scheme. Engineer Chris Southwell is at the throttle in May 2011. *Patrick Yough*

Headquarters: Falconer, NY

Years operated: 2001–present

Route mileage: 328 (2011)

Reporting mark: WNYP

Emblem: Circle with railroad name enclosing silhouette of locked Janey knuckle couplers

Primary locomotive shop: Alleghany (Olean), NY

Notable feature: Keating Summit (near Liberty, PA)

States served: NY and PA

◄ Western New York & Pennsylvania has paved the way for a renaissance of moribund former Erie lines between Hornell, New York, and Meadville, Pennsylvania. A WNY&P Alco looms out of the fog near Saegertown, Pennsylvania, in October 2009. *Brian Solomon*

In 2001, Livonia, Avon & Lakeville affiliate Western New York & Pennsylvania began operations on largely dormant trackage between Hornell and Olean owned by Southern Tier Extension Railroad Authority. A year later it extended operations to Meadville. In 2003, it upgraded track and began handling through Norfolk Southern unit coal trains. In 2005, it assumed operation of the former Erie Meadville Yard and Oil City branch. Then in 2007, it acquired from Norfolk Southern former Pennsylvania Railroad trackage between Machias and Olean, New York, over Keating Summit to Driftwood, Pennsylvania.

Like other LA&L railroads, it is largely operated with secondhand Alco and Montreal Locomotive Work diesels.

WESTERN PACIFIC RAILROAD

The twentieth century Western Pacific (not to be confused with the nineteenth-century railroad of the same name) was built to fulfill George Gould's dream of a transcontinental railway empire. Gould's lines, largely inherited from his father, Jay Gould, nearly reached coast to coast, yet gaps remained. The largest of these was between Salt Lake City and the Pacific. Despite cries of protest from his competition, Gould mortgaged his Denver & Rio Grande Western to fund the construction of the Western Pacific to fill the gap. WP's main line, the last transcontinental connection in the United States, was completed in November 1909—a half-century after the pioneering Central Pacific–Union Pacific's transcon route.

Benefiting from Gould's deep pockets, WP's route was a showcase for modern construction. Unlike earlier routes plagued by steep grades, this was a low-grade crossing of the Sierra using modern tower-supported plate-girder trestles, numerous tunnels, and the famed Williams Loop (near Spring Garden, California) to maintain a steady 1 percent climb. Although Gould penetrated right into the heart of Edward Harriman's Union Pacific–Southern Pacific empire, WP suffered from a dearth of online traffic and was symbolic of Gould's connect-the-dots approach to railroad building. A few years after WP's completion, Gould's empire unraveled, forcing WP's reorganization.

Actions during and immediately after World War I cured the WP of its flaws. The U.S. Railroad Administration's efforts to coordinate railroad operations included

► The WP reached California's Bay Area via Altamont Pass and Niles Canyon, and established terminals in both Oakland and San Jose. On December 6, 1976, the railroad's final four F7s lead the westward San Jose Turn near Altamont Summit. SP's original Altamont crossing can be seen on the lower level. *Brian Jennison*

the establishment of a "paired-track" arrangement between Wells and Winnemucca, Nevada, using the WP's and Southern Pacific's parallel single-track lines (in some situations close to one another, in others separated by more than a mile), thus giving the two railroads most of the benefits of double-track. Meanwhile, WP's acquisition of feeder lines, including Tidewater Southern and Sacramento Northern electric lines, addressed its traffic deficiencies. In the late 1920s, WP and Great Northern joined forces in construction of one of America's final mainline links, the so-called "Inside Gateway" that met at Bieber, California. WP's line north from Keddie, California, connected with the east–west main line on the Spanish Creek Trestle, which has been known as the "Keddie Wye" ever since.

Although primarily a freight railroad, WP is best remembered for the Budd-built streamlined domeliner *California Zephyr*, which connected Chicago and Oakland via the Burlington and Rio Grande and WP routes between 1949 and 1970. WP's famed Feather River Canyon route is among the most picturesque in the West; by contrast, its main line across central Nevada, which crosses broad expanses of open desert, remains among the least explored main lines in North America.

Headquarters: San Francisco, CA

Years operated: 1903–1981

Disposition: Merged with Union Pacific; most surviving routes operated by UP

Route mileage: 1,190 (c. 1952)

Locomotives
    Steam: 169 (c. 1929)
    Diesel: 152 (c. 1981)

Reporting mark: WP

Emblem: Rectangle incorporating feather, railroad name, and nickname (see below)

Nickname: Feather River Route

Primary locomotive shop: Sacramento, CA

Notable features: Arnold Loop at Silver Zone Pass (near Wendover, NV); Chilcoot Tunnel (Tunnel 37) at Beckwourth Pass (near Beckwourth, CA), 6,002 ft. long; Clio Bridge (near Portola, CA), 1,005 ft. long, 172 ft. tall; Keddie Wye (Spanish Creek Trestle, Keddie, CA), 105 ft. tall; Spring Garden (CA) Tunnel (Tunnel 35), 7,344 ft. long; Tunnel 7, 4,406 ft. long and Tunnel 8 (both east of Oroville, CA), 8,856 ft. long; Tunnel 43 (Shafter, NV), 5,676 ft. long

States served: CA, NV, UT

Major cities served: Oakland, Sacramento, Salt Lake City

Flagship passenger train:
    California Zephyr (Chicago–Denver–Oakland, operated with Chicago, Burlington & Quincy and Denver & Rio Grande Western).

Other name passenger trains: *Royal Gorge* (St. Louis–Kansas City–Denver–Oakland, operated with Missouri Pacific and D&RGW) and *Zephyrette* (Salt Lake City–Oakland)

Notable freight commodities: General freight and perishables

Principal freight yards: Oakland, Portola, and Stockton, CA

◄ *California Zephyr* advertisement, November 1953.

◄ WP employed the domeliner concept in its legendary *California Zephyr* services in an attempt to attract vacationers and travelers to its scenic routes. *Voyageur Press collection*

99

WISCONSIN CENTRAL RAILROAD

Wisconsin Central Limited (WC) was the most dynamic of the midwestern regional spin-offs. In the 1990s, it demonstrated the capabilities of a medium-sized line when creatively managed and freed from traditional restraints.

The railroad began operations in August 1987 when it acquired the Soo Line's Lake States Transportation subsidiary. This short-lived division had been created in February 1986 after Soo Line merged with Milwaukee Road, and it effectively represented the core of the pre-merger Soo Line network, which included the historic Wisconsin Central route (operated as part of Soo Line since the early years of the twentieth century). The genius behind Wisconsin Central Limited was Ed Burkhardt, who had cut his teeth on Chicago & North Western and was well familiar with the territory. Over the next decade WC made a series of strategic acquisitions, including routes to Superior, Wisconsin, in 1991 and 1992; the Fox Valley & Western (a C&NW spin-off in Wisconsin) and Green Bay & Western in 1993; Ontario's Algoma Central in 1995; and in 1997 former C&NW lines serving the

▼ In the 1990s, Wisconsin Central enjoyed robust and growing traffic, which it moved with a well-maintained fleet of secondhand Electro-Motive diesels. On March 23, 1996, a pair of WC SD45s leads train No. 50 at Byron, Wisconsin. On the adjacent track a former Algoma Central SD40 on a set of helpers drops downgrade after assisting a loaded iron-ore train. *Brian Solomon*

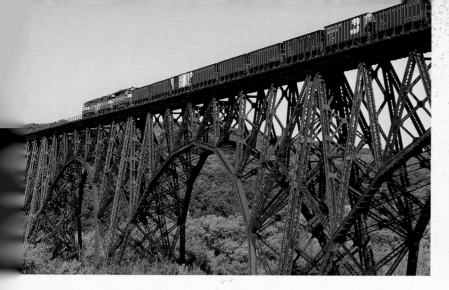

▲ A westward empty coal train crosses the former Soo Line St. Croix River Bridge. This massive five-span steel-arch was built by Minneapolis, St. Paul & Sault Ste. Marie in 1910 and 1911 as part of low-grade cutoff to connect its east–west mainline with the Wisconsin Central route to Chicago. The modern-day Wisconsin Central took its name from Soo's historical component. *Brian Solomon*

▲ Wisconsin Central assembled a large fleet of 20-cylinder Electro-Motive diesels cast off by larger railroads. In addition to dozens of SD45s, WC also operated six former Santa Fe F45s and one FP45s. *Brian Solomon*

Headquarters: Rosemont, IL

Years operated: 1987–present

Disposition: Operated as Canadian National subsidiary since 2001

Route mileage: 3,002

Diesel locomotives (1997): 217

Reporting mark: WC

Emblem: Badge-shaped shield with words "WISCONSIN CENTRAL LTD."

Primary locomotive shop: North Fond du Lac, WI

Notable feature: St. Croix River Bridge (near Stillwater, MN), 2,682 ft. long, 169 ft. tall

States and province served: IL, MI, MN, WI, plus ON

Major cities served: Chicago, Duluth, Milwaukee, Minneapolis/St. Paul

Principal freight yards: North Fond du Lac and Stevens Point, WI, and Schiller Park (Chicago)

Upper Peninsula of Michigan. In addition, WC was involved in a variety of overseas ventures, including operations in Australia, New Zealand, and the United Kingdom. Burkhardt's strategy attracted traffic to WC from myriad sources. While focusing on the Wisconsin paper industry, WC also moved large volumes of iron ore and developed a short-haul intermodal business. A haulage arrangement was signed with Canadian National in 1998, and in 2001 CN acquired WC and continues to operate it as a subsidiary.

WC's motive power strategy saw it acquiring large numbers of secondhand Electro-Motive diesels, focusing on 20-cylinder models such as the SD45 and rebuilding them at its North Fond du Lac, Wisconsin, shops. In this way, WC seemed a throwback to an earlier era, as few locomotives on the line were built more recently than 1972. Yet, by using modern technology and de-rating the 20-cylinder diesels, WC was able to achieve better fuel efficiency while improving reliability. The railroad maximized use of locomotives, crews, and track space by managing quick turnaround times, keeping trains moving, and running a scheduled railroad using yards at Stevens Point and North Fond du Lac as hubs. Pre-blocking of cars at Wisconsin yards simplified interchange arrangements in Chicago, while limiting the need to switch road freights en route. Finally, encouraging a positive employee attitude allowed the railroad to interact better with potential customers and find business previously ignored by railroads in the region.

▲ Wisconsin Central's shield adorns the nose of a former Algoma Central GP40. *Brian Solomon*

WISCONSIN & SOUTHERN RAILROAD

100

Today's Wisconsin & Southern is a loose network largely assembled from former Milwaukee Road lines in southern Wisconsin and northern Illinois, along with a few routes cast off by other carriers. This successful regional railroad, referred to by its reporting marks, WSOR (sometimes pronounced "Wissor"), had its origins in Milwaukee Road's 1980 reorganization. When the Milwaukee pared back operations, it spun off numerous secondary lines resulting in a host of new short lines. WSOR was formed in 1980 to operate a 147-mile cluster of state-owned former Milwaukee lines radiating from Horicon, Wisconsin.

William Gardner acquired the property in 1988 and under his administration the railroad has greatly extended its reach and increased freight business. WSOR's greatest expansion stemmed from its 1992 acquisition of the Wisconsin & Calumet (known by its reporting marks as the WICT, referred to by enthusiasts as "the Wicket"), a 422-mile short-line network. Among its other routes, it reopened the former Milwaukee line between its Janesville, Wisconsin, hub and Fox Lake, Illinois. This line, in conjunction with trackage rights over the Metra and Canadian Pacific's former Milwaukee Lines via Rondout, Illinois, has since served WSOR as a link to Belt Railway of Chicago's Clearing Yard. Another WICT line reached west from Madison, Wisconsin, to the Mississippi River

▼ A pair of Wisconsin & Southern GP38-2s leads a local freight across the Wisconsin River. While much of the WSOR network comprises former Milwaukee Road routes, it also operates sections of other lines, such as this former C&NW line from Madison to Rock Springs, Wisconsin. *Brian Solomon*

Headquarters: Milwaukee, WI

Years operated: 1980–present

Route mileage: 700+

Diesel locomotives (2009): 47

Reporting mark: WSOR

Emblem: WS topped with silhouette of flying Canada goose

Primary locomotive shops: Horicon and Janesville, WI

Notable feature: Lake Wisconsin Bridge (Merrimac, WI), 1,729 ft. long

States served: IL and WI

Major cities served: Chicago, Madison, Milwaukee

port at Prairie du Chien. The original WSOR routes are operated as its Northern Division, and former WICT lines constitute its Southern Division. Tracked rights over Canadian National's former Wisconsin Central link the two systems. More recent expansions have included operation of the former C&NW route between Madison and Reedsburg (still owned by Union Pacific as of June 2011); a branch to Cottage Grove, Illinois, in 1996; and the former Milwaukee Road branch between Madison and Watertown, Wisconsin, in 1998.

The railroad operates its freight network with a roster consisting largely of 1960s- and 1970s-era EMD diesels. It also maintains a classy A-B-A set of E-units for its business train.

▲ Wisconsin Southern's roster consists of various secondhand Electro-Motive diesels. No. 3805—an ex–Richmond, Fredericksburg & Potomac GP38—was photographed in Janesville, Wisconsin. *Brian Solomon*

◀ A former Union Pacific SD20 on the WSOR was photographed in June 2004. *Brian Solomon*

BIBLIOGRAPHY

BOOKS

1846–1896 Fiftieth Anniversary of the Incorporation of the Pennsylvania Railroad Company. Philadelphia: Pennsylvania Railroad, 1896.

A Century of Progress: History of the Delaware and Hudson Company 1823–1923. Albany, NY: The Delaware & Hudson Company, 1925.

Abdill, George B. *Pacific Slope Railroads: From 1854 to 1900*. Seattle, WA: Superior Publishing, 1959.

Alvarez, Eugene. *Travel on Southern Antebellum Railroads, 1828–1860*. Tuscaloosa, AL: University of Alabama Press, 1974.

American Railway Signaling Principles and Practices. New York: Association of American Railroads, 1948.

Anderson, Craig T. *Amtrak: The National Rail Passenger Corporation, 1978–1979 Annual*. San Francisco: Rail Transportation Archives, 1978

Anderson, Elaine. *The Central Railroad of New Jersey's First 100 Years*. Easton, PA: Center for Canal History and Technology, 1984.

Archer, Robert F. *A History of the Lehigh Valley Railroad: Route of the Black Diamond*. Berkeley, CA: Howell-North Books, 1977.

Armstrong, John H. *The Railroad: What It Is, What It Does*. Omaha, NE: Simmons-Boardman Publishing, 1982.

Asay, Jeff S. *Track and Time: An Operational History of the Western Pacific Railroad through Timetables and Maps*. Portola, CA: Feather River Rail Society, 2006.

Armitage, Merle. *The Railroads of America*. Boston: Little, Brown, 1952.

Austin, Ed and Tom Dill. *The Southern Pacific in Oregon*. Edmonds, WA: Pacific Fast Mail, 1987.

Baedeker, Karl. *Baedeker's the United States: Handbook for Travelers*. Leipzig, Germany: Karl Baedeker Publishing, 1909.

Bancroft, Hubert Howe. *History of California, Vol. VII: 1860–1890*. San Francisco: The History Company, 1890.

Bean, W. L. *Twenty Years of Electrical Operation on the New York, New Haven and Hartford Railroad*. East Pittsburgh, PA: American Society of Mechanical Engineers, 1927.

Beaver, Roy C. *The Bessemer & Lake Erie Railroad, 1869–1969*. San Marino, CA: Golden West Books, 1969.

Beebe, Lucius. *The Central Pacific and the Southern Pacific Railroads*. Berkeley, CA: Howell-North Books, 1963.

Beebe, Lucius, and Charles Clegg. *Narrow Gauge in the Rockies*. Berkeley, CA: Howell-North Books, 1958.

Bell, J. Snowden. *The Early Motive Power of the Baltimore and Ohio Railroad*. New York: Angus Sinclair Company, 1912.

Berton, Pierre. *The Last Spike: The Great Railway, 1881–1885*. Toronto: McClelland and Stewart, 1971.

Bezilla, Michael. *Electric Traction on the Pennsylvania Railroad, 1895–1968*. State College, PA: The Penn State University Press: 1981.

Black III, Robert C. *The Railroads of the Confederacy*. Chapel Hill, NC: The University of North Carolina Press, 1952.

Bradley, Rodger. *Amtrak: The US National Railroad Passenger Corporation*. Dorset, UK: Blandford Press, 1985.

Bruce, Alfred W. *The Steam Locomotive in America; Its Development in the Twentieth Century*. New York: Bonanza Books, 1952.

Bryant Keith L., Jr. *History of the Atchison, Topeka and Santa Fe Railway*. New York: Macmillan, 1974.

———, ed. *Railroads in the Age of Regulation, 1900–1980*. New York: Facts on File, 1988.

Burgess, George, H. and Miles C. Kennedy. *Centennial History of the Pennsylvania Railroad*. Philadelphia: Pennsylvania Railroad Company, 1949.

Burke, Davis. *The Southern Railway: Road of the Innovators*. Chapel Hill, NC: The University of North Carolina Press, 1985.

Bush, Donald, J. *The Streamlined Decade*. New York: George Braziller, 1975.

Byron, Carl R. *A Pinprick of Light: The Troy and Greenfield Railroad and its Hoosac Tunnel*. Shelburne, VT: New England Press, 1995.

Casey, Robert J., and W.A.S. Douglas. *The Lackawanna Story*. New York: McGraw-Hill, 1951.

Carlson, Robert E. *The Liverpool & Manchester Railway Project, 1821–1831*. New York: Augustus M. Kelley, 1969.

Castner, Charles B., with Ronald Flanary and Patrick Dorin. *Louisville & Nashville Railroad: The Old Reliable*. Salem, VA: TLC Publishing, 1996

Chernow, Ron. *The House of Morgan: An American Banking Dynasty and the Rise of Modern Finance*. New York: Grove Press, 1990, 2010.

Churella, Albert J. *From Steam to Diesel: Managerial Customs and Organization Capabilities in the Twentieth-Century Locomotive Industry*. Princeton, NJ: Princeton University Press, 1998.

Condit, Carl. *Port of New York: A History of the Rail and Terminal System from the Beginnings to Pennsylvania Station ,Vols. 1 & 2.* Chicago: University of Chicago Press, 1980, 1981.

Corbin, Bernard G., and William F. Kerka. *Steam Locomotives of the Burlington Route.* Red Oak, IA: self-published, 1960.

Cupper, Dan. *Horseshoe Heritage: The Story of a Great Railroad Landmark.* Halifax, PA: Withers Publishing, 1996.

Currie, A. W. *The Grand Trunk Railway of Canada.* Toronto: University of Toronto Press, 1957.

Daggett, Stuart. *History of the Southern Pacific.* New York: The Ronald Press, 1922.

Daughen, Joseph R., and Peter Binzen. *The Wreck of the Penn Central.* Boston: Little, Brown, 1971.

Del Grosso, Robert C. *Burlington Northern 1980–1991 Annual.* Denver: Hyrail Productions, 1991.

DeNevi, Don. *The Western Pacific: Railroading Yesterday, Today and Tomorrow.* Seattle, WA: Oblivion Books, 1978.

Dixon, Thomas W., Jr. *Chesapeake & Ohio: Superpower to Diesels.* Newton, NJ: Carstens Publications, 1984.

Doherty, Timothy Scott, and Brian Solomon. *Conrail.* St. Paul, MN: MBI Publishing, 2004.

Dolzall, Gary W., and Stephen F. Dolzall. *Monon: The Hoosier Line.* Glendale, CA: Interurban Press, 1987.

Dorin, Patrick C., and Robert C. Del Grosso. *Burlington Northern Railroad: Coal Hauler and Coal Country Trackside Guide.* Bonners Ferry, ID: Great Northern Pacific Publications, 1995.

Dorsey, Edward Bates. *English and American Railroads Compared.* New York: John Wiley & Sons, 1887.

Droege, John A. *Freight Terminals and Trains.* New York: McGraw-Hill, 1912.

———. *Passenger Terminals and Trains.* New York: McGraw-Hill, 1916.

Drury, George H. *The Historical Guide to North American Railroads.* Waukesha, WI: Kalmbach Publishing, 1985.

———. *The Train Watcher's Guide to North American Railroads.* Waukesha, WI: Kalmbach Publishing, 1992.

———. *Guide to North American Steam Locomotives.* Waukesha, WI: Kalmbach Publishing, 1993.

Dubin, Arthur D. *Some Classic Trains.* Milwaukee, WI: Kalmbach Publishing, 1964.

———. *More Classic Trains.* Milwaukee, WI: Kalmbach Publishing, 1974.

Duke, Donald. *Union Pacific in Southern California, 1890–1990.* San Marino, CA: Golden West Books, 2005.

Duke, Donald, and Stan Kistler. *Santa Fe: Steel Rails through California.* San Marino, CA: Golden West Books, 1963.

Dunscomb, Guy, L. *A Century of Southern Pacific Steam Locomotives.* Modesto, CA: self-published, 1963.

Encyclopedia of American Business History and Biography: Railroads in the Nineteenth Century. New York: Facts on File, 1988.

Farrington, S. Kip, Jr. *Railroading from the Head End.* Garden City, NY: Doubleday, Doran, 1943.

———. *Railroads at War.* New York: Coward-McCann, 1944.

———. *Railroading from the Rear End.* New York: Coward-McCann, 1946.

———. *Railroads of Today.* New York: Coward-McCann, 1949.

———. *Railroading the Modern Way.* New York: Coward-McCann, 1951.

———. *Railroads of the Hour.* New York: Coward-McCann, 1958.

Ferrell, Mallory Hope. *Colorful East Broad Top.* Forest Park, IL: Heimburger House, 1993.

Fitzsimons, Bernard. *150 Years of Canadian Railroads.* Toronto: Bison Books, 1984.

Frailey, Fred W. *Zephyrs, Chiefs & Other Orphans: The First Five Years of Amtrak.* Godfrey, IL: RPC Publications, 1977.

———. *Twilight of the Great Trains.* Waukesha, WI: Kalmbach Publishing, 1998.

Frey, Robert L., ed. *Encyclopedia of American Business History and Biography: Railroads in the Nineteenth Century.* New York: Facts on File, 1988.

Garmany, John B. *Southern Pacific Dieselization.* Edmonds, WA: Pacific Fast Mail, 1985.

Glischinski, Steve. *Burlington Northern and Its Heritage.* Andover, NJ: Andover Junction Publications, 1992.

———. *Santa Fe Railway.* Osceola, WI: MBI Publishing, 1997.

Grant, H. Roger. *Erie Lackawanna: Death of an American Railroad, 1938–1992.* Palo Alto, CA: Stanford University Press, 1994.

Greenberg, William T., Jr., and Robert F. Fischer. *The Lehigh Valley Railroad East of Mauch Chunk.* Martinsville, NJ: The Gingerbread Stop, 1997.

Grenard, Ross, and Frederick A. Kramer. *East Broad Top to the Mines and Back.* Newton, NJ: Carstens Publications, 1990.

Grodinsky, Julius. *Jay Gould: His Business Career 1867–1892.* Philadelphia: University of Pennsylvania Press, 1957.

Gruber, John. *Railroad History in a Nutshell.* Madison, WI: Center for Railroad Photography and Art, 2009.

———. *Railroad Preservation in a Nutshell.* Madison, WI: Center for Railroad Photography and Art, 2011.

Gruber, John, and Brian Solomon. *The Milwaukee Road's Hiawathas.* St. Paul, MN: MBI Publishing, 2006.

Hampton, Taylor. *The Nickel Plate Road.* Cleveland: Word Publishing, 1947.

Hare, Jay V. *History of the Reading*. Philadelphia: John Henry Strock, 1966.

Harlow, Alvin F. *Steelways of New England*. New York: Creative Age Press, 1946.

———. *The Road of the Century*. New York: Creative Age Press, 1947.

Hayes, William Edward. *Iron Road to Empire: The History of the Rock Island Lines*. New York: Simmons-Boardman, 1953.

Heath, Erle. *Seventy-Five Years of Progress: Historical Sketch of the Southern Pacific, 1869–1945*. San Francisco: Southern Pacific Bureau of News, 1945.

Hedges, James Blaine. *Henry Villard and the Railways of the Northwest*. New York: K. R. Smith, 1930.

Helmer, William F. *O&W: The Long Life and Slow Death of the New York, Ontario & Western Ry*, 2nd Ed. San Diego: Howell-North Press, 1982.

Hidy, Ralph W., Muriel E. Hidy, and Roy V. Scott, with Don L. Hofsommer. *The Great Northern Railway*. Boston: Harvard Business School Press, 1988.

Hilton, George W. *American Narrow Gauge Railroads*. Palo Alto, CA: Stanford University Press, 1990.

Holbrook, Stewart H. *The Story of American Railroads*. New York: Crown, 1947.

———. *James J. Hill*. New York: Alfred A. Knopf, 1955.

Holland, Rupert Sargent. *Historic Railroads*. Philadelphia: Macrea Smith, 1927.

Holton, James L. *The Reading Railroad: History of a Coal Age Empire, Vols. I & II*. Laurys Station, PA: Garrigues House, 1992.

Hofsommer, Don. L. *Southern Pacific, 1900–1985*. College Station, TX: Texas A&M University Press, 1986.

Hollander, Stanley, C. *Passenger Transportation*. Lansing, MI: Michigan State University Press, 1968.

Hoyt, Edwin P. *The Vanderbilts and Their Fortunes*. Garden City, NY: Doubleday, 1962.

Hughes, Sarah Forbes. *John Murray Forbes Letters and Recollections, Vols. I & II*. Boston: Houghton Mifflin, 1899.

Hungerford, Edward. *Daniel Willard Rides the Line*. New York: G. P. Putnam's Sons, 1938.

———. *Men of Erie: A Story of Human Effort*. New York: Random House, 1946.

Ivey, Paul Wesley. *The Pere Marquette Railroad Company*. Grand Rapids, MI: The Black Letter Press, 1970.

Jones, Robert C. *The Central Vermont Railway, Vols I–VII*. Shelburne, VT: New England Press, 1995.

Jones, Robert W. *Boston & Albany: The New York Central in New England, Vols. 1 & 2*. Los Angeles: Pine Tree Press, 1997.

Karr, Ronald Dale. *The Rail Lines of Southern New England*. Pepperell, MA: Branch Line Press, 1995.

Keilty, Edmund. *Interurbans without Wires*. Glendale, CA: Interurban Press, 1979.

King, Steve. *Clinchfield Country*. Silver Spring, MD: Old Line Graphics, 1988.

Klein, Maury. *History of the Louisville & Nashville Railroad*. New York: Macmillan, 1972.

———. *Union Pacific, Vols. I &II*. New York: Doubleday, 1989.

———. *Union Pacific: The Reconfiguration: America's Greatest Railroad from 1969 to the Present*. New York: Oxford University Press, 2011.

Lamb, W. Kaye. *History of the Canadian Pacific Railway*. New York: Macmillan, 1977.

Leachman, Rob. *Northwest Passage*. Mukilteo, WA: Hundman Publishing, 1998.

LeMassena, Robert A. *Colorado's Mountain Railroads, Vol. 1*. Golden, CO: Smoking Press, 1963.

———. *Rio Grande to the Pacific*. Denver: Sundance Limited, 1974.

Lemly, James H. *The Gulf, Mobile & Ohio*. Homewood, IL: Richard D. Irwin, 1953.

Leopard, John. *Wisconsin Central Heritage, Vol. II*. La Mirada, CA: Four Ways West Publications, 2008.

Lewis, Oscar. *The Big Four: The Story of Huntington, Stanford, Hopkins, and Crocker, and of the Building of the Central Pacific*. New York: Alfred A. Knopf, 1938.

Malone, Michael P. *James J. Hill: Empire Builder of the Northwest*. Norman, OK: University of Oklahoma Press, 1996.

Marre, Louis, A. *Diesel Locomotives: The First 50 Years*. Waukesha, WI: Kalmbach Publishing, 1995.

Marre, Louis A., and Jerry A. Pinkepank. *The Contemporary Diesel Spotter's Guide*. Milwaukee, WI: Kalmbach Publishing, 1985.

Marre, Louis A., and Paul K. Withers. *The Contemporary Diesel Spotter's Guide, Year 2000 Ed*. Halifax, PA: Withers Publishing, 2000.

Marshall, James. *Santa Fe: The Railroad That Built an Empire*. New York: Random House, 1945.

Marshall, John. *The Guinness Book of Rail Facts and Feats*. Middlesex, UK: Enfield, 1975.

McDonald, Charles W. *Diesel Locomotive Rosters*. Milwaukee, WI: Kalmbach Publishing, 1982.

McLean, Harold H. *Pittsburgh & Lake Erie Railroad*. San Marino, CA: Golden West Books, 1980.

Mellander, Deane E. *East Broad Top: Slim Gauge Survivor*. Silver Spring, MD: Old Line Graphics, 1995.

Middleton, William D. *When the Steam Railroads Electrified*. Milwaukee, WI: Kalmbach Publishing, 1974.

———. *Landmarks on the Iron Road*. Bloomington, IN: Indiana University Press, 1999.

Middleton, William D., with George M. Smerk and Roberta L. Diehl. *Encyclopedia of North American Railroads*. Bloomington, IN: Indiana University Press, 2007.

Mika, Nick, with Helma Mika. *Railways of Canada*. Toronto and Montreal: McGraw-Hill Ryerson, 1972.

Miner, Craig H. *The St. Louis-San Francisco Transcontinental Railroad*. Lawrence, KS: University Press of Kansas, 1972.

Moedinger, William M. *The Road to Paradise*. Lancaster, PA: Privately published, 1983.

Mohowski, Robert E. *New York, Ontario & Western in the Diesel Age*. Andover, NJ: Andover Junction Publications, 1994.

Morgan, David P. *Steam's Finest Hour*. Milwaukee, WI: Kalmbach Publishing, 1959.

———. *Canadian Steam!* Milwaukee, WI: Kalmbach Publishing, 1961.

Mott, Edward Harold. *Between the Ocean and the Lakes: The Story of Erie*. New York: John S. Collins, 1900.

Murray, Tom. *Canadian National Railway*. St. Paul, MN: MBI Publishing, 2004.

Myrick, David F. *Life and Times of the Central Pacific Railroad*. San Francisco: Book Club of California, 1969.

———. *Western Pacific: The Last Transcontinental Railroad, Colorado Rail Annual No. 27*. Golden, CO: Colorado Railroad Museum, 2006.

Nock, O. S. *Algoma Central Railway*. London: A&C Black, 1975.

Osterwald, Doris B. *Cinders & Smoke*. Lakewood, CO: Western Guideways, 1995.

Overton, Richard, C. *Burlington West*. Cambridge, MA: Harvard University Press, 1941.

———. *Burlington Route: A History of the Burlington Lines*. New York: Knopf, 1965.

Potter, Janet Greenstein. *Great American Railroad Stations*. New York: John Wiley & Sons, 1996.

Quiett, Glenn Chesney. *They Built the West: An Epic of Rails and Cities*. New York: Cooper Square, 1934.

Raymond, William G., revised by Henry E. Riggs and Walter C. Sadler. *The Elements of Railroad Engineering, 5th Ed*. New York: John Wiley & Sons, 1937.

Reed, S. G. *A History of the Texas Railroads*. Houston, TX: St. Clair Publishing, 1941.

Riegel, Robert Edgar. *The Story of the Western Railroads*. Lincoln, NE: University of Nebraska Press, 1926.

Rosenberger, Homer Tope. *The Philadelphia and Erie Railroad*. Potomac, MD: The Fox Hills Press, 1975.

Sabin, Edwin, L. *Building the Pacific Railroad*. Philadelphia: J. B. Lippincott, 1919.

Salsbury, Stephen. *No Way to Run a Railroad*. New York: McGraw-Hill, 1982.

Saunders Jr., Richard. *The Railroad Mergers and the Coming of Conrail*. Westport, CT: Greenwood Press, 1978.

———. *Merging Lines: American Railroads, 1900–1970*. DeKalb, IL: Northern Illinois University Press, 2001.

———. *Main Lines: American Railroads, 1970–2002*. DeKalb, IL: Northern Illinois University Press, 2003.

Saylor, Roger B. *The Railroads of Pennsylvania*. State College, PA: The Penn State University Press: 1964.

Schafer, Mike, and Brian Solomon. *Pennsylvania Railroad*. Minneapolis, MN: Voyageur Press, 2009.

Schrenk, Lorenz P., and Robert L. Frey. *Northern Pacific Diesel Era, 1945–1970*. San Marino, CA: Golden West Books, 1988.

Shaughnessy, Jim. *Delaware & Hudson*. Berkeley, CA: Howell-North Books, 1967.

———. *The Rutland Road, 2nd Ed*. Syracuse, NY: Syracuse University Press, 1997.

Shearer, Frederick E. *The Pacific Tourist*. New York: Crown, 1970.

Signor, John R. *Rails in the Shadow of Mt. Shasta*. San Diego, CA: Howell-North Books, 1982.

———. *Tehachapi: Southern Pacific–Santa Fe*. San Marino, CA: Golden West Books, 1983.

———. *Donner Pass: Southern Pacific's Sierra Crossing*. San Marino, CA: Golden West Books, 1985.

———. *Beaumont Hill: SP's Southern California Gateway*. San Marino, CA: Golden West Books, 1990.

———. *Southern Pacific's Coast Line*. Wilton, CA: Signature Press, 1994.

———. *Western Division*. Wilton, CA: Signature Press, 2003

Simmons, Jack. *Rail 150, The Stockton & Darlington Railway and What Followed*. London: Eyre Methuen, 1975.

Smalley, Eugene V. *History of the Northern Pacific Railroad*. New York: G. P. Putnam's Sons, 1883.

Smith, Warren L. *Berkshire Days on the Boston & Albany*. New York: Quadrant Press, 1982.

Snell, J. B. *Early Railways*. London: Octopus Books, 1972.

Solomon, Brian. *Trains of the Old West*. Metro Books: New York, 1998.

———. *The American Steam Locomotive*. Osceola, WI: Motorbooks, 1998.

———. *The American Diesel Locomotive*. Osceola, WI: MBI Publishing, 2000.

———. *Super Steam Locomotives*. Osceola, WI: MBI Publishing, 2000.

———. *Locomotive*. St. Paul, MN: MBI Publishing, 2001.

———. *Railway Masterpieces: Celebrating the World's Greatest Trains, Stations and Feats of Engineering*. Iola, WI: Krause Publishing, 2002.

———. *Railroad Signaling*. St. Paul, MN: MBI Publishing, 2003.

———. *GE Locomotives*. St. Paul, MN: MBI Publishing, 2003.

———. *Amtrak*. St. Paul, MN: MBI Publishing, 2004.

———. *Burlington Northern Santa Fe Railway*. St. Paul, MN: MBI Publishing, 2005.

———. *Southern Pacific Passenger Trains*. St. Paul, MN: MBI Publishing, 2005.

———. *CSX*. St. Paul, MN: MBI Publishing, 2005.

———. *EMD Locomotives*. St. Paul, MN: MBI Publishing, 2006.

———. *Railroads of Pennsylvania*. Minneapolis, MN: Voyageur Press, 2008.

———. *Alco Locomotives*. Minneapolis, MN: Voyageur Press, 2009.

———. *Baldwin Locomotives*. Minneapolis, MN: Voyageur Press, 2010.

Solomon, Brian, and Mike Schafer. *New York Central Railroad*. Osceola, WI: MBI Publishing, 1999.

Staff, Virgil. *D-Day on the Western Pacific: A Railroad's Decision to Dieselize*. Glendale, CA: Interurban Press, 1982.

Staufer, Alvin F. *Steam Power of the New York Central System, Vol. 1*. Medina, OH: Self-published, 1961.

———. *C&O Power*. Carrollton, OH: self-published, 1965.

———. *Pennsy Power III*. Medina, OH: self-published, 1993.

Staufer, Alvin F., and Edward L. May. *New York Central's Later Power*. Medina, OH: self-published, 1981

Starr, John W. *One Hundred Years of American Railroading*. Millersburg, PA: Dodd Mead, 1927.

Stevens, Frank W. *The Beginnings of the New York Central Railroad*. New York: G. P. Putnam's Sons, 1926.

Stover, John F. *The Life and Decline of the American Railroad*. New York: Oxford University Press, 1970.

———. *History of the Illinois Central Railroad*. New York: Macmillan, 1975.

———. *The Routledge Historical Atlas of the American Railroads*. New York: Routledge, 1999.

Swengel, Frank M. *The American Steam Locomotive, Vol. 1: Evolution*. Davenport, IA: Midwest Rail Publications, 1967.

Taber, Thomas Townsend, III. *The Delaware, Lackawanna & Western Railroad, Parts 1 & 2*. Williamsport, PA: Lycoming Printing, 1980.

Talbot, Frederick A. *Railway Wonders of the World, Vols. 1 & 2*. London: Cassel and Company, 1914.

Thompson, Gregory Lee. *The Passenger Train in the Motor Age*. Columbus, OH: Ohio State University Press, 1993.

Thompson, Slason. *The Railway Library: 1912*. Chicago: Bureau of Railway News and Statistics, 1913.

———. *Short History of American Railways*. Chicago: Bureau of Railway News and Statistics, 1925.

Trewman, H. F. *Electrification of Railways*. London: Sir Isaac Pitmand & Sons, 1920.

Turner, Gregg M., and Melancthon W. Jacobus. *Connecticut Railroads: An Illustrated History*. Hartford, CT: The Connecticut Historical Society, 1989.

Vance, James E., Jr. *The North American Railroad*. Baltimore: Johns Hopkins University Press, 1995.

Walker, Mike. *Steam Powered Video's Comprehensive Railroad Atlas of North America: North East U.S.A*. Feaversham, UK: Steam Powered Publishing, 1993.

Waters, L. L. *Steel Trails to Santa Fe*. Lawrence, KS: University Press of Kansas, 1950.

Weller, John, L. *The New Haven Railroad: Its Rise and Fall*. New York: Hastings House, 1969.

Westing, Frederic. *Penn Station: Its Tunnels and Side Rodders*. Seattle, WA: Superior Publishing, 1977.

Westing, Frederic, and Alvin F. Staufer. *Erie Power*. Medina, OH: Self-published, 1970.

White, John H., Jr. *A History of the American Locomotive: Its Development, 1830–1880*. Baltimore: Johns Hopkins University Press, 1968.

———. *The American Railroad Passenger Car, Vols. I & II*. Baltimore: Johns Hopkins University Press, 1978.

———. *Early American Locomotives*. Toronto: Dover Publications, 1979.

Williams, Harold A. *The Western Maryland Railway Story: A Chronicle of the First Century*. Baltimore: Western Maryland Railway, 1952.

Wilner, Frank N. *The Amtrak Story*. Omaha, NE: Simmons-Boardman Books, 1994.

Wilson, Neill C., and Frank J. Taylor. *Southern Pacific: The Roaring Story of a Fighting Railroad*. New York: McGraw-Hill, 1952.

Wilson, O. Meredith. *The Denver and Rio Grande Project, 1870–1901*. Salt Lake City, UT: Westwater Press, 1982.

Winchester, Clarence. *Railway Wonders of the World, Vols. 1 & 2*. London: Amalgamated Press, 1935.

Wright, Richard K. *Southern Pacific Daylight*. Thousand Oaks, CA: Wright Enterprises, 1970.

PERIODICALS

American Railroad Journal and Mechanics' Magazine. New York (published 1830s and 1840s).

Baldwin Locomotives. Philadelphia (no longer published).

CTC Board. Ferndale, WA.

Diesel Era. Halifax, PA.

Home Signal. Champaign, IL.

Jane's World Railways. London.

Moody's Analyses of Investments, Part I: Steam Railroads. New York.

Official Guide to the Railways. New York.

Pacific RailNews. Waukesha, WI (no longer published)

Railroad History. Boston (formerly *Railway and Locomotive Historical Society Bulletin*).

Railway and Locomotive Engineering. New York (no longer published).

Railway Age. Chicago and New York.

Railway Gazette. New York (published 1870–1908).

The Car and Locomotive Cyclopedia. Omaha, NE.

The Railway Gazette. London.

Trains Magazine. Waukesha, WI.

Vintage Rails. Waukesha, WI (no longer published).

Washington Post. Washington, D.C.

BROCHURES, TIMETABLES, AND RULE BOOKS

Amtrak. Public timetables, 1971–2011.

Boston & Albany. *Timetable No. 174*, 1955.

Boston & Albany. *Facts about the Boston & Albany R.R.*, 1933.

Burlington Northern Santa Fe. Annual reports, 1996–2004.

Burlington Northern Santa Fe. Grade profiles, no dates.

Burlington Northern Santa Fe. System map, 2003

Canadian National. Annual report, 2007.

Chicago, Milwaukee, St. Paul & Pacific. Public timetables, 1943–1966.

Chicago Operating Rules Association. *Operating Guide*, 1994[?].

Conrail. *Pittsburgh Division Timetable No. 5*, 1997.

CSX Transportation. *Baltimore Division Timetable No. 2*, 1987.

CSX Transportation. *System map*, 1999.

Delaware, Lackawanna & Western. *A Manual of the Delaware, Lackawanna & Western*, 1928.

Erie Railroad. *Erie Railroad: Its Beginnings and Today*, 1951.

General Code of Operating Rules, 4th Ed., 2000.

General Electric. *A New Generation for Increased Productivity*, 1987.

General Motors. *Electro-Motive Division Operating Manual No. 2300*, 1945[?].

Pennsylvania Railroad. Public timetables, 1942–1968.

New York Central System. *Rules for the Government of the Operating Department*, 1937.

New York Central System. Public timetables, 1943–1968.

NORAC Operating Rules, 7th Ed., 2000.

Richmond Fredericksburg & Potomac. *Timetable No. 31*, 1962.

Santa Fe Railway. Public timetables, 1943–1964.

Southern Pacific. *Pacific System Timetable No. 17*, Coast Division, 1896.

Southern Pacific. Public timetables, 1930–1958.

Southern Pacific. *Your Daylight Trip*, 1939.

INTERNET SOURCES

www.aar.org

www.ble.org

www.bnsf.com

www.cn.ca

www.cpr.ca

www.csx.com

www.durangotrain.com

www.fecrwy.com

www.fra.dot.gov

www.guilfordrail.com

www.gvtrail.com

www.gwrr.com

www.kcsouthern.com

www.lalrr.com

www.montanarail.com

www.nscorp.com

www.railamerica.com

www.uprr.com

www.vermontrailway.com

www.wnyprr.com

www.wsorrailroad.com

INDEX

ACKNOWLEDGMENTS

Compiling the data for this book was no small task. Aiding my efforts was previous research undertaken for more than three dozen railroad projects covering subjects as varied as signaling, preserved steam locomotives, bridges, and histories of Amtrak, BNSF, Conrail, CSX, and Southern Pacific. During the last 15 years, I've spent many thousands of hours scouring railway literature for information, and this work helped provide the data that appears within this volume.

My intent was to portray each railroad concisely, yet in a manner that gives more than just raw facts to convey the essential flavor of each company and its operations. My interest in railways stems from a fascination with the details of their individual histories and operations, and I hope that this text has benefited from my personal experiences.

In addition to library work, I've explored railroads across the continent in person and discussed topics with fellow researchers, historians, authors, photographers, and professional railroaders. While my name appears on the cover, this book could not have been possible without help from a great many people who have aided in my research, photography, and understanding of railroading over the years. Thanks to Mike Abalos, Howard Ande, Jim Beagle, Ed Beaudette, F. L. Becht, Marshall Beecher, Kurt Bell, Robert Bentley, Dan Bigda, Mike Blaszak, Scott Bontz, Jim Boyd, Philip Brahms, Robert A. Buck, Chris Burger, Joe Burgess, Ed Burkhardt, Brian Burns, Dave Burton, Paul Carver, Tom Carver, David Clinton, George C. Corey, Mike Danneman, Tom Danneman, Brandon Delaney, Tim Doherty, Oliver Doyle, Doug Eisele, Ken Fox, Michael L. Gardner, Colin Garratt, Chris Goepel, Phil Gosney, Sean Graham-White, Dick Gruber, John Gruber, J. J. Grumblatt Jr., Don Gulbrandsen, Chris Guss, Mark Healy, David Hegarty, Paul Hammond, John P. Hankey, Mark Hemphill, Tim Hensch, Mark Hodge, Will Holloway, Gerald Hook, T. S. Hoover, Thomas M. Hoover, Brian L. Jennison, Clark Johnson Jr., Danny Johnson, Bill Keay, Tom Kline, George W. Kowanski, Blair Kooistra, Bob Krambles, Mark Leppert, Bill Linley, Don Marson, Fred Matthews, Norman McAdams, Denis McCabe, Patrick McKnight, Joe McMillan, George Melvin, Hal Miller, David Monte Verde, Doug Moore, Dan Munson, Vic Neves, Claire Nolan, Colm O'Callaghan, Mel Patrick, John Peters, Howard Pincus, Candace Pitarys, George S. Pitarys, Markku Pulkkinen, Joe Quinlan, Paul Quinlan, Peter Rausch, Hal Reiser, Doug Riddell, Peter Rigney, Jon Roma, Brian Rutherford, Dean Sauvola, Mike Schafer, J. D. Schmid, Jim Shaughnessy, Gordon Smith, Scott Snell, Joe Snopek, Carl Swanson, Richard Steinheimer, Vic Stone, Carl Swanson, David Swirk, Tom Tancula, Emile Tobenfeld, Justin Tognetti, Harry Vallas, Otto M. Vondrak, John H. White Jr., Craig Willett, Matthew Wronski, Norman Yellin, Pat Yough, Nick Zmijewski, and Walter Zullig.

Special thanks to John Gruber for writing sections on Green Bay & Western, Milwaukee Road, and North Shore, and to Patrick Yough for sections on Bessemer & Lake Erie and Western Maryland. Thanks to Robert A. Buck, Chris Guss, George S. Pitarys, T. S. Hoover, and my father, Richard Jay Solomon, for aiding with proofreading final versions. Thanks to all of the photographers who participated in this project; their images are credited appropriately. Research facilities at the California State Railroad Museum, Irish Railway Record Society–Dublin, Railroad Museum of Pennsylvania, San Francisco Public Library, Steamtown, Wendt Library at the University of Wisconsin–Madison, and the Western Railway Museum at Rio Vista, California, were invaluable, as was access to private collections, including those of Thomas L. Carver, Tim Doherty, Doug Eisele, Patrick Yough, and my father. Of the hundreds of sources consulted, many of the most useful and most relevant are listed in the bibliography.

My editor, Dennis Pernu, helped me refine the concept and was instrumental in turning the facts, texts, and illustrations into the book you see before you. I've gone through great lengths to find or make the best possible images to illustrate each of the sections. I've sifted through thousands of images, hoping to find those that best represent the individual railroads and shed new light on an element of their history. Some images are iconic, others obscure. It is my hope that information presented here is both accurate and relevant. I've gone over the data and texts again and again to check, confirm, and reconfirm the facts within. I'm a believer in providing useful and detailed information, but by being specific, there's a greater risk of making mistakes, or repeating the mistakes of others. Whenever possible, I've qualified information so as to be more useful.

I hope that this book finds a treasured place upon your shelf and that future generations will turn to it again and again, as I have done with the great books on my own shelf.

Page 1: U.S. railroads played an integral role in the country's "arsenal of democracy" during World War II, a fact that many—including the Pennsylvania Railroad—portrayed in their advertising. *Voyageur Press collection*

Page 2: In a classic pose, Chicago North Shore & Milwaukee heavy-electric interurban cars pause for a traffic light on a rainy evening at Sixth and National streets in Milwaukee. North Shore brought passengers directly from downtown Milwaukee to the Chicago Loop in a fast service more convenient than anything offered today. *Richard Jay Solomon*

Page 320: Among Southern Pacific's icons were its Union Switch & Signal "Style B" lower-quadrant semaphores, which required two blades to display three aspects. Here, US&S semaphores protect the Golden State Route at Polly, New Mexico, at sunrise on January 17, 1994. While many were installed in the early years of the twentieth century, some survived until the end of SP operations in 1996. *Brian Solomon*

First published in 2012 by Voyageur Press, an imprint of Quarto Publishing Group USA Inc., 400 First Avenue North, Suite 400, Minneapolis, MN 55401 USA

Voyageur Press titles are also available at discounts in bulk quantity for industrial or sales-promotional use. For details write to Special Sales Manager at Quarto Publishing Group USA Inc., 400 First Avenue North, Suite 400, Minneapolis, MN 55401 USA.

To find out more about our books, visit us online at www.voyageurpress.com.

ISBN: 978-0-7603-4736-2

The Library of Congress has cataloged the hardcover edition as follows:

Solomon, Brian, 1966-
North American railroads : the illustrated encyclopedia / Brian Solomon.
    p. cm.
Includes bibliographical references and index.
ISBN 978-0-7603-4117-9 (plc)
1. Railroads–North America–Encyclopedias. I. Title.
TF22.S65 2012
385.097'03–dc23
                    2011039375

Editor: Dennis Pernu
Design Manager: James Kegley
Cover Design: Simon Larkin
Book Design: Wendy Holdman
Layout: Erin Fahringer

Printed in China

10 9 8 7 6 5 4 3 2 1